The Smog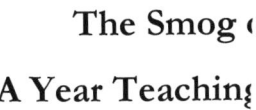
A Year Teaching

By Andrew Snape

Copyright © 2015 Andrew Snape

All rights reserved. No part of this publication may be reproduced, distributed, or transmitted in any form or by any means, including photocopying, recording, or other electronic or mechanical methods, without the prior written permission of the publisher, except in the case of brief quotations embodied in critical reviews and certain other non-commercial uses permitted by copyright law. For permission requests, write to the publisher, addressed "Attention: Permissions Coordinator," at the address below.
enquiries@inclined-publishing.co.uk

ISBN-13: 978-1508555025
ISBN-10: 1508555028

Acknowledgements

I would like to thank all those who have helped me put this book together, whether it be from allowing me to use their photos or for reminding me of some of the events that happened. Thanks to Julie, Jamie M, Tanja, Dani, Lisa, Miisa, Chris, Shang, Neighbour Amy and Jamie S. Without them, this book would have been a lot less interesting.

Dedication

This book is dedicated to all those people who have taken the plunge, foregone their comfortable lives and headed off to teach their language to people around the world, no matter what language that is.

Contents

Foreword 1
1 第一章 3
2 第二章 11
3 第三章 21
4 第四章 27
5 第五章 37
6 第六章 47
7 第七章 55
8 第八章 63
9 第九章 71
10 第十章 79
11 第十一章 87
12 第十二章 95
13 第十三章 105
14 第十四章 113
15 第十五章 121
16 第十六章 131
17 第十七章 139
18 第十八章 149
19 第十九章 157
20 第二十章 167
21 第二十一章 175
22 第二十二章 183
23 第二十三章 195
24 第二十四章 205
25 第二十五章 213
26 第二十六章 221
27 第二十七章 229
28 第二十八章 237
29 第二十九章 247
30 第三十章 257
31 章三十一章 267
About the Author 273

Foreword

There is a very important aspect of this book that needs to be made clear from the start: it may not be 100% accurate. I'm not talking about the specifics of conversations or particular actions I describe, I mean in general. You see, there are two things that have made this tricky to write. The first is that I never kept a diary of my time in China, which is an utterly shocking thing to admit as someone who has long held ambitions of being a writer. The second is that I failed to back up my lesson plans, and in late 2012 my laptop's hard disk failed and I lost them all. This has had a number of effects on this book, all of which I want to confess to you from the outset.

The first is that there are a number of people, mostly students, whose names I have forgotten. However, there are times where I still need to mention them, so I've made the names up. I haven't invented new people though. Everyone I mention is real.

The second is that I can't remember the syllabuses, so I have almost no idea what themes I taught and when I taught them. This will become obvious for any reader who has extensive knowledge of EF courses.

The third, coming off the previous, is that I can't remember what tasks and tricks I used specifically at these times. However, I do know what I used throughout the year, and I remember reactions and outcomes, so while I may have the timings wrong and the lesson themes wrong, the tasks and results are all real.

Also the reader will notice, as I have, that there is a considerably large number of mentions of certain corporations, so much so that as I've been writing, I've wondered if it could come across as product placement. I want to make it clear that I have not received any support or funding from any company, nor have I ever sought any, and that I only mention these companies because they are relevant to the events that happened. This, I hope, will be obvious when competing brands are mentioned.

This is not a self-aggrandisement tome, nor is it a way to discredit others. I have done the best I can to be fair and positive, as well as self-critical. There are events I could have mentioned that could be considered negative, both about other people and me especially, but I've left them out because, overall, I had a positive experience and look on everyone very fondly. This book is not about bigging-up anyone or putting them down, it's about my experience of teaching English in China, and I have only included events, reactions and feelings, as I see them, that are relevant to that function.

This is also not a tourist information book about China, nor is it a justification or attack on the people, culture or political system. If I give my opinion, I call it like I see it. I am not, nor have I ever been, a political or social activist, and I've never been employed as a travel writer either (although I have had articles published in print magazines). I have provided honest observations about the country, the people and the places I saw, and I make no apologies for what is in this book.

The point of this book is to give an account of my experience moving from a well-paid corporate job in the affluent West, into a lowly paid job in the developing world. It is not a recruitment brochure for TEFL, or any companies in the sector, nor a criticism, just an honest account of the pleasures and pitfalls that I experienced in my year doing this important profession.

1 第一章

My epic quest to educate the people of an unknown city thousands of miles from home began in a small office in an edge of town building in Brentwood, Essex, on 1st April 2009.

I used to work in the finance arm of Ford Motor Company and, if I'm completely honest, I was never a stellar employee. I did ok, sometimes badly, and sometimes well, but I was never a particularly dedicated worker and I never made much of a difference. I gained my first promotion in 2007 and became an internal controller, which was a great job as I got to travel to a few places in Europe and tell senior people what they could and couldn't do, but I wasn't exactly blazing a trail or impressing too many people.

On that memorable day, everyone in the company was to have a special meeting. Ford was going through some problems and had decided to instigate a massive voluntary redundancy programme and, to ensure no-one was put under any pressure, everyone was to be told what their package would be worth and if any restructuring would affect their job. I sat in front of my boss, in his tiny office, and he handed me the letter with the numbers and then revealed that, due to all data centre operations being consolidated in Germany and Spain, it was decided that there was no need to have a UK IT internal controller i.e. they wanted to get rid of my job.

I had two options; take the money and leave, or find another position within the company. The former meant leaving a good firm with great pay and benefits. The latter meant staying, but at the risk of not finding a new job and being made compulsorily redundant and getting a lot less money. I had two weeks to decide.

That evening, in somewhat of a panic, I tried to think straight. Part of me knew this was the opportunity I had been looking for. For years I had been doing the morning commute on the A127 and A128, from my small flat in Basildon to the office in Brentwood, wondering what I was doing with my life. I kept imagining doing something better and more valuable in the world; something more noble than IT for a motor finance corporation. However, the pay was very good and I had a mortgage, so I was always held back by the comfort and safety of my life. Now I had to make a decision. At home I had an idea.

Darren was one of my oldest friends, and we had gotten back in contact thanks to the power of Facebook. He'd talked about how he'd worked on cruise ships for a few years and was at that time teaching English in Prague, so I dropped him a note asking how to find out about working abroad, doing whatever. I also started crunching some numbers, knowing that something would have to be done with my flat. He came back pretty quickly with a whole bunch of links, all of them related to teaching English. I wanted to reply, asking him for more than one job, but I was just grateful he'd been so quick to help, and so I started digging.

What I was faced with was a revelation. If there was one job I thought ill-equipped for and uninterested in it was teaching. I've never seen myself as particularly confident giving a presentation in front of a group of people but, after reading some testimonies and watching a few online videos I suddenly had an epiphany; teaching may well be my future.

One site provided a video of an entire lesson being taught to adults and it looked great, even if the grammar being taught was beyond my poor understanding and the exercises he was giving were things I could never have thought of. Granted, it was obviously a staged lesson, probably edited and reshot, and the students were on their best behaviour, but something about it made me smile.

There was plenty of information on other sites, with lots of glamorous and exciting-looking pictures of people teaching children of all races, groups in foreign countries laughing together in over-zealous camaraderie, and people enjoying the travel benefits of living far from home. I wasn't stupid; I knew these images were overly romanticized, and I had enough of a mind to strip away the garnish and think for myself. It took a couple of days for me to truly decide that this was the path for me.

There were still issues to sort out. Over the next five days I ploughed through the material online and probed Darren about his life. I also went over the numbers again and again, knowing that I would have to rent out my flat for God knows how long. I also talked to my close friends at work. Stephen, Robin and Matt were guys I was pretty close to and they knew me very well. For them, there was no dilemma. They knew that I had not been happy for a long time and that this was a big chance to walk away with relative ease and money in the bank. Also, they seemed pretty unsurprised that I was looking into teaching. This was something that would come up time and time again; people seemed to think that I was well-suited to education.

It was a stressful few days, but in the end I had it all in my head. Two weeks after that initial meeting, I sat in my boss' office and told him the good news; I would take the money and run. The decision was made. There was no going back. I had decided to leave the comfortable corporate world and become a teacher of English as a foreign language.

That all sounds a bit rushed, doesn't it? It seems like I've skipped over what was a hugely important time in my life when I had to make a decision that was make or break, one that would change the course of my personal history. Well guess what; it was rushed. I had a grand total of two weeks to decide my future and everything in those fourteen days had to be done apace. That part of the story was short and rushed because that part of my life was short and rushed.

It wasn't as straightforward as upping sticks and leaving though. Yes, it was possible to make a few calls, get a job and get on a plane, but I've always valued qualifications. I have a BSc (Hons) in Applied Psychology and Computing and an MSc in Information Systems, so getting those pieces of paper has always been important for me. I wanted to do things properly, and one of my biggest concerns was to get a teaching qualification. Also, if I chose to do it long term, that piece of paper would be essential for earning the "big money".

It turned out that there were two main qualifications to earn; CELTA from Cambridge University and CertTESOL from Trinity College London. As far as I was concerned they were exactly the same and it made no difference to me which one I took. I'm sure certain schools have biases one way or the other, but overall these balance out around the world, so it didn't really matter. What mattered was money and location.

My first option was to look at courses in the UK, and they were all over the country in the big university cities. They were also expensive, with the cheapest costing about £1100. By then I would have left Essex and moved back home to Portsmouth, so Southampton would have been the nearest for me, but that course was over £1300. There were courses all over the world though, so I checked them out and boy, was I in for a surprise.

I couldn't believe how many in Eastern Europe were on for less than £1000 and in decent cities too, such as Krakow and Budapest. Even Western European courses were a couple of hundred less than Southampton, and I'm talking places like Berlin. That's right, Berlin was cheaper than Southampton. So the no-brainer was established; Europe it would be. Why commute from Portsmouth to Southampton when, for the same amount, I could fly out to a thriving European city to live and study? It would also be the kick-start for a little trek around the continent before having to get into the real world of work once again, only less formal, more stressful and insanely adventurous.

But where to go? I'm an avid traveller, so I was open to pretty much anywhere, but I still had to think about cost and liveability. The two cheapest courses I could find were on CactusTEFL and in Poland; Krakow and Wrocław. Krakow was my first choice at £749. It was already full by the time I applied so I chose the slightly more expensive city I had never heard of. Research showed I wasn't as geographically aware as I thought, as it is Poland's 4th largest city and was once known as Breslau. It wasn't just a simple matter of booking and flying out though.

With limited places and a fair amount of demand the school, International House (IH), couldn't just let anyone in. I had an interview to complete, but it wouldn't be like any I'd had before. It wasn't like I was a novice. There were a few at the end of university for graduate recruitment and some gruelling ones when I planned to join the Army, as well as those needed for internal job rotations at Ford and a couple for other companies. They were all the same really; give an example of this situation and what do you know about us and what kind of a person are you and what values do you think are the most important? For IH, it would be a lot different; this would be about linguistic knowledge and potential teaching skills. In essence, it would be an oral exam.

From their website I downloaded a bunch of material relating to the English language and teaching, and over a couple of evenings I ploughed through the lot, getting my head around grammatical structures I hadn't considered since GCSEs (much less understood). It seemed pretty straightforward enough, and a few days later I was put to the test. Mike was my interviewer, over the phone from who knows where in the world.

During that phone interview I had the material printed and laid out in front of me, covering every last inch of floor between my sofa and TV. He asked me about linguistics and teaching methodologies, and it was here that I got my first lesson in teaching. One question was about how I would explain some concept to students who had only the most basic ability. I tried to be clever, thinking of some solution that was innovative and tricky, but his response was simple. "All you need to do is draw it". It was no big deal though. On that call he approved my place on the course. In the next few days the payment was processed and that was it, I was heading to Poland to become an English teacher.

The next few months weren't nearly as strange as they could have been. Lots of people had chosen to take the money and were thinking about their escape, while others had been denied the chance to leave. It seemed mightily unfair, especially as some had plans to start their own business or travel the world and were specifically expressing their lack of desire to be there. On top of that, they weren't offered any kind of compensation for this restriction. Clearly, I was one of the lucky ones.

People congratulated me on my decision and seemed impressed I was making a complete change in my life and, if they had been 100% honest, they would have told me it was long overdue. I had never properly gotten the hang of corporate culture and had never been a major hard worker. I wasn't the kind of person to stay late for no overtime and there was much about that world I resented. For me it was always just a way to earn money, and so it was obvious and right that I would jump ship at such an opportune moment.

The schedule called for a quick departure; June 30th at the latest. With holiday time still owed to me I chose to go much sooner and so, on 17th June, I handed over my ID and corporate credit card to my boss, shook hands with my team, said goodbye to people I had known and worked with for some 9 years, and headed out of the building for the last time. That was it, my corporate career was over and I was heading for a new life as an English teacher.

It felt weird not going into work every day, or being in Essex. I had rented my flat out so I was out and back in with mum in Portsmouth. It was a good summer, but I wouldn't have that much time off. My plan for July was to do as little as possible, followed by a few days visiting Prague and then head off straight to Wrocław for the course. For the most part, it was nice and sunny for that month. I read up on some linguistics and spent a lot of time in coffee shops enjoying the free time.

It should have been the case that I felt awkward and empty, not commuting every day and sitting at my desk, reading and approving documents and taking calls from people asking about IT policy, but to be honest nothing could have been further from the truth. It was a blessed relief. I was still a little apprehensive about what I had let myself in for, but what was done was done; there was no going back. It was now all about making the best of it.

On the evening of Tuesday 28th July I spent a couple of hours with my dad. He wasn't a well man and had been in and out of hospital all year with various ailments, all connected with his age and years not taking care of himself properly. He was pretty upset when I said goodbye, because there was every chance I would not be back for a year or so.

We did what we normally did when I visited him – drank tea, watched TV, talked about what was going on in my life and about the news. It got late, and I had an early start. I kissed him goodbye that night, not knowing how important that evening would turn out to be.

In the morning it was much the same with mum. My suitcase and rucksack were packed and in the mid-morning she gave me a big, tearful hug and I left, heading for the train station for the two hour journey to Heathrow Airport.

A few hours later I touched down in Prague and began my long weekend break in the city known for its beautiful medieval architecture and popularity with drunk British men.

It was hot and humid for the whole trip, but it didn't slow me down. Prague deserves its reputation as one of the most beautiful cities in the world and I was dazzled by the heavenly spires, cobbled squares and elegant statues. The Charles Bridge is especially stunning, lined on both sides with 30 statues of saints. The Petrin Tower, a diminutive copy of the Eiffel, provides the most stunning views of the centre and the Museum of Torture shows tourists the macabre side of medieval (and surprisingly recent) European culture.

On the Saturday afternoon I met up with Darren, my old school friend who'd put me on to the idea. We had dinner in a local pub and caught up on the good old days of primary school, then headed to U Flecku, the oldest pub in the city, where he introduced me to his fiancée Gayathri. I had a pretty early train to catch in the morning so I chose to stay up all night, moving from bar to bar and wandering the streets trying not to pass out. The city looked as beautiful in the dawn as it did in the dark.

After dragging myself back to the hostel, I lugged by tired body and two bags down the hill to the train station, hauled myself onto the train, threw myself into the compartment that looked more in keeping with something from the 1940's, and settled down for the many, many hours to pass by. By mid-afternoon I was in Wrocław, being met by Ania, a receptionist at the school who took me to my small and sparsely furnished apartment on the outskirts of the city, my home for the next four weeks. This was it, the fun was about to begin.

1-4. Basildon, Essex, my home before my big adventure. 5-10. Prague, Czech Republic.

2 第二章

Without a doubt, the four weeks of the CELTA were the hardest four weeks of my entire life. For pretty much all of that time I had nothing else in my head other than that course. I've been through plenty of hectic times in education in the past. GCSEs and A-levels always provided a lot of exam stress and coursework deadlines were pretty tight. Both my degrees were pretty heavy too, but I got through them all. By the time I finished the CELTA I was more relieved than ever. No course I had done before had ever been so intense.

It started off on the Monday with a pretty standard orientation; a tour of the building's facilities and an explanation of how the course would work. I was sharing the flat with an English guy called Dominic, and the rest of the group were either Brits, North Americans or Poles. There was Patricia, Essex-boy Warren and Mark from Scotland. Jessie and Nomsa were Canadian and married and Stephen was American. Matt and Clay were also American but lived in Poland, thanks to meeting the loves of their lives there. Kasia and Woijcech were Polish with near-perfect English and a better technical understanding of the language than us native speakers.

It was during this orientation that I had my first eye-opener. There would be no slow build up, no easing into things. We would be teaching pretty much straight away. We were split into two groups who would take different classes of adult students, then each group would be split in half again; one half would give their first 30 minute lesson the next evening and the other half (my group) the night after. In reality, I had a day and a half to figure out how to be a teacher. Instruction started that afternoon and our tutors – Mike (my interviewer), Annette and Alina – took the first lessons for us in the evening.

The next day was more of the same, and the first group taught their lessons and, that evening, I had one of the most stressful nights of my life. Annette was assigned to my group, and she had given each of us some pointers for the following night, which was great, because I had absolutely no clue what I was going to do. Looking back, I find it amazing to think how much I fretted trying to plan those first thirty minutes of teaching. It's nothing really; now I could give a lesson that long on the fly, with no plans or even any real forethought (I hope). That evening though, those thirty minutes felt like I was planning to do brain surgery.

That day my nerves were up and down. Sometimes I was calm and in control, looking at my plan and feeling confident that I would pull it off. Other times I sat in the classroom, listening to Mike and Annette talk about the day's subject, and I could barely concentrate. I had given presentations at work before, and had facilitated a few meetings, but this was different; this actually felt important. Not only did a qualification depend on it but, to a certain extent, somebody's intellectual understanding of English too.

Eventually our teaching began, and while another student did their 30 minutes I paid barely any attention, spending my time going over my plan and the materials I had prepared. It was a hot day, and by the time I stood up for my turn I was sweating like I had completed the Great South Run.

Those thirty minutes were painful and dragged on forever. I felt nervous and awkward, and I interpreted the looks on the faces of the local students as gazes of bewilderment and contempt. It wasn't the nicest feeling I'd ever had, but eventually my turn was over. Everyone else did their bit and we finished for the day. I had a couple of beers that night and slept like a baby, knowing that I had a day's respite before doing it all over again.

As it turned out, I was incessantly self-critical (as I've been told I am all my life, probably because I'm an idiot). The feedback the next day was positive, and I'd done a really good job. Yes, my nervous tension was obvious and the beads of sweat had been noted, but the important thing was that I'd been given something to teach and I had taught it. My instructions were clear, the tasks were logical and related, the students understood what I wanted from them and in the end it was clear that they had learnt something. My shaking constitution had played no part in their assessment. Somehow, I had pulled it off and my God, I felt good.

We had another couple of lectures, then the other guys gave their lessons for that evening. I spent the night planning my turn, got up early the next morning to work in the school, gave feedback to the teachers from the previous night, had a couple of lectures that involved some practical tasks and then gave my own lesson. It had been a stressful first week, but somehow I managed to get through it without a hitch. That weekend we had an assignment to complete and were warned that it would easily see us holed up for the whole two days.

After hitting a nightclub with Dominic on Friday I was in no position to do any work on Saturday, so I popped into the city centre for a few hours, wandering the streets, taking in the architecture, sampling the food and drink and generally relaxing. It was nice to have a respite from the mental slog of the course. A few of us met up in the town square for more drinks and on the Sunday, I sat myself in my room in the morning and only left to get some supplies, working through until midnight on the assignment and lesson plan. It was a mental nightmare, one that I had no intention of repeating, but I got through it in the end.

For the next three weeks that was how life panned out. We planned our lessons, gave our lessons, observed everybody else's lessons, gave feedback on those lessons, attended our own classes, discussed theories and let our hair down when we could. It was often quite uncomfortable in the school. There was no air-conditioning and it was a particularly hot and humid month. One evening, four of us waited for the bus home and we stank to high heaven of stale sweat.

We had other assignments to complete and I managed to do 80% of mine on the Saturday mornings and then go out and enjoy myself, while others on the course spent almost the whole time in front of their laptops, struggling to get a single word documented.

It was pleasant spending a few hours around the medieval town square, taking in the eclectic architecture, browsing the shopping mall and, one day, checking out the motorbike festival (mostly Honda Goldwings). Wrocław is a lovely city, one that, up to then, hadn't been discovered by the hordes of screaming British stag parties looking for cheap beer and cheaper women.

After a couple of weeks the intensity of the course hit us all, when we all began reporting having freaky dreams, largely based on the course, as well as being unable to think about anything other than what we were there for. However, it was a lot easier to get through than I would have thought, mainly because it was only four weeks, and making such a solid, intense effort in that time was nothing really.

The last two days were momentous for all of us. It had been a hard slog, but eventually I gave my final, 1 hour lesson on the Thursday, and that night we were all ready to have a big release. Cheap beers in a couple of local pubs were followed up by a tram ride to the Wrocław Fountain, where the dancing spouts waltzed with a light show and music from a broad timeline of eras.

It was remarkably calming for all of us, who had just given our brains over to a single subject, and a single purpose, for four whole weeks, and were just about ready to explode. Now it was over. We still had one more day, but that would be taken up with the usual lectures and giving lessons on subjects of our own choosing that would not be under any kind of assessment. The course was over, and we could finally have some fun.

That weekend I moved out of that pokey little flat and into a hostel, where my travelling would commence. I finally got to see the city proper, spending more time wandering the streets, crossing the river to the cathedral and partying in the local nightclubs. It's a great city and I love it, one of the most underrated and undeservedly ignored cities in Europe. However, I was glad that it was ignored, as there were no crowds of drunken idiots spoiling the atmosphere. After a few days enjoying the city that had been my home for a month, I dragged myself and my gear to the train station and hopped into a carriage for the long trip to Krakow.

The old royal capital of Poland is pretty much what you expect it to be. It's become one of the most popular city tourism destinations in Europe in recent years, with its grand square and elaborate castle providing a postcard perfect destination for a weekend break. Sadly there were a few stag parties visiting too, and the prices were insanely high for Poland, but I did find a cheap little restaurant that served the best pierogi (dumplings stuffed with meat or vegetables) I have ever had.

Touring the castle, known as Wawel Castle, was like stepping into a city within a city. Sitting on the prominent Wawel Hill on the banks of the Vistula River since the 14th century, it was the home of Polish kings during the golden age of the nation, growing into a complex with a palace, armoury, treasury, gardens, defensive systems and church. In many parts of the Eastern Bloc, historic royal residences were demolished to make way for modern, Socialist statements (East Berlin anyone?) but, thankfully, the Polish Communists left this gem alone.

There is a pleasant Jewish district which, surprise surprise, is devoid of all Jewishness. The National Museum has a vast collection of Polish art, and at that time an extensive photographic exhibition (David LaChappelle's *Deluge* and Nobuyoshi Araki's marriage in photos stood out) and an exhibition of American graphic art from the mid-20th century. There is also the view from the Church of St Mary, looming over the main square, but the best views came from the tethered hot air balloon that rose 120m above the city, allowing me to take in every single historical spot my eyes could fall on.

I also took the essential opportunity to make the haunting and disturbing trip to the city's most famous neighbouring landmark, Auschwitz. It was a pretty unnerving and unpleasant experience on the tour. The second part of the camp, Birkenau, where people lived in the worst conditions and where the trains pulled up near the gas chambers, was surprisingly serene and pleasant. It was the first part of Auschwitz that provided the horrors, with the rooms displaying bundles of human hair, shoes and suitcases as well as haunting photographs of working prisoners and the selection process, where a doctor would assess each arrival and point left or right. One way meant "into the camp to die working" and the other meant "die immediately". Despite that, my days there were enjoyable and interesting, but I still much preferred Wrocław by every measure.

Another train journey took me back through my former home and onward to Poznán, where I spent a few days hanging out with Matt. We also hooked up with Dominic for a night out, and it was great to drink with these guys one last time before moving on with our lives. It was cold and wet for most of the time, but the city was pretty cool.

Much like Wrocław it had a quaint historic charm but was largely free from tourists, especially the cheap booze kind. Also, like Wrocław, its town square is marked out with one of the prettiest town halls in Europe. Completed in 1560 in the Mannerist style, it sees a crowd gather at midday every day, when two animated goats come out of the clock tower and put on a display of butting each other.

Matt told me the legend that the town was saved when someone was woken up by the noise of two goats fighting, and subsequently found the cattle market was on fire, although there are other stories around. We also visited the Poznan Uprising Museum, and institution dedicated to the much ignored and under recorded protests of 1956 that were the first major civil actions against the Communists. It was great hanging out with Matt, meeting his fiancée, getting a tour in the rain and necking a few beers with him and Dom before heading on my way, once again.

My next stop was Gdansk, the main port of Poland and the city where the end of Communism in Europe really began. It was a little unusual as it didn't have a main square, more like a rectangle that opened up from one, long street (where Costa Coffee had conveniently set themselves up). The riverfront was stunning, dominated by the remarkable Medieval Crane that is the symbol of this once dominant maritime metropolis. I visited the shipyard, the site of the first truly successful stand against Communism, where a strike led by Lech Wałęsa led to the first non-Communist trade union to be recognized. The tap had been opened and, nine long years later, the Communist Bloc collapsed.

My formative years were during this time, and the news back then was full of reports of the unrest that grew over the decade. A few years before, I had visited Berlin and was excited about seeing the Brandenberg Gate for this reason, but was disappointed by how small it looked. Not so with the ship yard. Its glory days are gone, but at least it's still functioning.

The city was also a host for the 2009 Eurobasket tournament, and in a bar one night I got pally with a bunch of Latvian fans whose one goal was to score some coke and drag me along with them. I managed to avoid the excursion thanks to my interest in some of the local Polish ladies.

I also took a day trip to the nearby town of Malbork. This small town is home to Malbork Castle, former headquarters of the Teutonic Knights and still the biggest castle in the world by surface area, and the largest brick building in Europe. I'll be honest, I've seen more impressive looking castles in my time. It reminded me of the Forbidden City in Beijing – a large complex of buildings that, put together, deserved their reputation, but individually were not that special. It had been worth the visit though.

A long overnight bus journey took me across the old Iron Curtain into Germany. Hamburg was my destination for a few days, where I stayed in a mega hostel with hundreds of guests, a big reception, a large canteen and rooms with en suite facilities and a TV.

The city was heavily bombed during World War II, so it's not exactly the chocolate box utopia of medieval Teutonic perfection. It has its canals and the redeveloped warehouse district, but the heart is the Reeperbahn, the old rope making centre that is now the party hub; both mainstream and illicit. For me, the highlight was La Paloma, a small bar just off the main drag. There seemed to be no concept of health and safety, as the crowd was packed in so tightly it was difficult to lift one's glass to one's mouth, but the DJ played *We Didn't Start the Fire* by Billy Joel, one of my all-time favourite songs. Any bar that plays that song is the kind of bar I want to spend the night in.

Despite its sordid reputation, none of the city felt sleazy. There's the little side street where the women in the windows tout for business, but both entrances are partitioned off for privacy, and women are banned. Some working girls hung around these entrances, trying to bully passing men into choosing other "delights" but on the whole, the area was a fun place to be. After all, if it was good enough for The Beatles………..

After a couple of days, I hopped on another bus and headed for Frankfurt, the home of European finance. I had been looking forward to this the most, as I have a more than passing interest in skyscraper architecture. My hostel was in the area between the train station and the financial quarter, which I soon realized partially comprised the red light district.

Sadly, the city was a bit of a disappointment. The skyline was impressive but the actual financial district was pretty boring, not like Wall Street or the City of London. Everyone seemed to be holed up in their offices and no-one was passing through on foot. It actually felt quite dead, like an out of town business park, but in the city centre.

There was a pretty old square (restored in 1984), a nice river, and most streets were clean and pleasant, but it didn't give me the buzz I had hoped for. I met a couple of US airmen in the hostel bar and we went out for a few beers, managing to avoid the "hostess" bars with the aggressive women sat outside who were overly keen to get us in. There was also a lot of open drug taking, including in the daytime, right outside the international train station, right in front of the police.

My next stop would be one of the most memorable visits to a foreign city of my life, but for the wrong reasons. The long train journey to Luxembourg City was one of the most beautiful journeys I had ever taken. I passed through some stunning valleys and rural plains for hours on end; nature at its finest, even if I generally don't care about such things.

When I arrived I called home to let mum know I was safe. That was when she told me dad was back in hospital. He'd been in and out all year, but I had thought he was getting better, so this admission was somewhat of a blow. She reassured me that it was no different to the other visits and I took her word for it, but in the back of my mind I knew I was kidding myself.

The next day I took my tour. The city seemed to be in three parts. The first is along the river, which resembles a quaint French village with its tiny cottages and delicate looking church. The river cuts through a gorge and on top is the modern city. On one side is the ultra-modern zone where European institutions have chosen to set up shop, and on the other is the heart of the city, a micro-Paris/Berlin/London/Brussels with grand palatial buildings, high-end shopping, cultural institutions, public squares and government offices, all crammed in to what is basically a small town.

After the sightseeing and museum visiting I settled down in the restaurant in my hostel. It was 6pm and I was ready to tuck into a spaghetti Bolognese when my phone rang. It was my sister, and she had bad news. Dad had taken a turn for the worse, and when she'd told the doctor about my trip, he'd suggested to her to call me home.

My brain pretty much shut down and I just couldn't figure out what to do. I was hundreds of miles away, with the English Channel like a watery wall, blocking an easy escape. Thankfully I had purchased a train ticket to Amsterdam for the morning, so I decided to stick to that; get to Amsterdam and get to Schipol Airport and onto the next flight I could find. I didn't eat the food, but I did go out and have a few pints, just to calm myself down.

It wasn't such a big surprise really. Dad had been in and out all year and I'd been with him in hospital when he'd been coughing up a lot of blood. He'd had mobility issues for years, thanks to arthritis of the spine and some unhelpful weight-gain, but before I had left he'd been a lot more mobile and had spent a lot more time at home, actually making an effort to eat proper meals at the right time of day.

Weirdly, it was at this time that I knew he didn't have long. I had visited him at his home and he was doing ok, still watching the TV a lot but getting up a lot more and moving around. He was in the kitchen, sitting on the seat of his walker eating lunch. As I walked out of the kitchen I turned around and looked at him. He was rubbing his forehead, like he had a headache or was trying to solve a difficult problem. For some reason, it was at that moment that I knew he didn't have long left, that at some point in that year we would lose him. Now that portent was coming true.

The next day was one of the longest days of my life. I got on the train and it left on time, heading for its connection at Brussels Midi. Everything was smooth and uneventful and, as we entered the Belgian and European capital, I was actually feeling relaxed.

I arrived at Brussels Centraal station and that's where things started to go wrong. Belgium is bi-lingual – French and Flemish – and so my brain told me 'Centraal' was the same as 'Midi'. When I left the platform and entered the main concourse I realized how wrong I was. This was not the same station I had visited three years before. I'd gotten off too early.

I tried to stay calm and headed outside, looking for the taxi rank. Amazingly, there didn't seem to be one, and so my heart started racing and the early stages of panic took hold. I didn't exactly have a lot of time left, and in my state of mind the thought of negotiating any metro system was terrifying.

Eventually, I found the taxis and was whisked through the streets to the right station. I texted a couple of friends to let them know what was happening and they replied with offers of whatever help they could give. I grabbed some food, then hopped on the train to Amsterdam.

That was where the second stress hit me. As we approached the Dutch capital there was an announcement that there had been a last minute change. The train would not be stopping at Schipol, so we'd have to hop off at a stop before then. The station seemed to have been in a village, but it was so modern that it seemed out of place in such a quiet setting. The next train came and I made it to the airport.

Then the third stress hit me. The first desk I saw was Lufthansa, a dead cert if ever there was one. Shockingly, they had no available seats on any flight to England, but they sent me to BMI who, God love them, helped me out, even giving me a discount on my excess baggage. I was going home and so, air side, I downed a couple of beers and got online to let more people know. More offers of help flooded in, but in reality none of them would make much difference. Eventually I queued up to board.

Then the fourth stress slapped me round the face. Take off was delayed by an hour and a half due to some engine issue. Somehow, I didn't completely lose my mind and was able to get something to eat. With everything fixed and ready, we boarded and headed to Heathrow. Thankfully, the flight was uneventful, and even a little bit early, and I was able to catch the bus and train back to Portsmouth without any hitches. I got home at about 1am and, after a quick change of clothes, I headed to the hospital.

When I got there my half-sister was with him. He was still awake and talking, and his face genuinely lit up when I arrived. I was tired and upset and just wanted to sleep, but there was no way that was going to happen. We talked about my time away, and some of the things I had seen and he was keen to hear it all, but it was clear that his mind was rapidly deteriorating. I had a couple of hours of lucidity with him before it became clear he wasn't with it anymore. I managed a couple of broken hours sleep before my sister Caroline came to take over, sending me home to freshen up and get a real kip.

After a shower and a few hours of sleep I woke up to the sound of the phone ringing. Before my mum answered it, I knew what it was and was dragging myself out of bed. By the time I got to the hospital my sister, half-brother and uncle were at his side. Dad was breathing heavily and laboriously, his gaze straight ahead and unfocussed. All we could do was sit, watch and wait, hoping that he knew we were there with him at the very end. He was sat up in his 'thinking' pose – his left arm resting on the bed rail and his index and middle fingers laid on his temple.

For two hours we sat there, talking to him, doing whatever we could to make his passing easier. Eventually, at about 7:25pm, he shifted, turned and looked in my direction, made a noise like the movement was a struggle, his facing turning a hint of grey and he slipped away. His final moments were pretty uneventful, but it was all over.

1-2. Wroclaw. 3. Krakow. 4. Auschwitz. 5. Poznán. 6. Gdansk. 7. Malbork. 8. Hamburg. 9. Frankfurt. 10. Luxembourg City.

3 第三章

Ten days later it was my birthday, a weird one considering we'd lost dad. It was pretty quiet; dinner with Mum and Caroline and meeting up with Jamie, an old school friend who shared the same day. Not long after, we had a cremation service for Dad that included a Royal Marine bugler playing *The Last Post*, and a good wake, and then it was all over. I hung around for a few weeks, lounging in coffee shops and looking into where I wanted to teach, and then I decided, before I had to get out there and work, I needed to finish the trip I'd had to rush away from.

I arrived at Helsinki Airport as the sun was coming down in the early afternoon. Waiting for me at arrivals was Miisa. We had met on one of those Facebook apps that get people together, and we had been talking for months, originally planning to get together before I had been called home in September.

It was great to see her and she was everything I had hoped; intelligent, athletic, beautiful, friendly, talkative and with a lovely smile. I stayed at hers for a couple of nights and she showed me round the city, even taking me to a concert by her favourite band, Apulanta. She and her friend became particularly teenager-ish when, in the bar, the lead singer came out of a back room and chatted to the manager. Apparently this guy is a huge sex symbol in Finland. As soon as he was done, they leapt up and, almost bouncing like Tigger, asked him for a photo, which he duly obliged. They were immediately followed by a couple of actual teenage girls who did exactly the same.

I'll be honest though, I wasn't so impressed with Helsinki. I had been once before, for a day from Tallinn, and I had thought it was boring then. Don't get me wrong, it's not an ugly or nasty city, but it didn't give me that buzz I always look for. The Design Museum was pretty interesting though, and I especially liked the 1960 Solifer moped, a Finnish brand with the most beautiful design. If I ever make money (thanks for buying this book by the way), I will get my hands on one of those for sure. It was mostly cold in the city, and the significantly earlier sunset probably didn't help my mood. Miisa's company made it fun though, and when I left I hoped, somehow, that I would see her again.

My flight landed in Oslo in the afternoon, and the ultramodern and clean train took me into the cold, dark city centre. I had set myself up for an expensive few days, and I wasn't disappointed. Oslo has some of the most interesting museums though.

The Viking Ship Museum is stunning, displaying a number of perfectly preserved, real Viking long boats and all the amazing trinkets found on them. It's incredible to think that such simple, minimalist and flimsy looking constructions could have carried people and plunder across the vastness of the Baltic and North Seas, and even the Atlantic Ocean, with all their storms and destructive waves.

The Folk Museum has an eclectic mix of displays from all periods of history. The stave church (a traditional multi-tiered, wooden construction) is a unique sight in Norway, and the toy gallery showed the current generation what they could have enjoyed had the Xbox not been invented. My favourite part was the 80's exhibition, displaying all sorts of finery from my childhood such as original Transformers, fluorescent clothing, newspaper headlines of the day and a small, portable TV, playing the video for *Take On Me* by A-Ha on a continuous loop. When I was leaving I realized that that song could be heard – just about – by the poor person working on the front desk ALL DAY!

The Kon-Tiki Museum is devoted to the Kon Tiki expedition, an experiment led by Thor Heyerdahl to show how ancient South American people could have settled Polynesia. It is also home to one of the few Oscars on public display in the world, thanks to the 1951 winning documentary.

The highlight of the city for me was the National Gallery and its Munch Room, home of *The Scream*, although the portrait of his sister Inge was far more beautiful and striking than anything I had ever seen before. It actually made me stand and just look at it for a long time, which is something I rarely do.

I also enjoyed the beautifully bleak view of the harbour from the Akerhus Fortress, took tea at the painfully elegant Café Royal (favourite haunt of Henrik Ibsen), ate an elk burger from the Christmas market and dined at a Caribbean-themed Thai restaurant. Oh, and I spent a hell of a lot of money and had very little to show for it, especially in a yuppie nightclub on top of a department store. Oslo lived up to its billing.

A fantastically comfortable coach took me into Sweden and the city of Gothenburg. I was really impressed with the coach; there were only three seats to a row, and with fewer rows the seats were bigger and had more leg room than I had experienced before. It was the perfect coach for an overnight trip. Sadly, it was during a bright, sunny day. It had turned icy cold and the streets were slippery and dangerous, but I stayed warm enough and safe. It looked like a mini St Petersburg with its canals and striking 18th century facades. It wasn't the most exciting or memorable city, but it was clean and pleasant and had a nice, relaxed feel to it.

The Lisberg amusement park was closed, but it was still worth a visit just to see the Walk of Fame, with stars for such luminaries and legends as ABBA, Anita Ekberg and Ace of Base. Close by is the statue of Poseidon, with its cleverly crafted attack on prudish artistic censorship of the time (all I will say is 'fish penis'). I spent most of my time very cold though, a really icy chill that made my skin tingle. I didn't experience much of the nightlife either, preferring to get back to the warmth of my hostel before the cold night set in.

Another coach journey took me into the national capital, Stockholm. What a stunning sight it was from the dining room of the floating hostel on the opposite side of the Mälaren to the island of Gamla Stan. This was very different to Gothenburg. Gothenburg was built from nothing in the 17th century and has a distinct new town feel. Stockholm dates from the time of the Nordic sagas, and its medieval-spired heart still stands out loud and proud ahead of some ugly post-war updates.

Top of the attraction list is the Vasa Museum, an exhibition of the eponymous warship that sunk in 1628 and was raised in 1961. There's a similar exhibit in Portsmouth Naval Base for the Mary Rose. I've seen it a few times and it's impressive, but that's less than half a ship, whereas the Vasa is almost completely intact. To be fair though, I prefer the Mary Rose because it looks like a proper wreck, but the Vasa is still stunning and impressive to behold. It's perfect, almost too perfect. Looking at the Vasa one gets an exceptional, first-hand representation of what warships were like to live on. The Mary Rose tells you what they were like to die on.

My one big night out there was originally going to be at an 80's-themed club, but the queue was long. I got chatting a few local people and they got bored waiting, so dragging me along we headed back to near my hostel, and partied until the early hours on one of the boat nightclubs on that side of the water. After a couple of hours sleep I spent my last day being lazy. Sadly, I missed out on the medieval crane, but my brain wasn't exactly in the right way, let alone my body.

I took a night coach to Copenhagen, suffering a restless sleep that was finally killed in Malmö, when we crossed the Oresund Bridge and into the Danish capital. I had a stressful time with my hostel as none of the main staff were there when I arrived, and no-one seemed to be in charge. I finally got hold of the sick manager on the phone and he got me sorted.

I had arrived at the start of the Earth Summit, a gathering of world leaders and experts to discuss and raise awareness of the dangers of climate change through the power of flashy and gaudy lighting, a dazzling rock concert and thousands of people arriving by plane. It was a decent enough city, but it was spoilt by some clichéd and boring speeches and street performers who didn't do anything to change my opinion of climate protesters; noble, worthy but ineffective and unappealing. I could have spent a whole day browsing the Taschen shop though. I love their books and this was my favourite place in the city, far better than the Little Mermaid statue and the Christiania hippy commune.

Copenhagen fell firmly into the same type as the other Scandinavian cities I had been to, including Helsinki (Finns can be very touchy about the whole Scandinavian thing). It was a lovely environment. The streets were clean, the people were friendly and it was easy to get around. Copenhagen is especially famous for cycling, and there they have proper cycle lanes that run for miles, are separate from the car lanes and connect cyclists easily to every part of the city. In Britain they are all painted (badly), make no sense and seem to be done to meet some sort of government mileage target, rather than functioning to provide better transportation routes and promote a viable alternative to cars. However, it wasn't a stunning city either, and I didn't come away with any sort of wow factor that would make me go back in a hurry.

I arrived in Hannover, and Miisa came soon after. She had suggested joining me for a few days and so, after dumping our bags, we headed to the Christmas market. We spent the evening warming up on mulled wine and rum in the most impressive temporary keller I had ever seen; two floors and tiered like a wedding cake. I explained how the British Royal family heralded from this city and how I wanted to reclaim all the good bits for the Queen, while leaving the ugly Brutalist crap for the locals (it's the least I could do, Gawd bless 'er!).

The next day we wandered the city in the most constant and hateful drizzle ever. We took in the remains of the Aegidian Church, with its bell donated by the city of Hiroshima and, to get a respite from the rain, took a browse round the Lower Saxony Museum, home to some of the finest works by Rubens, Rembrandt and Dürer, as well as a bog body (ancient body preserved in remarkable condition in peat), known as Red Francis. There was also the palatial New Town Hall, and the endless stalls of Christmas markets to enjoy, with gallons of delicious mulled wine just begging to be necked by frozen tourists like us.

The next day we took a train to the chocolate-box perfection of Hameln, site of the mysterious event immortalized in the fairy tale of the *Pied Piper of Hamlin*. The earliest written record from this town is dated 1384 and simply, and hauntingly, reads "It is 100 years since our children left". A few decades later, a stained glass window (now gone) depicted an early incarnation of this legend, and it has remained a European favourite ever since. If ever there was a place that embodied the rest of the world's idealized image of Germany, it was Hameln.

The next day, Miisa and I parted at the train station on happy terms, both of us feeling more confident that we would see each other again.

The train took me into Amsterdam without a hitch. It was a symbolic arrival, as it had been to this city that I had rushed when I needed to get home quickly before Dad passed away. The city is one of the most chilled out and welcoming I had ever been to. I spent a few good hours in one café, chatting to the barmaid who had to put up with all the cannabis fumes, despite not being a smoker herself. I actually got a little high and had to go out for an hour just to stay conscious.

De Wallen is the well-known red light district and it was a sight to behold, with all the women in the windows trying to beckon all and sundry to enjoy their pleasures. These women are generally young and pretty, with a variety of body shapes, hair colours and ethnicities, but I noticed that during the daytime the women tended to be a lot older.

The Sex Museum was an eye-opener, but the highlight was the Ann Frank House, the home of two Jewish families hiding from the occupying Nazis during the War until being betrayed and dying in concentration camps. Her diary is one of the most important pieces of literature of all time, and it was an eerie experience to see one of the very volumes on show.

My final stop was a return visit to a place important in my childhood. Rather than fly home, or take the Channel Tunnel to London, I chose the more direct route; a train to Paris, then a train to Le Havre. When I was 12 I did a week-long school trip to France and we stayed in there, a decent sized town on the Normandy coast and one of the ferry destinations from Portsmouth.

It was genuinely great to walk around the town again, rediscovering the park with the small lake, the school where we stayed along with a bunch of other kids from Southampton, the "Rocket Tower" church, the playground on the seafront, the civic centre, the opera house designed by Oscar Niedermeyer and the "Bouncy Bridge".

It was freezing cold, and the skin on my legs was cracking in the dry air, but it was worth it to reminisce about one of only two foreign trips I did as a kid. We didn't have much money then and so, while my friends often went on summer holidays to Spain or France, we did day trips to places like Arundel or Windsor. The only holidays we actually did were week-long summer trips to Wales and a week in northern Italy. Now I was the hard-core traveller.

The following day I hopped on the ferry, and settled in for the six hour trip across the English Channel, back home to Portsmouth, enjoying a view of my hometown from the sea for a very rare occasion. I was home, back in Old Blighty, for the time being.

1. Helsinki. 2. Oslo. 3. Gothenburg. 4. Stockholm 5. Copenhagen. 6. Hannover. 7. Hameln. 8. Amsterdam. 9. Le Havre. 10. Portsmouth.

4 第四章

The fun as over. I'd had an up and down few months, full of elation and loss, hard work and hard partying, travelling to new lands and lazing around at home. Now it was time to get a job. I had my eyes set on one location, Vietnam.

  Like most people in the West, most of the images of Vietnam I had seen were connected to the war with America. I knew there would be much to see and experience and learn that the great film directors had missed or blatantly ignored. *Top Gear* had done a special episode there, where the three presenters had biked up the country from Ho Chi Minh City to Halong Bay, and every scene was in a setting of exciting urban chaos and stunning rural beauty.

  I was determined to get there, and so sent my CV to every school in Vietnam I could see advertising. I also uploaded a CV to TEFL.com and forwarded it for jobs in various other countries. I wasn't going to tie my whole existence to one place; the more jobs I applied for the more chances I had.

  Sadly, it seemed all the schools in Vietnam were working to strict criteria; every job seemed to have a two-year minimum experience requirement. I heard nothing, absolutely nothing from any of them, not even a polite rejection. I wouldn't say it was depressing, just a shame. Like I said, I wasn't tying my whole future to a single country, but Vietnam was the one place I wanted to go to more than any other.

  I applied for jobs in South Korea, Taiwan, Chile, China, Brunei, Japan, Indonesia, Hong Kong and Thailand, and there was a mixture of rejections and "We'll get back to you" responses as well as some unsolicited enquiries. It was a positive start and I expanded my search to other sites, such as Gold Star, CactusTefl, BridgeTefl, TeflJobsAsia, EslCafe and ITeachNTravel. Eventually, three responses came that were of particular interest, responses that offered interviews on the phone.

  The three responses had two things in common; they were in China and they were with EF (Education First, often referred to as English First), one of the biggest players in the world of TEFL. It's also the biggest in China, so big in fact that it was one of the official sponsors of the 2008 Beijing Olympics.

  One was in a place called Xiaoshan, a city/overspill near Hangzhou. Another was in the city of Urumqi, the capital of the Muslim-majority Uighurstan province. At the time there were major riots taking place by the ethnic Uighurs who felt marginalized by the immigrant Han Chinese. The third was in the city of Chongqing. I knew a tiny bit about this place, thanks to two factual TV series; *Paul Merton in China* and *The Ascent of Money*. A bit of research told me that it was a huge city that had largely escaped the attentions of the outside world, other than for its lack of profile and its heavy pollution.

  I had phone interviews with each one and it wasn't long before I had decided on my destination. The first was with Xiaoshan and it went well for the most part. I liked the sound of the Director of Studies (DoS) who interviewed me and the school sounded like a good place, but I was turned off when he described the place as having "not much", mainly a "residential district" and "not very exciting". A big cross was written across Xiaoshan in my head.

Then I spoke to the DoS from Urumqi. Sadly, she was up against it from the get-go, as the city was on the news on a daily basis at that time. The city had been pretty much shut off from the rest of the world, save for a few foreign TV crews, but she put a brave face on it, although to get any Internet access she needed to travel to a nearby town. I could easily have seen myself there had it not been for all that trouble.

Then there was Chongqing. I spoke to an Englishman called Theo, and the interview progressed just like the others had. He talked about the school, the curriculum and the working conditions. I asked him about the city and his description of it was very positive; no political problems, lots to see and do and plenty of alternatives for a desperate foreigner. To me, it seemed pretty obvious; out of the three, Chongqing was the one. I gave it some thought but eventually decided for sure, and gave Theo the wonderful news.

The weeks leading up to my departure were a mixture of eventful and lazy. One weekend in December I travelled to Bournemouth for a university reunion. I hadn't seen these guys in 12 years so it was great to see how little they had all changed. Then Christmas came, and it was the usual period of shopping, wrapping, exchanging, eating and drinking. It was the first Christmas Day where I hadn't popped round to visit my dad, and that felt weird.

After Christmas was when I had to get properly sorted. I headed into London with all the necessary documents to get my visa. Thankfully the Chinese had improved the process, and there was no queuing up on the street for three hours like I'd had to endure before my trip in 2007. They had a new visa application office in Holborn, with a seated waiting room and central heating and, when I arrived, it was almost empty.

When I handed the English woman my documents she quickly handed them back, saying I had the wrong ones. Suffice to say that I was furious and, leaving the office, called Theo to find out how they had screwed up. I'd filled out the requisite application form properly, and EF had sent me the necessary forms from their end by email. I had even made sure they were printed in colour. Apparently, the office needed the originals, which could only have been sent by post. How could EF have messed up like that? They hadn't.

A diplomatic spat was on between the UK and China. UK citizen Akmal Shaikh had been convicted of drug trafficking in the country and, despite protests and claims he was not mentally competent, was executed on the 29th December. The UK government did what it could to "kick-off" and the Chinese responded in kind and that's why I, somehow, "didn't have the right documents".

So, no work visa, no teaching in China. Theo had a solution; I would get a three month tourist visa and then, while there, they would sort out the proper one. It seemed a bit risky, but apparently it was a common thing to do, so I trusted him, and a week later made the trip back to London, when my application was accepted, my passport taken and I could finally relax. My passport came back in good time and there, covering an entire page, was the glorious visa that signalled the reality of what I was doing.

The 12th January saw a day like no other, when a deluge of snow dropped on the entire country, producing a now legendary satellite photo of Britain completely white. Never had it felt so good not to have a job, but it did raise a concern for me. It took a long time to clear, and during that week the streets were icy and dangerous. Despite my hiking boots (which I thought were the most appropriate footwear) I managed to fall over a few times. Mum was forbidden to leave the flat and that was fine. I was there so I could get everything that was needed, but what if it happened while I was away?

A week or so before leaving, mum arranged a party, just to say goodbye, with a few family, friends and big pile of home-cooked food. I really think that my leaving was a bigger deal for her than it was for me. She was from a generation where to travel you had to be either military or rich, and holidays for most people were in Bognor Regis or Skegness. For my generation, travelling to the other side of the world has become no big deal.

Then, once all was quiet, I had to start preparing. I spent a few days getting all my clothes together and packing the books I thought I would need for the coming year. On my final evening in the UK I had a full suitcase, a holdall stuffed with a few books and extra clothes and a small rucksack with my laptop and a few more books and clothes, all laid out in the living room, ready to be dragged outside the next morning.

The day I left was grey and murky. It was a cold morning as I lugged my bags on to the street, ready for the taxi to take me to the train station. As expected, my mother was pretty tearful at me leaving. I had been away plenty of times before, but at least with university it was no trouble for me to come home. Now I was heading thousands of miles away to the other side of the world, almost certainly not to return for at least a year, maybe even for longer. I had no idea either, and for me that was part of the adventure, but for mum it was the source of her anguish.

The cab arrived, I stacked my bags in the boot then received a tearful, crushing bear hug from her as I said goodbye, knowing that for at least another year we would not see each other. It's amazing how strong a woman in her seventies can be in such situations. At 8am on the dot I climbed into the taxi and we drove off.

The trip to Heathrow was smooth and uneventful; taxi to Portsmouth Harbour, train to Woking and connecting bus to the airport. After checking in and passing through to departures I sat down in one of the pubs and feasted on one last full English breakfast, and then I settled myself down, waiting for the moment we all wait for in those lounges. After a couple of hours of reading, wandering, browsing and sitting, my flight was called and, at about 1:30pm, I strapped myself into my cramped seat on Aeroflot and was lifted into the heavens to my first stop en-route to my new life.

Moscow Sheremetyevo is, for me, the single worst airport in the world. Whenever I have been there it has always been in Terminal F, a miserable, grubby, downtrodden, poorly designed and ugly terminal building, not to mention the crappy services on offer. This was to be my fifth visit to the airport and, thankfully, scaffolding and screens were up, signifying that the building was undergoing some sort of major renovation. Not a moment too soon, but thankfully I had barely an hour to hang about before jumping on the next national carrier to the other side of the world.

Despite being a seasoned traveller, long haul flights were still a novelty for me. I'd done Aeroflot before and was unimpressed by the crummy excuse for in-flight entertainment, but at some point there'd been an upgrade and I got to watch a couple of films before drifting off into a typically broken and uncomfortable sleep. *Déjà Vu* was surprisingly entertaining and *Whiteout* was a generally run of the mill crime thriller, bolstered by the ever-delightful presence of Kate Beckinsale.

The timing of the flight was pretty perfect. When I woke up we must have been over Chinese airspace, and a decent breakfast was served. It was early morning and I felt a tiny bit refreshed with a body clock seemingly in perfect balance. The plane touched down in Beijing on a freezing cold Thursday morning. I collected my suitcase and lugged myself out into the icy cold air, where I jumped on the shuttle bus that took me to one of the most incredible buildings in the world.

Terminal 3 is the second largest airport building on the planet after Dubai International Terminal 3, but it's hard to imagine anything being more impressive. Unlike Heathrow, the check-in area is more like a public square; wide open, airy, lined with shops and restaurants and crowded with people. Check-in was pretty quick and, after a browse of a few shops, some snacks and some light reading, I headed upstairs to begin my acclimatization with some local cuisine.

Time was ticking by. Airside, I started to get anxious, sitting at the gate as my fellow passengers crowded into the plush seating of the ultra-modern terminal but eventually, with my belly full of weirdly-seasoned meat and nervous tension, we boarded the plane for the final leg. As I looked around the passengers I noticed one thing; I was the only non-Chinese person on the flight.

This leg turned out to be the most nerve-wracking flight I had ever taken. Now the barriers to my new life were coming down. I was no longer sitting in a connecting hub, wandering around shops, eating and drinking and waiting to get going. I was in the air, heading towards something unknown, something exciting and something weird.

There was a film showing on the communal screens, but it was a Chinese historical epic, so I pushed in my earplugs and put the mask over my eyes, hoping I would drift off and the painful few hours would fly by. Sadly, my body clock was fighting against me, and no matter how tired I felt it wouldn't let me nod off. Eventually the plane touched down, we all stepped off, edged through passport control, claimed our baggage and walked to the exits. I was finally in Chongqing.

My arrival turned out to be one of the easiest I'd ever had to a destination. At first I was apprehensive as I headed out of the baggage claim area and through customs because, in all the excitement at the thought of getting here, I had forgotten to ask who was picking me up. I could only hope that I would stick out like a sore thumb and, as it turned out, they did too.

My first view of the city was the crowd of Chinese people waiting for their friends and family and, at the back, towering over them by at least a head and shoulders, was a white guy with glasses and a big smile, waving at me. As I got past the crowd this friendly, beaming face was joined by the equally friendly and beaming face of a white woman with a mass of long, curly, jet black hair. Their warm and enthusiastic welcomes fitted perfectly with their strong American accents. This was Julie, the DoS and Rory, the Senior Teacher and without further ado, we headed into the cold afternoon and into a taxi.

My first impression of Chongqing was one of greyness, all over. The airport was at the edge of the city but it was still pretty crowded in the local area. There weren't any high rises, but the nearest buildings were a few storeys taller than the homes of the habitual whingers on the outskirts of Heathrow. Our taxi took us along a major highway that seemed pretty new and was devoid of any potholes or mad pedestrians.

Rory spoke the lingo, and I noticed there seemed to be little hassle telling the driver where we needed to go. On my trip to China in '07 I'd had horrendous problems with taxi drivers in Beijing and Shanghai. In the former we drove around for ages until we stopped off at a Novotel and got directions from the reception, while in Shanghai I had to direct the guy to my hotel.

We headed down an almost endlessly straight highway, passing the pylons of what I was told was the incomplete metro system, and forests of skyscrapers rising up from the mud as the city expanded to house the countless thousands of new arrivals looking for a new life, like me.

The network of new roads was like a snaking monster, feeding off the fumes of the cars and trucks that crawled along its spine. Thankfully there weren't that many vehicles, and we cut through the metropolis with relative ease. I wanted to spend the whole time gazing out of the window, taking in every sight we passed, but I didn't want to be rude to my new friends. Rory and

Julie were from Missouri, married and had been in Asia for a few years working as teachers. They worked at one of the two EF schools in the city, one that they said was located in a shopping mall, the last place I would have expected to find any sort of productive establishment.

The population became gradually denser, with more high rises crammed in and more people milling about on the pavements. Pretty much every tower had shops and restaurants on the ground floors, each one adorned with gaudy signs in flashy Mandarin script and, occasionally, some typically funny attempts at English.

The road turned into a bridge, crossing a river at least as wide as the Thames at a height greater than the towers on Tower Bridge. Rapidly, the road artery narrowed and the traffic intensified. We made a right turn and were in a normal, residential street; normal for China that is. It was heavily shadowed, thanks to the high rises on both sides and trees all the way up its slope. The taxi made a left turn and we were in a back street at the entrance to the courtyard of three of those towers.

We were finally at where I would be calling home for the next twelve months. The three towers were connected on the lower floors by shops and restaurants on the street side and the shared recreational space at the back. In the lift I saw the floor numbers went up to 33, but we stopped at 9, dragged my bags down a dark, narrow corridor and into the apartment. It had been 25 hours, almost to the second, since I had given my mum a hug and a kiss, but I had finally arrived.

Inside was a middle-aged man with a smiling face and healthy stature. He was Theo, the man who'd given me the chance to change my life, and I was so grateful to see him. Also there was a young, ginger-haired lad. This was Dave, my new flat mate and a born and bred Essex boy, from Chelmsford. It was great to be sharing a place with someone who knew the places I knew. It felt so strange being there, in the flat, in that city, in that country, knowing that I wasn't on holiday and there was no travelling on the cards any time soon, nor going home for the time being.

My room had everything it needed; a large bed, a heater/air-conditioner, a bed side cabinet and a large fitted wardrobe. The large windows looked on to the street where, for the first time, I got an actual sense of where I was. The opposite side of the street rose up a small hill where, on the short summit, three high rise apartment buildings were going up. In front of them were a row of downtrodden, miserable and dirty mid rises, with locals hanging out their washing in the filthy smog or beating the dust out of rugs. It was a busy scene down below, and noisy too. The glass wasn't double glazed and the frames didn't look like they'd been fitted flush either.

The kitchen was small, just a corner of the large living room with a floor to ceiling glass screen/box separating it. They'd bought me some food to help me out; milk, cola, some tubs of instant noodles and some fruit, so I was sorted for a couple of days. It was a pretty nice flat, and the street below seemed to have everything I needed. Now it was all about settling in.

Then came the first shock of my stay, one that would cause me concern for the entire year. Just before leaving the flat Julie did the normal thing and popped into the toilet. Then she, Rory and Theo left, and it was time to settle in. I unpacked a few items; t-shirts, underwear and socks were stacked on the wardrobe shelves and shirts were hung; my first major purchase would be coat hangers. I was tired, sweaty and stinking and my guts hadn't had a proper clear out in a day so, with towel and washing gear in hand, I headed into the bathroom for a shit and a shower.

My first problem was that I couldn't see the toilet. I was sure Julie had gone in there, but I couldn't see it anywhere. The bathroom was an open box with a shower head opposite on the wall and a porcelain hole in the floor, shaped like a toilet bowl. I looked at it, looked around the rest of the room, left the room and felt the wall next to the door just to make sure there was no other room I had missed. I was confused.

"Dave," I asked tentatively, and a little bit embarrassed. "Where's the toilet?"

"It's in the bathroom, it's a wet room." He replied.

"But, I don't understand. There's no toilet in there."

He smiled and stifled a laugh. David was already a veteran. He'd worked the previous year at the EF school in Urumqi. He already knew everything that was freaky about China and it quickly clicked what was on my mind.

"It's on the left" He said. "In the floor."

"Oh." I replied, trying to come up with a way not to lose face. "Fine, okay, right."

I shut the bathroom door and looked at it, my enemy. The bowl itself wasn't exactly deep, which made sense since it was buried in the floor, and the cistern attached to the wall should have been the big bloody giveaway in the first place. My one thought was *'How am I supposed to sit on it?'* It was clear that sitting was never going to happen, but I had no idea what else to do. My stomach was rumbling and I needed to go, pronto, so I had to improvise. I pulled my jeans down, squatted, put my hands on either side of the bowl, stretched my legs out in front (to keep my jeans and pants away from danger) and, praying I had enough strength to hold myself up, let nature take its course.

It was one of the least pleasant experiences of my life. My arms ached like hell and it was clear that the bowl was far too shallow, especially if I ever picked up a nasty shitting bug. I was terrified that they would give out and collapse and that my arse would be covered in my own shit for the first time since I was a toddler. I was going to need a new strategy. I showered, dressed, shaved in the wash basin just outside the bathroom and made myself a coffee.

"That was awful." I told Dave, sitting on the sofa. "How do people shit like that? My arms are killing me?"

"Why would your arms hurt?" He asked, looking confused.

"Well, I had to hold myself up or I'd have been sitting in my own shit."

"Why do you need to use your arms in a squat toilet?"

It was that word, 'squat', that switched on the light bulb in my head. I was supposed to squat. For the first time since I was a toddler, somebody had to show me how to use the bog. Dave assumed the position over the bowl for me. I felt pretty bloody stupid that I hadn't worked that out, especially since I was well aware of Asians habit of casually squatting when hanging around somewhere. I have always admired the strength and suppleness in their legs that allow them to make an almost 180 degree bend in their knees and not fall over, but I still had a problem.

There was no way I could squat that far, so there was still a danger of shitting on my jeans and shoes. How would I use public toilets if I got caught short? What if the trots really slapped me in the arse out of the blue? Either I developed new leg strength and flexibility pretty bloody quickly or learnt to hold it in. It required some serious consideration.

That evening we had a welcoming meal for me. Dave and I headed round to the front of the building to one of the restaurants on the ground floor. He pointed out the pharmacy, the basement level CBest supermarket and a couple of hot pot restaurants that would become very familiar over the year. Rory and Juile were already there, along with a Filipino woman called Maria and an American woman called Sandra. Soon we were joined by another American, Tanja, and Karen and Susan (both Chinese).

That meal we had was my first actual taste of Chongqing. It was known as chuancai, the genuine local cuisine originating from the neighbouring province of Sichuan. It was a mixture of spiced and non-spiced dishes, all laid out buffet style on our table, looking both enticing and odd at the same time. I've never really been the most adventurous food traveller, but I've always made a point of giving local things a go at least once.

This wasn't travelling though; this was living, so I tucked in. It all tasted a little unusual but still good. The chillies were especially odd. Again, I'm not an avid foodie, so my descriptions will probably be lame, but the chillies were not the same you get in Tesco's. These were smaller, had a darker red colour and had a hotter, sharper and I think bitter taste than at home.

It was the usual couple of hours eating piles of food, drinking some pretty ropey local lager, trying to remember everyone's names and answering the usual questions about my background and why had decided to teach English and why China and why Chongqing blah blah blah blah blah. I also did my best to find out about them, but it was futile for me. They only had to remember shit about one person while I had to memorize a basketball team. I gave up pretty quickly and just decided to eat the food and drink the beer. We didn't stay out late though, and by 9 o'clock I was back in the flat and in bed, thinking about how best to get comfortable on such a hard mattress. My first day in China was over. Only another 364 to go.

1. The tower blocks at the end of Huayi Lu. 2-3. Huayi Lu from my balcony. 4. Me in my lounge. 5. The squat toilet – my mortal enemy. 6. My apartment block.

5 第五章

Before going any further, a little explanation of Chongqing is in order. Chongqing is one of the four municipalities of China – effectively an independent city governed at the same level as a province – along with Beijing, Shanghai and Tianjin. It was created in 1997, separating it from Sichuan province along with a number of smaller, satellite cities. It has a population just south of 30,000,000 people, although the city itself is home to about 7,000,000.

The city is located in a sub-tropical zone, between the Yangtze River region and the Qinghai-Tibet Plateau. The municipality has an area of 82,000 squared-kilometres, bordered by the Dabu Mountains in the north, the Wu in the east, the Wuling in the southeast and the Dalou in the south. The Yangtze runs through from the west, through the Three Gorges Dam (the Qutang, Wuxia and Xiling gorges) and joins the Jialing at the Yuzhong Peninsula.

The city has a humid, sub-tropical climate, influenced by monsoons, with short winters and long summers. Average temperatures range from 8 Celsius in January to 29 Celsius in August, with an all-time low of -3 and high of 44. However, located in the Sichuan Basin means that it has one of the lowest totals of sunshine in the country. It's also known as the "Fog City", and in January 2013 was rated by the Asian Development Bank as being in the top ten of the most polluted cities in the world by air quality.

It's history dates back to before unification, and is usually associated with the State of Ba, who may have established the settlement in the Spring and Autumn period (771-476 BC), naming it Jiangzhou. It was conquered by the Qin in 316 BC and was known by a number of different names over the centuries; Chu (Southern and Northern Dynasties), Yu (Sui Dynasty). It was named Chongqing in 1189, in honour of the newly crowned emperor, who described his coronation as a "double celebration" (*shuanchong xiqing* or *chongqing*).

It then became a popular capital for rebellious kingdoms. In 1362 it became the capital of the Daxia kingdom under the peasant rebel leader Ming Yuzhen, and in 1621 was the capital of Daliang, under She Chongming. Its last period of homing rebels came in 1644, when it was captured by Zhang Xianzhong after the fall of the Ming. It was soon recaptured by the Manchu Qing Dynasty, who supported mass immigration to the region.

After centuries of isolation, China began a slow opening up to the world, and in 1890 Chongqing became the first inland port open to foreigners, with Britain, Germany, France, Japan and the USA opening consulates. It first became a municipality in 1929, but during the 2nd Sino-Japanese War (1937-1945), it acted as national capital under Chiang Kai-Shek and the Kuomintang. It became the main Allied base for resistance to Japan, with an international force led by Chiang and General Joseph Stilwell, which led to the city suffering heavy bombardment from the air. Because of this, Chongqing became known as the "City of Heroes".

After the war though, the Kuomintang and Communists fell into conflict. US-mediated peace talks were held in the city, but to no avail, and in 1946 the seat of government moved to Nanjing. In 1949 the Communists established a military and political commission there, and the Kuomintang was forced to flee, eventually settling in Taiwan and ushering in the current era of Communist rule.

It became a provincial city within Sichuan in 1954, and a rebuilding process took off, with setbacks in the Great Leap Forward and the Cultural Revolution. In 1983, it was included in the group of cities to enjoy economic freedoms and more foreign trade, and in the 90's it was classed as an open city, thanks to the development of trading on the Yangtze River. Eventually it regained its independent municipal status, and since then the city has grown at an exponential rate.

Today, the city is still growing – economically, socially and physically. For a number of years it was one of the hubs of organized crime, but in 2009 a concerted effort was made to crack down on the gangs, led by party secretary Bo Xilai, with some 5,000 gangsters arrested and imprisoned, allegedly with the help of torture. More recently though (after my time there), the city was in the news for the murder of British citizen Neil Haywood. Bo's wife, Gu Kailai, was given a suspended death sentence, while Bo was found guilty of various charges of corruption.

Thank you Wikipedia!

My first morning in Chongqing started with the beeping of the alarm on my mobile, followed by the sound of someone calling out on a megaphone. I opened the curtains to see rush hour on Huayi Lu, my street for the next year. It wasn't a main road, but there was plenty of activity. That calling out continued and I soon realized two things; it was coming from the three-towered construction site across the road, and it was a recording on a loop. I doubt if I could have handled something so annoying, but I guess it was supposed to be motivational for the workers.

I ventured into the wet room and, completely naked, made my first attempt at using the toilet properly. I couldn't squat like an Asian; my leg muscles were neither strong enough nor flexible enough, so I squatted as much as I could and knew immediately that I could never do this with any clothes on; the height of my arse above the bowl would have created dangerous splashing, not to mention shitting on my jeans. In my mind I knew one thing; I could NEVER use one of these away from the flat for anything other than pissing. My most important goal was to locate the seated toilets: there had to be some.

I answered the knock on the front door to a typically small, pretty and stern looking Chinese woman. Her name was Fei Ling and she worked for EF as some sort of administrator. Her job for the morning was babysitting a giant, clueless white man. I bet she thought she had hit the career jackpot.

We headed to the bus stop round the corner. The traffic was murder and the air was so thick with pollution I could see it as a fine mist in front of me. I could see the Jialing River through a gap in the buildings, but the other side was almost completely obscured by the air. The bus was heavily packed like nothing that would ever be allowed back home. There was certainly no visible sign that looked like it said "58 passengers max. 35 seated, 23 standing". Fei Ling told me an interesting fact.

"You will be working in the New York New York building. It's the most beautiful building in Chongqing."

Wow! How awesome did that sound? The most beautiful building in the whole city? I couldn't wait to gaze upon a work of such architectural genius and grace. What wonder of human creation was I about to see? My mind raced through its potential peers around the world; the UK Houses of Parliament, St Peter's Basillica, Hagia Sofia, Sydney Opera House, the Louvre, the Empire State Building, the Burj al-Arab, the Forbidden City. I didn't expect it to match them, but China has a good history of creating beautiful architecture, so I knew I was in for a treat. We crawled up the main road that snaked its way up the hill and, in just a couple of short minutes, we alighted, crossed through an underpass and were in the main city centre.

The melee of people milling around looked like Portsmouth city centre at Christmas, but there was no special occasion. The buildings were tall, really tall, and closely packed in. We arrived in Monument Square, a crossroad of pedestrianized streets with a monumental clock tower in the middle - the recognized focal point of the city. Surrounding us was a forest of modern towers, all tightly packed in and hogging what little space was available. I gazed up at the not-so-gleaming spires, catching the signs for Starbucks, MacDonald's, Pizza Hut and KFC and wondering if any of them had my beloved seated toilets. These skyscrapers would have cast major shadows had there been any kind of sunlight. The sky was a thick grey and not a single ray was getting through, and I wondered if this was as bad as it got. We took a left and Fei Ling pointed at one of the buildings.

"There it is." She said. "The New York New York building. Isn't it beautiful?"

I followed the direction her small, stubby finger pointed at, but I didn't see anything of any noteworthy aesthetic quality. The only building that stood out was a bland-looking 50-ish storey block that tapered at the top to form a sort of jagged pyramid, like a childish copy of the Chrysler Building in New York.

It took me a few seconds to put two and two together. This ugly-looking plagiarized design was the New York New York building, the most beautiful building in Chongqing. China is well-known as being a great centre of copyright and intellectual property theft, but that has mostly been limited to CDs and DVDs, with cars being added to the list in recent years. Now it seemed that buildings were fair game too.

We entered the small lobby area and waited a few minutes for one of the lifts to get down to the bottom. It was a gleaming, polished area, but not the kind of expansive, open entrance I had expected from such a building. The lift wasn't exactly large either, and I wondered what it would be like in the morning when a crowd of people were trying to cram in. At least it was air conditioned.

We came out of the lift and went straight into the lobby of the school. Despite the company's logo being blue and white, the main colours in the reception were green and teal. Fei Ling took me into the room on the right, the teachers' room. Actually it was a back room where teachers shared the tiny space with admin, sales and a storage corner. I was introduced to Audrey, the business manager of the school. She was Chinese and seemed physically different to all the other local women present. She seemed taller and more muscular, whereas the others seemed petite and as delicate as porcelain. She certainly wore the boss hat well.

Theo introduced me to some of the local staff. There was a large group of sales agents, but the really important ones were the PA's, all women, all with excellent English, and all wearing dark blue uniforms emblazoned with the EF logo. Really, "TA" would have been a better acronym, as they were essentially teaching assistants, but their job was to liaise with the students and parents, passing feedback between the two and making sure everyone was happy. He also introduced me to Yogi, the head of all the PA's. Like Audrey, she wasn't just fluent in English, but also physically different to the other staff – taller and more imposing than the average petite Chinese woman at the school.

Then he explained the courses. He had told me some of it on the phone, but I hadn't really listened. I was more concerned about getting the job than what to expect when I got there. Students were split into four age groups: Small Stars aged 3-6, High Flyers aged 6-11, Trailblazers aged 11-16 and Real English aged 16+. Each one was split into sub levels based on ability (except Small Stars which was strictly age). Each sublevel had its own course book with a set curriculum to follow and a set time to be completed.

Along with normal lessons were Life Clubs, a free form lesson designed to encourage students to produce what they knew. Themes could be anything and the main idea was to have fun outside the more formal class. He also mentioned something called *The Marco Polo Project*, which was a series of videos made with a couple of EF teachers designed to give teachers more materials for the clubs.

He took me on a tour. The big room behind reception was the Life Club Zone, a special room in every EF school specifically designed for more fun activities than the standard, run of the mill lesson. The Zone was a larger room with no furniture, so that teachers were encouraged to keep the sessions active. There were blue boxes on one wall, labelled A to Z and with sliding doors, the idea being to reveal new language in whatever fun way the teacher could think of.

Then there was the whiteboard above the stage. Actually this was the whizzy part. It was an IWB (interactive whiteboard), with a projector fixed on the ceiling and a PC at a desk in the corner. The projector showed whatever was on the PC, and with the help of super-duper special technology, the desktop could be controlled via the board, either with a stylus or a non-greasy finger.

The stage had two panels in front of the IWB. We lifted them off to reveal what looked like the two largest Playstation controllers in the world. They consisted of arrows and buttons and were there to play games created just for EF. Essentially, they were dance pads, and I assumed they were primarily for kids. I could see a lot of technical carnage if teens and adults were allowed to stamp on them. It looked pretty cool though. EF was clearly a company that spent whatever it needed to stand out.

Outside the Life Club Zone was the reception area. Apart from the reception desk there were a couple of sofas and, set into the wall above, was a flat screen TV. It was showing a cartoon that looked like something from the 1940's, like old *Tom and Jerry*, but with text and voice explanations of what was going on. This was obviously an educational tool, but later in the year I would find out just how bad it was for us to use.

There were a couple of small rooms that were designed for one-on-one lessons, classrooms in the green and teal with tiny plastic tables and chairs for the really young students, and a bunch of other rooms, mostly painted in orange, for the rest. There were no desks, just American style chairs with tiny little boards attached to an arm. I could see the point of these chairs in this school – the classrooms were pretty small so space was at a premium – but I've never understood them in a normal one. What's wrong with an actual desk? I can only assume class sizes in America make the problems in the UK seem petty and not worth bothering with.

For the first week and most of the second I was just to be observing lessons, and I started with Theo's Small Stars Blue class (3 year olds). It was a little shocking to see such young mites sat in a class being formally taught a subject for reasons they probably couldn't understand. It's not that it's wrong, it's just that you don't see it back home, which is probably why countries like China are rapidly taking over the world.

He was pretty good. The kids were engaged and they seemed to have a lot of fun, although a couple did randomly start crying and have to leave. He was using the Life Club Zone and it probably didn't help that the parents and grandparents were standing right outside the glass partition, looking in intently. Having an audience was not something I had expected.

After the lesson I felt my stomach rumble, so I headed to the toilet and, much to my horror, both cubicles had been fitted out with the dreaded squatters that I had begun to fear already. This was not good. I had assumed that, being a company employing a significant number of Westerners, they would have chosen a location fitted with familiar facilities. What was I going to do? I had an idea. I headed to the nearest Western outlet, Starbucks, and gloriously, the toilet was there, just inside the entrance and before the counter, so I could sneak in for a quick drop and sneak back out without having to buy anything. Heaven.

That was it. I left soon after, taking a short tour of the city centre to see if I could get my bearings. I managed to find my way to the main road the bus had come up, and I headed back to the flat. On the way I popped into the Cbest supermarket under the building. For the most part it was no different from anything back home. It had its home and clothes cleaning section, rows and rows of Coke Cola, Pepsi and other soft drinks, shelves stacked with big tubs of instant noodles, confectionary, pick n mix, chilled counters for meat and fish and a fruit and veg section.

Two things were very different. One was a section of large open boxes containing condiments such as salt, sugar and MSG (monosodium glutamate) that the customers scooped into plastic bags to be weighed. The other was the section of large fish tanks containing live fish and crabs, just waiting to be picked and slaughtered. What was lacking was bread. There was some, but not a lot and not much I was used to.

Thursday and Friday were pretty much the same. I was able to sleep funny hours to get my body clock in sync so I could go to school late to observe the one lesson I had scheduled. On the Saturday I watched David's HF00 class, a boisterous group of boys who didn't seem to want to be there. He was quite softly spoken and young, only just over a year out of university, and I wondered if it was his youth, inexperience or his personality that held him back from stamping his authority. I just hoped that I could put my foot down when it was needed.

At the end of the lesson he picked up a pile of what looked like brightly coloured school exercise books, making marks in each one and handing them to the kids as they left. These were the report books. In each there was a section for each lesson, with a graded row of emoticons – from big smile to big frown – to show how the student had behaved. The space below was for any special notes about their behaviour or progress – good and bad.

Then I sat in on a *Marco Polo* demo Theo gave. This was a sales pitch for prospective students and parents and I got to see a video for the first time. It featured two EF teachers; Coco, a Frenchman, and Christina, a Chinese

American woman. Each video had a different theme (food, clothes, sport etc) and each one was set in a different city around the world. They would talk about the subject for a while, act out some sort of scenario and that would be the first part. The second part would depend on the level of the students; there were three videos that would be played where Coco and Christina asked various questions. Then the third part wrapped everything up. There were some standard lesson plans, but the main idea was to give teachers an extra resource to play with any way they could think of.

Lunch was taken in the local branch of Starbucks. I'm a coffee whore, so it was good to know that I could get a decent one in the city. I'm not saying it's the best in the world, but it'll do for the most part. Sadly the food offerings here weren't up scratch. There were muffins and pastries but only two paninis; tuna mayonnaise and ham and cheese. The latter was my only option, as it would be for the whole year.

When I got back to the school, Maria came up to me with one of the PA's, slightly giggling and looking shy. Maria said the PA, Jennifer, wanted to ask me something, but when her big moment came, she lost her bottle and started giggling in that manner that is such a horrid stereotype of Chinese women. She whispered into Maria's ear, who passed the message on.

"Jennifer wants to know how tall you are." Maria said, sounding like she was trying to hide a hint of sarcasm.

"Six foot two." I said, without thinking. The blank looks on both their faces made me do a quick calculation. "One hundred and eighty-eight centimetres."

Jennifer looked shocked and said "Oh, so tall!" It was an odd thing to say with such a surprised tone, considering she was standing right in front of me and could see whether or not I was tall, short or unremarkable.

In the afternoon I observed Maria giving an adult lesson to 2 teenagers. The class should have had about 10, but the majority seemed to have been far too busy to show up. During the break she explained that she was having to change the plan on the fly as it had been set up for a full class. It was pretty normal though. Apparently adult classes often had attendance problems.

Then there was Theo's TB class. Here, the school seemed like a state school, and Theo a traditional teacher. He was strict with them, even sending one student out to complete his homework. He was also strict with manners and etiquette, especially when students decided to talk to each other or started slouching or were just generally uncooperative. I wasn't looking forward to TB's after this.

After sitting in on a one-to-one lesson with Theo (and taking over for a bit) I sat in on Maria's RE Life Club. It was about superheroes, and she tried a simple elicitation task by getting the students to ask 20 questions, but they didn't get it and they seemed more confused than educated. She stuck some pictures of famous heroes on the wall and, after getting the students to do some tasks based on what they saw, asked me to explain each one's back story and their super powers. It had been my first actual full day of work since arriving, and had actually involved me doing some teaching.

The next day, the first task was to observe another Theo TB class, this one about geography, although the subject eventually changed to me as they were encouraged to get to know me. At least these guys were well behaved and engaged and made me prejudge their level a little more positively than before.

Then I had a long lunch. I needed a few more groceries and some stationary, and Theo recommended shops for both. I quickly forgot the directions and got lost though, so I ended up back in Starbucks where I tried and failed to use some Chinese for the first time. While enjoying my latte I found myself being the centre of entertainment as a baby, maybe 6-9 months old, found my mere presence so wonderful that he couldn't stop laughing hysterically.

That afternoon I observed Karen give an RE lesson where she did something that I thought was a major no-no. One of the central tenets of TEFL is that one teaches without using the local language, as this would encourage translation rather than genuine understanding. Using the local language in class is a big controversy, but most teachers tend to stick to English 100% of the time, almost always because they can't speak the local lingo. Karen was Chinese though, and she spoke to the students in Chinese more than once. Personally, I'm on the strict side: use the subject language the whole time and communicate through gestures and pictures. That's how children learn, and that is the whole point of the communicative approach. Then there was Maria's HF class to watch and that was it. My first working week in China was over, and I had barely lifted a finger.

1. New York New York. 2. The Monument. 3. The rapidly growing Xinhua International Building. 4. World Trade Centre on the left. 5. Metro Mall. 6-7. Corners of Monument Square. 8. Food Street.

6 第六章

I had survived my initial few days in China, and so far there were no regrets. It's not that Chongqing looked like an easy city to live in, but it didn't seem unworkable either. My first Monday morning started in the usual way; car horns beeping outside and that incessant loudspeaker blasting out encouragement (or threats) to the workers on the high rise construction site across the street. It was time for my first day out in the city.

Fei Ling met me at my flat and we hopped in a taxi, heading for my first official appointment. It was a requirement for me to have a physical and, when we arrived at the medical centre, there was already a crowd waiting their turn. I gave a blood sample, a urine sample and had an ENT, an ECG and an X-Ray. Outside one room I noticed a sign with a crude picture of a hand, the fingers curled into a fist except for one sticking out with the tip covered in lines. I was not looking forward to that one; not because I was against a rectal exam, but because I already had a handle to the concept of hygiene there, and having one of those fingers up me – gloves or no gloves - was not appealing. As it turned out, it was the room for blood pressure. The eye test was interesting too. Instead of letters decreasing in size, there were blocks of three parallel lines either vertical or horizontal and I had to indicate which way.

Back at the apartments, Dave and I hooked up with Theo and Maria and we headed on the local bus going away from the school, ending up at what looked like a palace, sat on a mound as if to dominate the local skyline, despite being overshadowed by all the high rises. This was Chongqing City Hall, and opposite the expansive square was a noticeably modern building called the Three Gorges Museum, dedicated to China's impressive construction not too far away. We headed round the corner and met up with Karen in a local restaurant to grab some amazing tasting dumplings for lunch. Any apprehensions I had about the local cuisine were gradually fading.

Then we hopped on a bus and began what turned out to be a long trek, most of it standing up and feeling very squashed. Despite the lack of health and safety, I was beginning to like the buses. The main plus point about them was the cost. Each journey was a whopping 2 yuan, about 20p. 20p to get from one end of a city of 7 million people to the other. In the UK, 20p probably won't get you to the next stop, and there is the idiotic obsession of paying an exact fare for an exact journey.

This is especially dumb when you consider rush hour and a long queue of people, all waiting to tell the driver the exact place they want to go, and then the driver having to calculate the cost, not to mention people buying weekly and monthly tickets. No wonder buses in the UK are always late. True, day tickets exist, but they are very much the exception. Everywhere else I've been in the world uses the same principle; you pay a single, fixed fare and that takes you as far as you need to go. It makes it cheaper for people to go longer distances, thereby reducing the excuses for driving, and it speeds everything up; you get on the bus, pay your fare and then the bus goes. No hanging around, no fuss, the only delays due to heavy traffic.

As the bus passed through various avenues, different landmarks were pointed out to me, including the uninspiring but large convention centre. By then we had crossed the mighty Yangtze River and I had lost all sense of where I was in relation to home and work. We were soon joined by what seemed like more passengers than the bus could safely hold, but I was already resigned to the fact this would be happening on a regular basis throughout my stay. It's no reason to look down on Chinese attitudes though.

Currently, they are in a state of economic and social change very similar to Europe and North America in the 19th century. The annals of industrial history for that time are littered with cases of idiocy and inhumanity that make our enlightened eyes weep with despair, but without those attitudes we may not have the same lifestyles we have today. China is just going through those growing pains, and with each catastrophe and mass loss of life they will change, just like we did. But until then, there will still be public buses jam-packed with more people than is sensible.

There was another big difference between Chinese and British buses – the TV screens. It seemed that nowhere was sacred enough to avoid loud, annoying adverts. In Britain, the insides of buses are often emblazoned with small posters, but they are generally unobtrusive and avoidable. Not so in China. The TV screens were small, but they were located so that no-one could miss out on all the delightful commercial offers: the services of a local private hospital, the refreshing taste of JDB (Jiaduobao, tea in a bright red can), the latest martial arts historical epic from the native cinema, a new holiday resort on the coast, the latest offers from Cbest or the latest technology from Lenovo or Midea.

It took an hour, but we finally arrived at our destination, Foreign Street. I had been under a certain misunderstanding. When I had been told we were going to Foreign Street I had assumed it was like a Bar Street or some zone where expats could get the things they liked from home. This was something else altogether; it was a theme park.

My first impression wasn't exactly favourable. The landscape of its setting could have done with a bit more landscaping, and tarmacking for that matter. The path from the bus stop into the park was just dirt and a small lake/large pond at the bottom of a slope looked in serious need of de-silting. There was a scale model of the more famous part of the Great Wall of China and, sat in a little alcove, was a small Buddhist shrine, resplendent in a golden cloak and little swastika on its chest.

The further we got in, the more confused I became. It actually turned into a pretty decent theme park; the rides weren't exactly spectacular but they weren't tame either. There was a tall vertical drop, a large music stage, a track that looked like part of a rollercoaster, some swinging rides, a canal boat ride, dodgems, a couple of long and scary-looking death slides and a ton of prize games in little marquees.

The highlight had to be the actual Foreign Street, which I think was designed to show the locals how some people lived in the West. It was both impressive and hilarious. Some of these buildings had been built on a small canal network, where boats could be hired out for a short ride. There was also a model of the "New York skyline", which looked more like a very bad copy of the New York New York Hotel in Las Vegas. None of us felt any compulsion to go on the rides, or try any of the games; it just wasn't our scene. Despite being a family-friendly place there was still space for politics, with a large billboard displaying a message over the Stars and Stripes. Its translation almost made sense:

"There are more than 200 million people who occupy half of the world's resources in United States. Of course it's not the God's truth. In this state, it's not just worthy to be proud of and shown, but it's a kind of immoral behaviour".

TAKE THAT AMERICA!

After having our fill of a Chinese amusement park, we decided to make our way back. Maria suggested going for a pizza so she, David and I grabbed a taxi and we wended our way through the streets once again, my bearings in a total mess. We were dropped off in another commercial district and headed into a huge, new mall where, in the lowest basement floor, we ended up in a branch of Papa Johns. I had only had pizza from one of those places once and, to be honest, I wasn't exactly dazzled by them. It was still decent enough though, and it meant there was another option available to me in case I got sick of the local stuff after a while. Then it was back home, another day done and dusted.

The next day began with more officialdom. Fei Ling met Dave and I at our flat and we took a walk towards the centre, turning off the main road and walking up a steep set of steps, cutting through a crowded housing estate and ending up on a main road, with more uphill walking ahead.

We eventually ended up near a large brick gate, one of the last remnants of the old city walls. Nearby was the police station, where David and I had to go through some sort of bureaucratic registration process. We had to wait what seemed like an unnecessarily long time, and it was pretty cold in the building, but I was already prepared for this sort of nonsense, and David was a veteran, so we just sat it out, filled out our forms and eventually escaped without too much hassle.

After popping back home I took my very first proper excursion around the city, trying to get my bearings in the centre near my apartment block. From

Huayi Lu I walked across Yihao Qiao (Number 1 Bridge), a short crossing over a shallow gorge that exposed the solid rock of the plateau the city was built on. The road, the same that had taken me to the school, was winding and steep and it passed a number of small manufacturing shops, an unthinkably large Internet café, some grubby looking restaurants with live ducks and chickens tied down outside, some food stalls selling stinky dofu and other revolting looking and smelling delights (e.g. ducks faces), some market stalls selling old books and a lot of other crap, and what must have been a broken sewer, judging by the smell of human shit.

The traffic was crazy in places, like every stereotype of a large, Asian city. On the main roads it was jam packed on the tarmac, mostly with old, locally built and filthy buses and cars. There were some newer, Western models, but only for the lucky few. Yellow taxis flew through the streets, and there were also little three-wheelers, like tuk-tuks but covered and less romantic-looking. They looked pretty flimsy too.

Controlling the traffic at key points were specialized traffic police. There are three important facts about them. They wore uniforms that looked more suited to horse riding (including hat and tunic), they used rigid, sharp, rapid and robotic hand gestures to direct vehicles, and they were all very beautiful, young women.

It's not like I'd never been around vaulted skylines before. I'm an avid traveller and by then I had visited New York, Shanghai, Chicago, Nanjing, Frankfurt and Hong Kong, so I was pretty much used to being in an environment where the buildings shot up like Saturn 5s and much of the street life was cast in shadow. The difference was that I had only ever been in those places for a few days at a time and, despite my appreciation for skyscrapers, I had never really been tested. Now this sort of place was going to be my home, and I had to get used to it pretty quickly.

For the first time, I could take in Monument Square without worrying about having to get back to the school. Considering the construction it had been subjected to it had a pretty open feel to it. The buildings on the corners of the intersections were relatively low, with the tallest being a 10-storey-ish shopping mall. Opposite that was a large department store with three residential towers on top, and opposite that was the block with New York New York. Coming round almost full circle was what passed for the signs at Piccadilly Circus.

Here was a Chinese fast food outlet called CSC and the life-saving branch of Starbucks (and its toilet), on the first floor and with a long window giving perfect views of the masses below. At the other end of this block, a mighty construction was well under way. It was just a concrete shell, covered in netting and looking like it had a few more floors to go. It was pretty big – well over 200 metres and probably closer to 300, but I had the feeling I would get to see it finished before I left. Things get done quickly in this part of the world.

Other neighbouring streets were not so lucky, with skyscrapers rammed at the edges casting shadows over the narrow pedestrian paths – or at least they would have if there had been any kind of sun light poking through the pollution. It was insane. I had been there a week and there had been no sight of the big yellow disk in space, nor any of the stars visible at night. I knew Chinese cities could be heavily polluted but what I was experiencing was way beyond my imagination.

There was something in the centre that I had never seen before – or should I say, someone, or some people – something that seemed to connect this city to its traditional past; the bang-bang men. 'Bang' (depending on the vowel inflection and symbol), means 'stick', in this case a long, thick, bamboo stick. Despite the rapid modernization the city had seen in recent years, it still relied heavily on these amazing men, work horses in the extreme. For most of the day, they just hang around the streets, either alone or with other bang-bang, almost always smoking, waiting and ready to pounce.

They are delivery men, in the traditional sense. If someone comes off a bus with a heavy load of shopping they are there, ready to offer their insane strength to carry whatever load is in front of them. They tie the loads to looped ropes attached to each end of their sticks, and then transport the loads on their shoulders, wherever necessary.

These men are not huge meat heads; they are usually of average height and build for China, but they are like worker ants when they tie up boxes and bags to their sticks. It's not just people's shopping. I saw one bang-bang carrying four boxes loaded with bottles of beer. Another carried a bunch of sacks of vegetables. Another had boxes of electrical appliances on his stick. Just carry one full box of beer, or one sack of potatoes, then imagine four, five or six. It's incredible. I saw an article in *China Daily* about their plight and it had a picture of a scrawny looking man with a fridge-freezer on his back.

'Plight' is an apt term. For all their efforts, all their superhuman feats of strength, they earn, on a good day, maybe £10. These men are rural peasants who have moved into the city to earn some money to send home. They live in normal apartments, but ones that have been converted to house perhaps 20 of them. And it's hard. I don't just mean the heavy lifting though; when they see a bus pass, and it's clear someone has a lot to carry, they are on it like a shot, banging on the doors and shouting to make sure they get their hands on the goods and the Yuan. If they see a removal truck outside an apartment block, they just hang around, waiting to be called on to lug the items up the tens of floors. It's a hard life for them, but Chongqing could not function without them. One wonders how long they will last in the new China, and whether it would be a loss to see them go.

After checking out the central streets and another shopping mall, I headed back the way I came and further along the road I had taken from my apartment. I ended up on an open platform, looking out across the Jialing River. There was another Starbucks, a Subway and a statue of houses piled on top of each other like something out of the mind of Tim Burton. The oversized model of a pirate ship hanging over the edge topped off the weirdness. I looked over and realized I was standing on top of a stepped building that headed down the side of the shear face of the plateau, all the way to a main road that headed into a tunnel. The river flowed by below, heading towards its conjunction with the Yangtze. What was most shocking was what I saw across the river.

In fact, it was more what I didn't see. I knew I had been on that side when the taxi had taken us from the airport, so I knew that over there, very close, was a forest of skyscrapers. What I saw was beyond belief. I saw next to nothing. I could just about see the riverbank and a couple of vague shapes – one that looked like a boat on the land. Other than that, the part of the city I had driven through just a few days before, home to maybe a million or so people, was completely shrouded by the poisonous smog that engulfed the city.

It wasn't like the river was that wide either; not much wider than the Thames at Westminster. Imagine standing at the London Eye and barely being able to see the clock face of St Stephen's Tower (referred to as Big Ben by idiots). That's how bad the pollution was.

The building I was standing on was called Hongyadong, a new "traditional" building that had been built onto the old Hongya Cave dwellings where people had once lived in houses built onto the cliff face.

I carried on along the main road, passing the oh-so essential Carrefour and finding a local temple. My plan had been to head to the tip of the Yuzhong peninsula, Chaotianmen, where the Yangtze and the Jialing met. I was told there was a clear line of delineation due to one having more silt than the other. However, as would happen for a good few months, I got my bearings all wrong.

I headed down a series of steps and ended up on the river side and, without the map I had been given, made a decision and turned right. It turned out I was walking along the Yangtze in the opposite direction and this side wasn't exactly the most awe-inspiring site I'd ever seen. I did see, through the smog, a twin towered skyscraper that was coloured in the gaudiest gold it was possible to get away with. Even in the thick atmosphere it stood out.

I eventually gave up, crossed the road and tried to find my way back. I wasn't worried about getting lost, after all I had nowhere I needed to be and plenty of time to escape. A few streets and steps later and I was looking up at an archway with the English name "Nanjimen Medicine City" emblazoned across it. I assumed it was a small district that specialized in traditional Chinese remedies, but it was hard for me to tell. It seemed a lot of shops supplied at least some sort of herbal medicine, and this street didn't look like it had anything special.

Somehow, maybe through a latent attuned sense to magnetic fields, telepathy or just blindly walking in a vaguely reasonable direction, I saw a couple of buildings that looked familiar. I was back in the city centre, on a place called Food Street. I wouldn't say it was anything special from a culinary perspective. There were plenty of stalls selling all kinds of snacking delights on sticks – some appealing and some revolting. There were some restaurants too and, not to be left out, a MacDonald's.

It was the statues that were the highlights – bronzed vignettes displaying quirky street scenes such as the laughing fat man eating hotpot and the group of young women striding along listening to music. A crowd of people were standing in one place and voices were raised, and as I got closer, I saw a couple of girls wiping tears from their eyes. When I checked out the scene I saw an old man, remonstrating about something with even more tears flowing. In his arms was a dog, its head lolled and its tongue hanging out with a wound in its body. I left the sad scene, hoping there was some compassion in the local people.

I was back that evening, and what had been a dull, overbearing graveyard of monolithic construction had been transformed into a dazzling cacophony of neon and LEDs. The pollution still obscured the sky, but the lack of stars didn't detract from the illuminations at ground level. Strips of light ran up the sides of the tallest buildings, and the adverts glowed as they vied for the attention of the masses on the ground.

Everywhere, Chinese script dazzled my eyes, whether static or flashing, and I was reminded of one thing as I walked through the streets: *Bladerunner*. Everything about this city reminded me of Ridley Scott's classic (the director's cut, not the one with the stupid ending). The polluted atmosphere, the lack of sun, the over-bearing buildings enclosing the streets, the Chinese writing, the sharp illuminations at night. It was as if science fiction was coming true, once again.

1-2. Foreign Street. 3. Bang-Bang man. 4. Hongyadong sculpture. 5. Smog-shrouded view across the Jialing. 6. Hongyadong from the street. 7. Nanjimen Medicine City. 8. Statue on Food Street. 9-10. The neon lights of JieFangBei.

7 第七章

My second week started with a bit more work. Theo gave me an induction sheet with a list of questions about the school and teaching in general that I had to research in books and by asking the local staff. It was all very officious, and I should admit to a certain amount of naiveté.

When I had decided to become an English teacher I had thought it would be a glorious life of seeing the world and earning easy money without the stresses and petty pressures of the corporate environment. After the CELTA course I knew it was actually a lot of work to do it properly, but after a week at EF I knew it was far more corporate than I had accounted for.

It was a slow day, but at least I had a timetable and I could start planning for some lessons during the week, even though there was only one and it wasn't until the weekend. I was also shown TeacherPages, EF's online admin application where we could keep course progress up to date and make notes about students. More processes to follow, just like at Ford. There were a couple more lessons to observe and then it was back home, but by then I was feeling a bit off colour.

The next day I didn't feel good at all. It wasn't like I was puking my guts up or in intense physical pain, but I was feeling very lethargic and had a raging headache. Guiltily, I called in sick and tried to rest it out on the sofa. It wasn't like I had any lessons to teach though, so I spent the day watching some of the Winter Olympics on CCTV (Chinese Central Television) and, after a few coffees and a pot of noodles, I headed downstairs to the Internet café.

In Britain (and I expect most other countries in the developed world), Internet cafés tend to be a café with a few PCs and a printer/scanner/copier. Here, the cafes are vast rooms, sometimes with a hundred terminals and no barista in sight. These are places where the youngsters spend what little free time they have playing online MMORPG's on proper broadband connections with screens that would cost up to a year's wages for their parents. All I wanted to do was send a few emails.

Back in the flat I signed up for a very expensive online Mandarin course. Dave recommended it, so I thought I'd give it a go, but from the outset the language didn't seem to be set out logically. I tried not to be too negative though. I was keen to learn, and I also had m *Teach Yourself Mandarin Chinese* course on hand.

The next day I was still feeling the same; not exactly ill, but very run down. Theo sent the ever-diligent Fei Ling to take me to a local hospital where, after waiting in a not so clean corridor, I was seen by a young doctor who recommended a combination of pharmaceuticals, traditional Chinese herbal medicine and more sleep.

I didn't understand the prescription. If traditional Chinese medicine is so good, and its veracity so rock solid that trained medical doctors are willing to prescribe it, then why not prescribe only that and stick two fingers up to 'Big Pharma'? Personally, I think the problem was a combination of latent jet lag and my body adjusting to the hideous environment, with its thick pollution and germ-ridden poor hygiene.

Later that day a guy came round and installed our Internet connection. I then downloaded a proxy application to get round the "Great Firewall of China" and I was fully online, free from the hideous, dictatorial restrictions on my free speech.

I also watched a few episodes of a freakish cartoon about talking goats and dogs. It looked like a cruder version of the cartoons I watched as a kid, like *Dogtanian and the Three Muskahounds* or *The Mysterious Cities of Gold*, and it had quite an anarchic feel to it. One episode had one of the sheep seeing something weird and looking at the bottle he was drinking from i.e. the sheep was drunk!

The show is called *Pleasant Goat and Big Big Wolf*, and is the most popular TV show for kids in the country. It's set in the 31st century, where goats and wolves live in a human-less, rural utopia. The premise of each episode is pretty much the same: the wolves want to eat the goats and the goats take great pleasure in evading them.

The show is huge in China. The merchandising is everywhere and on many occasions in the year I heard kids in the school humming the annoyingly catchy theme tune. As of writing, Wikipedia states that there are 1,222 episodes and four successful feature films and yet, no-one has thought of exporting this proven successful franchise to the West. Shame on you media buyers!

The next day I made it in. Theo had made arrangements for Sandra to take my RE7 lesson the following day, as he wasn't confident I would be able to plan it in time. I probably could have, but I guessed he was being extra cautious with my introduction. I observed his SS class and helped him prepare some materials. For lunch, we all treated ourselves to a Subway from the branch at Hongyadong, next to Starbucks, but weirdly it wasn't very tasty.

I had a lot more time, so got myself a latte from Coffee, a coffee shop across the road from New York New York which made a decent cuppa. I sat outside, listening to the *Teach Yourself* audio and trying hard to burn the language into my brain. It was hard, and not helped by the distraction of a controlled explosion from one of the nearby construction sites that shook the ground, but I was slowly getting there.

When I headed back to the school I saw something quite shocking. On the ground floor of New York New York was a wedding dress shop, ready to make the dreams of millions of young Chinese women come true. I could only assume that their dreams were full of gaudy colours and garish patterns, because the dresses were horrendous. I'm no fashion expert, but even I could tell just how bad they were.

Bright pink gowns, purple and green flowing trains and flowers stuck on from veil to hem. Imagine the more infamous celebrity weddings, such as Posh and Becks or whichever of Jordan's is relevant. Now multiply the sickness. That's what this shop was. As the months passed though, I realized it was perfect for the style sensibilities of the women in Chongqing. Ugly for the West, but beautiful for the East.

The rest of the day was more observations; 3 OPT's (assessments of new students to put them in the correct level), Maria's TB3B class (where one student, Tim, revealed himself to be a thief and a womanizer) and Karen's HF1A, where I had to sit back and not help her while she had to deal with one of the biggest brats I've ever encountered. At home that evening I was finally able to get on MSN and talk to Miisa on camera. We had been keeping in pretty much constant contact, and I genuinely missed her, and was as happy I could talk to her as much as any of my friends and family back home.

On the Sunday, Sandra took what would have been my first class, RE7, which I observed in preparation for my long awaited turn. Lunch turned out to be a delight as I found that Coffee made a good bacon and egg sandwich on a crusty roll, but sadly they hadn't thought to import any brown sauce, the only liquid condiment that should ever go near bacon. Then I observed another rowdy kids lesson, this time Maria's HF1A. So far the kids seemed to be a bit difficult to handle, but there was no use fretting over it. Either I could deal with them or I couldn't. I would soon find out.

Another weekend had arrived and another day out was on the timetable. Dave and I walked up the main road towards the city centre, my leg muscles slowly acclimatizing to the hilly topography. I had lived for a year in Sheffield, and that city was pretty hilly too. It caused problems with my knees at the time, thanks to my pampered upbringing in the dead flat city of Portsmouth, so I knew the pitfalls of living in such an undulating environment.

We entered QiQi Hotpot, one of a small chain of hotpot restaurants that are considered the best in the city. Every part of China has its own version of this meal, but Chongqing's is widely regarded as the daddy of them all. It's a simple principle; there's a gas hob in the middle of the table, you pick the items you want from a tick list, they bring out a large bowl filled with a broth of water, various herbs, spices, vegetables, oil and tons of chillies, it gets heated on the hob and then your choices are brought out for you to cook as you like them.

Julie and Rory were already there, and in a few quick minutes our table was resplendent with meat and vegetable dumplings, plates of thin slices of beef and lamb, quails eggs, shrimp balls, slices and chunks of dofu, crab sticks, rice, noodles and even more things that were impossible to identify, but essential to try. It felt like a royal feast, grabbing a sample of every item, dropping it into the boiling broth then hunting around the bowl with chopsticks to find the damned thing before pulling it out and tasting its spicy, numbing delightfulness.

In fact, Chongqing hotpot is known as "ma la", which means "numb and spicy".

Once we were full of stingingly hot food and cheap, Chongqing 1958 lager, we hopped into taxis to make our way to our day out. We were swept along the length of the Jialing River, the towers of the adolescent metropolis following us like watchful spies. The tracks of the metro monorail system stood above us too, as we crossed inland and wended our way through more residential and commercial zones until we arrived at an outpost of low rise tradition, relatively free from the pollution of traffic and people.

Chongqing is a city that has rapidly and unashamedly ripped up its historical heart, but it's had the good sense to keep something of the old in place. CiQiKou could be described as "Chongqing Old Town". It dates from as early as the 10th century, and was once a separate port and market town until being absorbed by its larger neighbour. Now it's subject to extensive and rigorous preservation; even the ever ambitious local officials who want to ingratiate themselves with Beijing by building and building have had the good sense to maintain a sense of the old world.

We walked through the main entrance and into a narrow and crowded street. The smell of stinky dofu was already hitting our senses as we negotiated our way through the crowds, taking in every shop we saw on both sides. A popular theme was Maoist memorabilia; how ironic that people were making money from selling trinkets glorifying the anti-capitalist ideology that allegedly shaped their lives. I bought myself a copy of the iconic "Little Red Book", and there were other books too, written by and about other notable figures from that era, and eclectic collections of posters and postcards depicting people in heroic poses, urging the citizens to strive to do more for their country, to sacrifice themselves for the greater good.

Other shops weren't so patriotic. There were jewellery shops, a couple of shops that specialized in old-timey books - which included bizarre photo story books from the seventies where the heroes were all bushy-haired white guys - and musical shops that specialized in traditional instruments. One was a wind instrument called a hulusi; it's like a recorder but the mouthpiece looks like a pear, and there's a stop at the end of the pipe that can be removed to change the sound.

The main avenue was more of the same, with the trinket shops joined by vendors selling clothes, fireworks, cheap toys and even panda merchandise. Stinky dofu was still hanging in the air, and it was making me wretch. I hate that smell; it's the worst food smell in the world and I curse the soul of whomever it was who invented it. This was clearly meant to be a mecca for traditional crafts and it didn't disappoint. One shop was particularly popular with spectators, all crowded round to watch the man make their precious noodles with a strainer and his bare hands.

At the end of the main avenue were steps that led down to a plaza, dotted with food stalls and covered seating. At the end was the Jialing River and what looked like a sandbank littered with rubble. This, apparently, was the beach, and people were using it as such, but I didn't see anyone going in for a dip. Clearly the water and the air had a symbiotic relationship. At the top of the steps was a hostel, and we stopped in for a good coffee and a bite to eat, before heading back out to catch the bus home. On the way I bought a cheap hulusi, with every intention of teaching myself how to play.

That night a few of us headed into JieFangBei. In one of the smaller streets, lined with clothes shops and food stalls, we headed up a few steps and into an Indian restaurant. It felt great knowing that I could get a good curry here, and the staff were Indian too, so I was expecting something splendid. The menu didn't have many familiar dishes, but it's normal for Indian restaurants to adapt their meals for local tastes, so I played it safe and ordered the beef vindaloo. Shockingly, this vindaloo didn't destroy my taste buds or make me sweat pints out. In fact, the most prominent ingredient seemed to be cheese, and not even good cheese.

After the meal, I broke away from the group and headed for another night time walk around the city. It looked incredible, with all the buildings lit up and glowing under the canopy of a sky choked with poison and dust. The light seemed to reflect off the thick cloud, giving it a shimmering glow of its own. There was not a single star visible, but there was still a strange, misty beauty to it.

I headed back up, wending my way back through the streets in the centre, still feeling like I hadn't seen enough. I walked along a smaller road around Monument Square, lined on one side with the modernity of the new China, and on the other with the crumbling facades of the old. There was a side street where every market stall sold fresh flowers, with fallen petals strewn across the street and the smell of a garden centre thick in the air. I passed the Marriot Hotel and soon realized I was in the party hub of the city.

On the first corner was the Cotton Club. It was the only night venue I had read about, and it was the popular haunt for local expats. The entrance to the building was covered in glowing, neon signs, and one intrigued me more than the others – Haoledi KTV. What TV channel was that? What did they show? I carried on, and found myself back on one of the roads that went straight back to the square. Now I could tell I was in the party hub. The nightclubs were congregated on one corner, and they looked as glitzy and as gaudy as it was possible to be. There were signs like Babyface, Soho and Bar 88, all flashing and dancing to get the young, upwardly mobile punters in.

For no particular reason, I chose Bar 88. This wasn't like a British nightclub. It was more like a bar. There was no dance floor, the bar was in the centre, and all around it was pretty much standing room only, with everyone crowding round high tables. On each one there was a bottle of some sort of spirit and a jug of something else, something mysterious. I got a bottle of Heineken and was shocked that it cost pretty much the same as it would back home. The music was loud and the crowd was rowdy, but it was all good natured.

  A few locals approached me with their glasses to raise a friendly toast, and then headed straight back to their precious tables. It was a nice little courtesy, and it made me smile. One group who toasted me then invited me to join them. I'd had a couple of beers by then (on top of the ones with dinner), and the drinks they offered me meant that, sadly, I have no idea who they were or what they looked like. What I do know, is that the mysterious liquid in the jugs was cold, Chinese tea, used as a mixer with the spirits. It actually made Jack Daniels drinkable, but didn't really lessen the effects.

  I managed to find my own way home in the early hours, sadly without being able to devour a kebab. I walked down the back road, past the flower market, a few late food kiosks, a couple of DVD shops, and a couple of sex shops. One was just a big kiosk, staffed by a young woman with her kid in the back watching TV. Another was more like a real shop, though it was just a corridor with a counter at the back. I had a little peak in, and the woman came to help. I tried to tell her I was "just looking", but she seemed to get the wrong idea. Soon a guy appeared and asked, in basic English, if I was "looking for a girl". That phrase means the same thing everywhere in the world, so I decided to leave.

  I crossed the road through the underpass, taking in the open sewer and distinct smell of human faecal waste. There were small retail units there too, and people seemed to be sleeping in them. Annoyingly, I dropped my phone and the glass screen cracked. It wasn't a small crack, but it didn't totally fuck it up either. The last thing I wanted to do was buy a decent new phone on the low salary I was earning. I could tell I was going to have enough expenses with all the eating and partying the year was going to bring.

Oh, and as for the hulusi, well it didn't happen. It had a look online and couldn't find too many resources for learning it. There were a few videos on YouTube, but they weren't made by experienced teachers, and in the end I gave up. It spent most of the year in the drawer of my bedside cabinet, un-mastered.

1-8. CiQiKou Ancient Village. 9. The neon lights of the Cotton Club and Haoledi KTV. 10. Bar 88.

8 第八章

The next day Dave and I met up with Fei Ling again. I imagined she was getting sick of the sight of us, having to take us around the city for one bureaucratic procedure after another. This time she took us to the Foreign Experts Bureau. Everything about it shouted officialdom nonsense. It was located in a monolithic building that must have housed countless other equally useless government departments. We were interviewed by an official whose job it was to make sure we were actually qualified to do our jobs. Dave had no teaching qualification, and he was given a particular grilling, but it seemed to be a waste of time. There was no legal requirement to have a qualification after all. The official barely took any notice of me.

Then he pulled out a magazine I had seen in Starbucks and Subway. It was called *Chongqing Currents*, an English language magazine printed by the bureau we were sat in. He was keen for us to write articles for it, and we nodded with feigned enthusiasm, but it didn't appeal to us, not even to an aspiring writer like me. One thing I had noticed about it was that, in each edition, there was an article about how beautiful the women of Chongqing were, including photos of local women in the city who probably had no idea their faces were in print. There is an obsession in Chongqing about how beautiful the women are there; they claim to have the most beautiful women in China. For me, the jury was still out.

Across the road we headed to another, smaller office, where Fei Ling performed more of her bureaucratic heroics to sort out my new visa. In an hour or so I had filled out the new forms and they had eventually been checked. I didn't feel too great about leaving my passport with them, but I didn't have much choice in the matter either. At least it would get sent back to the school, and Fei Ling would be on the case if there were any problems. Soon I would have the sticker letting me stay in the country.

Back in the city centre I chilled out in Starbucks before doing some shopping, something I'm always loathe to undertake. I managed to find a thin jacket that would do me well for the spring, and a new satchel, so I didn't have to use my small rucksack everywhere. Neither was cheap – £30 each – and I probably could have found cheaper had I shopped around, but I hate shopping that much that I was ready to buy the first things I liked that did their jobs. Remember, £30 in China is more like £100-£200 in the UK, so I was really splashing out.

I popped into a big electrical department store for a bit of a browse, and made a beeline for the audio-visual section. Like HMV, it was crammed full of the usual Western offerings, but with plenty of Chinese films and albums too, and no "world cinema" or "world music" section.

There was another room, where the DVDs looked different. Instead of the standard cases, these were in envelopes with the normal covers printed on the front. It was odd, and I would see this in other big shops too, such as Sunning. I also saw these enveloped DVDs on sale in the little, grubby DVD shops in the city's backstreets. As it turned out, these were all pirated DVDs (not all Hollywood, they even pirated their own cinema). It was amazing enough that people ran seemingly legitimate businesses in the open selling them, but they were also on sale in major retailers.

That evening I had my first taste of expat night life. David and I headed back into the city, but instead of heading through the underpass to JieFangBei, we crossed over the road, to a modern building with traditional looking towers on each corner. I'm always in two minds about such decoration. A lot of people only want buildings to look old, which is idiotic. Likewise, some people never want restoration – if it goes then it's gone. This is also stupid: look at how Central European nations rebuilt their historic city centres after World War II, compared to what we did in Britain. But should traditional elements be used in modern design? Isn't that just Mock Tudor?

It was only a few storeys high, but was built on the cliff face of the plateau the city sat on, so there were more floors going down. We climbed the outer steps and found ourselves on Datang Plaza, which was basically the roof of the building, Kui Xing Lou. Here was a huge Internet café, and our destination, Ci Ci Park. It was as if it was trying to be a hippy/dive/drug bar. It served a locally brewed dark bottled beer, had chill out music and big, comfy sofas. It was pretty dark inside, and not very full, but it had a relaxing atmosphere and outdoor seating. There was another Westerner there, and it looked like he was rolling a joint. If not, then his fag was bigger than normal (that's not a sexual joke America!). Maria and Tanja joined us, and we played some of the little gambling games the bar had for a few hours, before we remembered we had work in the morning, and headed home.

On the Monday, during hotpot, Julie had told me that it had been decided that I was needed at the other school in JiangBei district more than New York New York. I had been near it in a taxi on one of my official trips with Fei Ling, but I had no real idea where it was or what to expect, other than that it was in a shopping mall. So on the Wednesday morning I got up earlier than normal, as I was due in at 10. I was ready at 9 and was out on the street, my right arm cocked and ready to hail a cab. Julie had texted me the street name, and all I had to do was read it correctly.

For a good 10 minutes there were no cabs heading down my street. I wasn't worried though; I had plenty of time to get there. A few more came and went, all full, then another with its light on, but the driver seemed oblivious. One going the other way saw me and shook his head, as if a U-turn was above his pay grade. Others were hailed by people in more fortuitous positions, and by 9:30 I was really pissed off. I hate being late for anything; if I make arrangements to be somewhere at a certain time I do everything in my power to be there on time, and I expect the other people to do the same. It's simple courtesy.

A little further up the road a woman hailed down another taxi that wasn't coming my way, as she got in she waved to me to come over. It turned out she was heading in the same direction, so we shared the cab and I was finally on my way to my new job in my new school. After a few minutes winding through the streets, down a tunnel and over a bridge across the Jialing, the taxi pulled over and she paid her half of that trip and I was off.

When we arrived at my destination the driver pointed at the meter. It had continued running from the moment I'd gotten in and the full fare was there, despite the woman having paid some of it. He must have thought it was his lucky day. I had no way to argue that I should only pay for half the journey up to when she had left, and the whole of the rest. It was best for me to just hand over the money and go.

Bei Chen Tian Jie – North Phase Paradise Walk, my new place of work. It was a pretty new shopping mall, six storeys high of glass, steel, a massive video screen and people moving in and out clutching bags from major international brands. On the ground floor was another branch of Starbucks, as well as a Häagen Dazs, with a Sephora, some local brands and a Cbest in the basement. I headed up the escalators and was soon in the reception of the school. The local staff at the desk, all women, knew who I was straight away and one took me to the teachers' room where Rory, Julie and Audrey were already busy at work.

And so I was taken on a tour of the school. It was smaller than New York New York, but it was still basically the same; same colour in the reception area with a flat-screen TV, big Life Club Zone with sliding glass doors and an IWB, a few desks with PC's for the kids to play with before class and in breaks, normal classrooms and Small Stars rooms, same one-to-one rooms, same furniture, same teachers room.

This time, Rory gave me a proper demo of the IWB, where he actually got me to try it for myself. We even had a go on a few of the games for the dance pad controller. The Teachers' Room was a lot bigger and, just like New York New York, had three offices; one for the DoS, one for Audrey, and a tiny, cramped one for the accounts administrator. This one was home to a typically pretty and petite local woman called Sherry, who looked a lot bigger than she was thanks to her cramped workspace.

The rest of the day was just as it had been at New York New York. I had been given a schedule, and on that Saturday I would be teaching my first lesson, a HF00 class, so I had an easy few days to prepare and get myself psyched up, but before that were a few more observations.

The next day we had a teachers meeting, and I got my first glimpse of how Julie was as a boss. When I had discussed lesson planning with Theo, he had been pretty relaxed. I had been taught a very strict process on the CELTA course; a front sheet detailing the lesson theme, student's level and any observations needed to be kept in mind, a language analysis sheet that broke down the grammar and syntax, the step by step lesson plan itself, replete with stage timings, instructions and seating arrangements, and a board plan for anything that needed to be drawn on the whiteboard. I had asked him about that and he was pretty apathetic; his main concern was that the lessons were good enough. Paperwork was not his thing.

Julie was completely different though. She wanted every lesson planned properly. She wanted a clear view of what we were doing, especially if things weren't going well. Some of the other teachers griped about it after the meeting; they didn't like the idea of being forced to compile so much documentation which, in their eyes, wasn't much value and would only mean more work. I wasn't overly thrilled either, but that was mainly because it still took me a long time to plan a lesson and I knew it would cause me stress. The principle was rock solid though. If a parent or adult student raised concerns about the teaching, Julie or Rory could look through the lesson plans to see if there was anything obvious that needed addressing. It also made it easier to share ideas.

Like every other area of professional life, teaching can be very territorial, parochial and selfish. A teacher can spend a long time planning a lesson and then resent the idea that another could pick up that plan and use big chunks of it for themselves, thereby making their lesson planning much, much easier. I have some sympathy with this outlook; it would be galling if some people were doing all the work and coming up with all the ideas, while others were just cherry picking from those plans, but that's not the reality in the overwhelming majority of cases.

People go into teaching English because they have a passion not just to educate, but to educate their way. Making lesson plans available to everyone makes it easier for everyone, including the really hard workers who want to keep it all to themselves. Julie's goal was to foster an environment of cross-cooperation, where everyone helped each other. The paperwork was just the small downside to the larger benefit.

For lunch, Tanja took me to one of the many food stalls in the street outside. Paradise Walk was a partially pedestrianized street that now looked more like an open square. There were modern shops and offices all round, with a construction site growing floor by floor, adding to the city's vast and rapidly expanding real estate portfolio. There was one corner that was still old and grubby, and here was a location with a number of street stalls and small "greasy spoon" type restaurants that were packed out with locals. Tanja recommended a stall that specialized in cold, spicy noodles and they certainly didn't disappoint. The cardboard bowl was small, but the noodles had a mighty kick.

To sooth my tongue, she took me to a bakery called Qin Yuan. I had seen a couple of outlets elsewhere in the city, but I didn't much fancy the weird looking baked products on offer. Thankfully, they made small sugared ring doughnuts, croissants and coffee, so I bought one of each and was pleasantly surprised that they tasted ok, and they were cheap too. It was also located opposite the bus stop I would be using, so my emergency breakfast spot was now sorted.

The rest of the day was admin, some work on my lesson plan, a trip to a local bookshop with Tanja - where I bought some Chinese writing exercise books for kids - and then a lesson observation. This one was different though. It was Julie's HF00, but this one was called an "open door". The first half was pretty standard stuff – a mixture of games and exercises. When the kids shot out for a break, we had to do a bit of furniture arranging. Extra seats were needed for the parents, the ones with the money. At regular intervals in each course the parents were invited to observe and ask questions. The more I saw of the place, the more like a normal school it seemed.

Paradise Walk had something wonderful. On the school's floor and the floor below; the ladies' and gents' toilets had a seated shitter each. It needed to be christened. I headed to the gents at the opposite end, passing a beauty parlour with a TV screen mounted just behind the glass wall. On screen was a pop video featuring an Asian girl band with nine – that's 9! – members, each one wearing tiny little hot pants and high heels and doing a dance routine that was more restrained than their Western counterparts, and yet, a lot sexier. The toilet was good, although it smelt a bit funny, and when I returned to the school the parlour was playing a different video by the same girl band.

I later found out that they were a Korean pop group called Girl's Generation. Korean pop (K-Pop) and Japanese pop (J-Pop) are huge in China, more than their own, Mando-Pop artists. Tanja had already warned me about a particular song called *Nobody*, by The Wonder Girls. In her opinion, it was the single most annoying song ever written. As the months passed by I had to admit, she was kind of right, though I would be inflicted with something much worse.

By this time in my life I had pretty much given up on popular music. Ever since *Kerrang!* Magazine went through a period where every front cover featured My Chemical Romance, I have been decidedly disinterested in what's going on in the charts. I'd vaguely heard of some kid called Justin Bieber, but I didn't really know much about him, until I came to China and heard his nasty, weedy, putrefying little voice from loud speakers in department stores, the mall, cafes and nightclubs. This was back when he was just a whiney little shit-ball – annoying but harmless. Guess how I feel about him now.

The rest of the week, for the most part, was pretty much the same. I only had one class to actually teach, so there was plenty of time to get the plan done. On the Friday I sat down with Julie to review my all-important first lesson plan. She didn't have any big concerns, but I'm pretty sure it wasn't perfect either. I guess she was avoiding any kind of hand-holding.

Afterwards, Sandra took me to one of the local grubby places for some glorious-tasting spicy beef noodles. It's a bit of an old travel cliché, but it is true that if you want to have good local food, always eat where the locals eat. These places were pretty dirty looking, and I mean significantly worse than a British greasy spoon in the days before health and safety became a real thing.

Then I observed Rory's RE Life Club where, despite it supposedly being a fun session, he insisted on making the students sit in groups of his choice. His rationale was simple; he wanted to get them together based on what he saw as their strengths and weaknesses. Despite it being a relaxed and less formal session, it was still part of their learning process, and they still needed to learn. Another day was over, and the big one was coming up; the one where it would all begin in anger.

1. Ci Ci Park. 2. Kui Xing Lou. 3. Top of Hongyadong. 4. Paradise Walk. 5. Hotpot. 6. Hongyadong from the main road. 7. Pirate ship on Hongyadong. 8. Memorial at Chaotianmen.

9 第九章

Saturday came, and it was another busy day for everyone else. Once again, I didn't have a lot to do, but I was still nervous. That evening I would be teaching my first class, HF00, and I was feeling just as apprehensive about it as that first lesson on my CELTA course. However, there was still a whole day to get through.

I arrived at the bus stop and, having missed breakfast, headed to the big M. I took the long way round the towering building and was greeted with a strange site. There was a group of young people, all wearing the same short-sleeved shirts, lined up in three rows, military style. One guy was talking to them and then, out of the blue, they all cried out the same chant, pumping their fists in the air three times. They looked like staff from a cheap restaurant, but they were acting like a cult.

In the morning I observed Rory's SS Orange class, and what a horrid eye-opener that was. I don't know if it was my presence in the room that did it, but the kids were an absolute nightmare. Rory seemed like a cool guy – pretty laid back and in control – but these "Little Emperors" seemed hell bent on making his day a misery. They were restless, overly excitable, loud, disruptive, rude and almost uncontrollable. Rory had to pick a couple off the floor and sit them back in their chairs and speak sternly to them. Even when speaking an alien language it's possible to give someone the third degree, but these kids seemed immune to his discipline.

Then, out of the blue, he cracked. He walked to the door and, as hard as he could, slammed his hand on the light switch, sending the room into pitch black.

"SMALL STARS ORANGE QUIET!" He shouted at the top of his voice with what sounded like more than a hint of real anger.

The kids went quiet immediately. After a few seconds, he switched the light on and the kid's faces were pictures of stunned innocence. He picked up their report books and, one by one, went to each student.

"Good? Bad?" He asked, giving a thumbs up and down. They knew what he was doing and, amazingly, each one gave him a thumbs up.

"No!" He continued, making the mark in their books.

Each one had been given a cross next to the frowning face in their report book – even the one or two kids who hadn't been that bad. It was unashamedly collective punishment, and it seemed to work. For the remainder of the lesson they were as good as gold. I had seen, for the first time, just how horrific teaching kids could be. Back in the teacher's room, Rory seemed embarrassed and apologetic, but it didn't worry me. I was fascinated by his discipline technique. True, it was extreme, and he admitted to making mistakes by not doing certain things earlier, but it did its job in the end.

The minutes and hours ticked by, getting closer to that momentous event. I wanted an extension socket, so I picked a small one up at the basement Cbest. At the till I managed to ask for a bigger one, and so another assistant when off to look. 15 minutes later she was nowhere to be seen, and the woman at the checkout seemed disinclined to ring the bell again, so I just left. I was late for a Life Club observation, and still down a few sockets.

The time had come for my job to begin in earnest. Before the class, I set up the furniture in the room. I had a maximum complement, 15 students, but I had a decent sized room with a full length and width window looking out over the street below. All my materials were in the room; course book, lesson plan, three different coloured markers and cue cards for a few nouns and verbs. The PC next to the whiteboard was switched on, and all I had to do was wait.

This is what it all came down to, this was the moment when my risk would start to pay off, or fail miserably. It had been nearly a year since I'd walked out of the office in Essex, leaving a well-paid job with great benefits and a well-trodden career path. Now I was living in a smog-choked megalopolis, unable to speak the local lingo (although the same could be said for Essex), getting ready to give my first lesson to a bunch of kids who could be a dream or a nightmare.

I popped out to the lobby and it was full of kids running around or playing on the PCs, with their parents and grandparents sitting on the sofas or trying to keep the unruly little angels in check. Eventually Linda, the PA assigned to my class, started gathering kids up in a group, and I knew that was my cue. I headed back into the classroom to wait. A minute or so ticked by, and the kids started coming in, excitable and hyped up, as if they had genuine enthusiasm for what was in store. Eventually, every seat was occupied by a child between ages 6 and 11, some so young their feet didn't quite touch the floor. Julie came in and, with Linda's translation, gave them a little pep talk to welcome them and tell them a few house rules. Then Julie and Linda left, and I was on my own.

Kids aren't stupid; they can see weakness, but they aren't so quick to play their hand. I had my plan in front of me, and all I needed to do was start as I meant to go on, with total and incontrovertible confidence. They were quiet at first, and compliant. When I waved the course book in front of me, they got theirs out of their bags. When I opened it to the first page of the first chapter, they opened it to the same.

I presented the words, demonstrated the verbs and got them repeating the phrases. We played a game or two, and I got them doing more formal writing. One girl, Lucy, took out her mobile phone at one point to read a text, so I gave it a little tap and she put it back in her pocket. A couple of times they got a bit rowdy, but nothing special.

At the end of the lesson I marked my opinions in their report books. Every one of them had been well behaved, so I put a tick next to the smiley faces and a little note, to the effect of "Well behaved" or "Good work". When the time was up I opened the door and they bundled out giggling. Lesson one was over. I had survived.

It had gone as well as I could have expected – nothing spectacular but nothing bad either. I put the seats back against the walls and put all my kit back in the teacher's room. My new job had started for real, and I was relieved. A mass of tension was finally released. I headed home, grabbing a Big Mac meal before getting on the bus, then buying a few beers from Cbest under the apartment building.

Then came Sunday, the end of another week. I had no lessons again, so I woke up late with a mild hangover and didn't get to school until midday. It was another day of lesson observations; Rory's TB Life Club about the Winter Olympics and Tanja's HF00. It was a bit of a problematic one for her. As with everyone else she had a lot planned, but it depended on them remembering what she had taught them before. She did a brief review session, but the kids didn't show one single iota of learning. This was where her experience kicked in. She had to make changes on the fly to get them up to speed and it seemed to work quite well.

Then she gave them language bingo cards, but the kids looked baffled. They basically understood that they had to match spoken words with pictures, but the whole line completion element seemed to be well above their heads. They also had more on their desks than they needed, and they fiddled with everything. Pens, rulers, erasers, phones, bingo stuff, whatever was there they played with. Another lesson learned; don't let the kids have anything on their desks that they don't need for the class.

And so another week passed. Monday and Tuesday were quiet, as no-one had suggested a day out and I couldn't be bothered anyway. There was laundry to do, and I was still getting my bearings around the city. The washing machine was a very simple affair. It was sat on the balcony and was a top loader; a real blast from the past. It was simply a case of putting the clothes in, adding the powder and softener, and then pressing the button. Simple stuff, except for the fact that all the labels next to the buttons were in Chinese, and we hadn't been given a list of translations. At first it had been a pain to figure out. David had already used it, but even he struggled to remind himself of what was what. We got there in the end though, and another round of clean pants were on their way.

Then there was cleaning the apartment. The floors were tiled in the lounge and wooden in the bedrooms, so no vacuum cleaner had been provided. Instead, we were given a long handled dustpan and a tall brush to clean up the dust. I'd never used one before, which sounds pretty weird, but I'd always used a vacuum for the floor and dustpan and brush (short handles) for tops or awkward corners. I'd never even seen the tall handled one. Throughout the year, that was all I ever saw being used to clean dust and crumbs off the floor, whether in shops, restaurants, or when I passed the wide open door of a neighbour. Vacuum cleaners seemed alien.

I've always considered myself pretty good geographically, but I was finding the city centre a little bit problematic. The focal point was the Monument, and from there I knew exactly how to find my way to the places I needed the most; Carrefour, Starbucks, MacDonald's, Pizza Hut, the nightclubs, Coffee, New York New York, Hongyadong, CSC and home. Most were located on or just off the square, but going beyond those streets was a little tricky.

I managed to find my way to Chaotianmen, but going in the opposite direction got me confused. I was so sure it would give me an easy route back to the flat, but instead it took me to the Yangtze, to a square overlooking an old and rundown district on the river bank. I had plenty of time to figure it out though, and it was giving me some interesting views of my new home.

Dave, Maria, Tanja and I headed to Ci Ci Park on the Monday for a few more chilled out beers. The women left early, so Dave and I headed to the nightclub on the plaza, which had been squeezed into a small corner, and stretched over four floors. It was glitzy and gaudy inside, with plenty akin to a German strip club (yes, I have been!). After a couple of hours not enjoying the club we headed home, where we spent a mild early morning on the balcony, emptying Dave's collection of bottles of the Korean drink Soju.

The new week began with a couple of easy Life Clubs but no observations. My main job was to plan for my second class; SS Orange on Friday evening. The course book was completely different to HF00. The HF book had been more about pictures and suggestions for activities, with a very basic plan that just needed fleshing out.

The SS Orange book was a collection of complete lesson plans that could have been followed without any need for the teacher to do any planning, theoretically. Despite still being in the novice stage I knew it could never be that simple, and I wanted to be completely responsible for what I taught. I still took a couple of hours of planning to come up with eighty minutes of lesson, but at least I had plenty of time to do it.

For lunch, Rory and Julie introduced me to something new and interesting – Chinese fast food. I had seen the signs in a few places. CSC stood for "Country Style Cooking", and was a local restaurant chain using the fast food principle. This meant that it was in no way set up to accommodate foreigners, so ordering food required me pointing at the menu boards behind the counter and the staff pointing to confirm.

I chose what Julie told me was a bowl of beef and noodles in a spicy broth, and it was ready in just a couple of minutes. It was arguably the best fast food I have ever tasted. The beef was well cooked and juicy, and the broth was stinging on the tongue. The main thing was that it was filling, and didn't make me feel like I needed a huge shit later in the day.

It also sold lots of other dishes, including what looked like beef with a fried egg and chips, another beef in broth dish with a hard-boiled egg, crispy shredded meats of other kinds with noodles and rice, and various other vegetable offerings that looked less than appealing to me. At least I had more options though. Ordering food was probably the thing I worried about most (other than taking a shit).

Every school has a star pupil, one who excels in pretty much everything they do and is a favourite of the teachers. EF Chongqing Paradise Walk was no different. I first encountered her while lesson planning in a quiet teachers' room. I heard running footsteps in the corridor outside and a little voice shout "Julie!". In ran a very pretty girl, smartly dressed with a beaming smile. She confidently walked around the desks, like she belonged there, and Julie came out of her office to pick her up and give her a big hug. The girl was called Aurora, and she was a special, one on one pupil of Julie's.

Her parents were pretty affluent – her mum was a bank director and they lived in a house – but she seemed like a genuinely sweet girl. Chinese kids can be very spoilt, thanks to the one child policy and rapidly growing wealth, but Aurora didn't come across like that. Julie was genuinely fond of her, and the girl had a basic grasp of conversational English that belied her young age – she was technically a Small Star. Julie had set rules about students coming into the teachers' room, but Aurora was the exception.

Friday arrived and I was as ready as I would ever be for class number two. Once again I prepped the room in advance of the kid's arrival. Despite being Small Stars they would be in a normal classroom; the special rooms were reserved for the Blues and Greens, the very little ones. I had been buoyed by my good start with the HFs, and the hand-holding level of information in the course book made me feel pretty confident about this one too. At 6 o'clock my class PA, Kathleen, ushered in the kids and then gave them a pep talk about the rules before leaving me to it.

And so it began. I had taken a leaf out of Theo's book and started the class by teaching them the *EF Small Stars Song*. It was cutesy, light-hearted and with a silly little dance routine. All I had to do was throw myself into it 100% and not let them think I was in anyway scared. They were a little tentative at first, but once the music started playing and the big white giant at the front started singing and making hand gestures, they got excited and gleefully copied my actions.

I tried to introduce myself, pointing at my chest and saying "Andrew" and writing it on the board. Then I pointed at the boy nearest me, but he looked at me in silence. I pointed at myself again and repeated my name, using the universal symbol for 'name tag' (finger drawing a line across one side of my chest). Still nothing. I tried again, and then, nervously, the boy said "Tim". I gave him a big smile and stuck my hand out for a high five. His name went on the board and I went to the next one. Each kid gave me their name and I wrote it on the board. First job, done. Then I got into the lesson.

It was all very basic. "Hello", "What's your name?", "I'm…". I also introduced them to the EF cartoon characters through their puppets. There was Roddy, the face of EF's SS and HF courses. He was basically a benevolent Stewie Griffin dressed in the colour scheme of Bod. There was Ben, a big fat bear in pyjamas. The kids found him particularly funny, because one of the meanings of 'ben' in Chinese is 'stupid'. Mel was a bright blue bird with glasses and a scarf, a wise old owl I guessed. Vic was a hedgehog in an apron and a straw hat. Finally there was Kev, a frog in snorkelling gear. The kids instantly connected with them.

The lesson went really well. It was hard to say whether or not they learnt anything, because they were so young, and I had no idea what to expect. They could have picked it up instantly or not until the very last lesson for all I knew. My main concern was that I got through the class without any major screw ups, panics or awkward silences. When the class was over everything seemed ok, and I gave every kid a tick next to the smiley face in their report books. Class two was done, and all was well.

SS Orange and HF00 had been a good introduction to the job and, despite a couple of minor stress-inducing mishaps, I felt surprisingly good about myself. I hadn't been looking forward to teaching the youngsters but it turned out not to be nearly as scary as I had first imagined. I was still looking forward to an adult's class most. Before that though, I had another new experience to deal with: teenagers.

1. Cinema. 2. Department store abseiling window cleaners. 3. Night time lights. 4. Cable car to Nan'an. 5. Round the corner from Chaotianmen. 5-7. Main road in JiangBei. 8. Statue on Hongyadong.

10 第十章

I was a pretty moody teenager, and I'm sure most people have their own horror stories about those fragile, formative years. In Britain, teenagers don't have the best reputation. Even though they are generally well-educated, enthusiastic, hopeful and open-minded they are often portrayed as violent, arrogant, bullying and unreasonable. I haven't had a lot of contact with teens since I stopped being one, so I had no idea what I was letting myself in for, but it was going to happen one way or another, so I just had to get on with it.

I was given a brand new group of TB3As. This is an intermediate level, so they had decent conversational and survival English. My SS and HF classes had been basic levels so I had started from scratch, but this would be jumping straight into the middle. I didn't worry too much about that though; at least with intermediates I had a bit more flexibility as I could just talk to them about whatever if the lesson plan didn't work out.

So, on the Sunday morning, barely a month into my stay, I arrived at the school and set about planning my lesson. I set the course book on my desk, opened it to the first chapter, browsed the material and then checked out the sample lesson plan. I'd been warned that the samples usually didn't fit the actual length of a session, but I used it as the baseline and added a few extra tasks to fill in the gaps. I was still getting used to lesson planning, so I wasn't exactly speeding through the process, but I wanted to make sure I got it right.

My lesson plan gradually built up, each stage filled with almost narrative detail as I made sure every task was clear to me, that I noted down every particular phrase I needed to convey, that every step followed a logical order and that the tasks were easy for the students to understand. I thought very hard about each step, wondering about time, relevance, order and engagement. I gave that plan so much thought over two and a half hours but, eventually, I had a lesson, in glorious detail, laid out in front of me, ready to dazzle the new batch of students.

I ate the sandwiches I had made that morning, then took a brief walk outside. My eyes were hurting a bit, and it had been mentally exhausting, but I was feeling supremely confident. I sat back at my desk and looked at the super-detailed plan, running through it step by step, making sure that it was in my head enough to at least be able to fake self-confidence. It all seemed pretty good to me and so I sat back, took a deep breath, and relaxed.

Then I saw the top corner of the plan, the cell that displayed the name of the class. For some stupid reason I had typed "TB3B". What a tit! I changed it and sat back. It then occurred to me that, despite the plan being so well written and so detailed, I would still need the text book, so I grabbed it from the shelf. I sat it on the desk and was immediately confused; it had changed colour, from pink to red. I opened it to the first chapter and didn't recognise a single page I had been looking at earlier. I looked at the shelf and saw the pink cover of the book I had been using. I took it out, set it on my desk and looked at them both.

"Oh fucking hell!" I said, loudly and with terror. "I've used the wrong bloody book!"

I'd been using the book for the next level up. I had spent two and a half hours planning a lesson from the wrong shitting book and I only had half an hour before the lesson started. I began to feel light-headed as the blood drained from my skull with the sheer terror of knowing that I was utterly screwed.

Tanja was at her desk next to me and Julie was sorting something out on the book shelves. They immediately kicked into action. They picked out some of the materials that others had already made and, using the correct sample lesson plan, set out a new lesson for me to teach. In ten minutes I had it, hastily scribbled on a sheet of A4 paper. I had materials, the correct book, a couple of alternative ideas in case things didn't work out and the knowledge that I just had to get through the first session and use the break to dig out something else. And so, with just a few minutes prep time, I entered the classroom in a mild panic.

Almost immediately, the beads of sweat began to trickle down my temples. I introduced myself and kicked off the lesson by trying to get them to find out information about each other. It was a struggle to get them started, but eventually the mingle task ticked along and they were talking to each other and finding out personal details. It had started well, but my nerves were still on fire.

I began giving the formal lesson, the one I had had less than half an hour to review and prepare for. I was completely unfamiliar with the content, and my hastily written lesson plan was scrawled in a font that could best be described as "Times New Unreadable Sans Serif or Care". A couple of times I even began explaining something only to find that I had missed something out all together, and so had to go back and start again. I was in a real state of stress and the sweat didn't let up. At one point the only boy in the class, Henry, looked at me and then looked at his fellow students as if to say *"Who is this joker? Is it just me or is he an idiot?"*

I got through the first forty minutes and then headed back to the teacher's room. Julie reassured me that it would be ok, giving me a couple more suggestions to add to my scribbled list. I survived another forty minutes, taking another break and then getting through the last forty minute session. It was the only lesson I had that day, but I was exhausted by the time I got back to my desk. I was sweating and breathing heavily but, somehow, I had managed to complete a detailed lesson with intermediate-level teenagers with almost no preparation time, pretty much on the fly, without it being a complete disaster.

My relief was palpable and we had a good laugh about it in the end. Rory reassured me that these things happen and that it wasn't the big disaster

I had thought. They had all done it, or something like it, but at least it happened sooner rather than later. The main thing was that, despite the funny looks, the kids had engaged with the tasks and done what I had asked of them. The result of the debacle was a decent enough lesson. It was the end of my week, so I headed out, treating myself to a stress-relieving MacDonald's on the way to the bus stop and home.

So I'd had my first disaster, or near disaster as it had turned out. The job had started well, in fact I had been blessed. HF00 had given me two good classes, the adorable little ones in SS Orange had been very kind to me and the Life Clubs I had done went quite well too. TB3A was my first wake up call, but I had dealt with it well, and I was raring to go for another week.

Eye-opener number two came around very quickly, and looking back on it, I think I handled it badly. It was my second SS Orange lesson, and this time it felt very different from the start. First of all, there was a new kid, called McQueen. Secondly they were more hyper, and McQueen was right at the heart of it.

We started with the EF song, which with hindsight was probably not the best thing to do. By the time I was ready to start the lesson they were already bouncing around, like they'd just jacked up on Coke Cola and Skittles. I asked them their names and wrote them on the board, but it was a lot more trying this time; if they weren't making silly noises they were shouting their names at the tops of their voices. Then reintroducing them to the EF characters got them even more excited. McQueen jumped off his chair to grab one and I sternly said "No!".

And then it kind of went downhill from there. I was getting one, major, reality check from these kids. They kept talking to each other and giggling, so I was constantly trying to get them to be quiet. Sternly saying "No!", clapping my hands loudly and going "sssssssssshhhhhhhhhhhhh" hard didn't seem to work, in fact, they just repeated what I was doing. I tried just carrying on with the lesson and not giving them the attention they craved. That wasn't exactly successful either. It seemed they weren't really out to get my attention but were dead set on pissing about as much as possible.

I was getting a headache fast, but I tried to keep my cool. The last thing I wanted to do was to lose my shit completely and turn into a raging ogre that the kids were scared of. I just had to grin and bear it. I just had to get through the lesson without too much going wrong.

Then it did go wrong. I had put some cue cards on the floor and got the kids to identify the objects. I struggled through the task, trying not to lose my mind as the kids continued to make my lesson plan a mockery. As I gathered up the cards, McQueen jumped out of his chair, took the few steps toward me with purpose and focus, and delivered a swift and hard kick to my leg.

Now don't get me wrong, it didn't hurt in any way, shape or form, but it was the line, and it had been crossed. I was genuinely shocked that he had kicked me. When I was a kid it never occurred to me to ever do that (although I once called a supply teacher a 'silly cow' – nearly got suspended for it) and I had naively though that children were under a lot more control in China.

I wasn't letting him get away with that. I said his name as sharply as I could without shouting, put my hand on his back, and ushered him out of the classroom. I took him to the reception, where Kathleen and Linda were chatting away. I told them what had happened, left him with them and then headed back in.

Looking back on this I can say, with total conviction, that I handled it completely wrong. In fact, I had gotten all my class control wrong from the start. I tried to be cool and tolerant at first and then suddenly shot to stern and strict, then dropped back to tolerant and patient. Shoving McQueen out of the room had been bad, especially as I had no idea what the PA's were dealing with at the time. They may have been too busy to take him off my hands. Plus, I effectively showed the kids that I didn't have full control or authority in the classroom. All in all, a pretty crappy way to deal with misbehaviour.

Back in the classroom though, the kids were a little better. The ringleader of the trouble had gone and they were a lot calmer. I carried on with the lesson, but they were still playing up a little bit. It wasn't too bad this time though, and eventually Kathleen brought McQueen back who, through pouting lips, said sorry, and returned to his chair. I was so relieved when that class was over. It had genuinely worn me out.

Julie and Rory sympathized with my plight as they had been there many times. They did make one major suggestion – actually a decree. Keep disciple "in" the class. Whatever the kids did, it had to be dealt with in the classroom; that was my domain. Don't get the PA's involved during the lesson. At the end of each lesson I would have to make a tick by the right face in their report book and, if necessary, write a note. That way, when the kid's parents saw the bad tick and the note they could ask the PA to translate, who could then come back to me if there was any dispute or need for clarification.

It seemed bureaucratic, but it made sense too. The PA's were there to liaise between teacher/school and parent/student, and they needed to know what was going on in class too. They had to report feedback from students to teachers, and even sat in on lessons if needed. They also needed to know what the students were doing, so this seemingly long-winded, circular process was the best way to keep them informed and keep everyone happy.

My first adult lessons came in quick succession, and they were vastly different from each other. The first was an external corporate class, where I had to take a taxi ride to the offices of Ericsson some 30 minutes away. It was only for just over an hour, and only six students showed up, and their English was already pretty good, but they didn't seem very enthusiastic. I tried to get on their side by telling them my corporate experience, but they clearly didn't give a shit and had better things to be doing.

Back at the school I talked about the class with Julie and she told me how much she hated it, and how she was just waiting for that contract to finish. It had been a pain in the arse from day one, mainly due to poor attendance and repeated class cancellations by the customer. She told me about a similar situation she'd had at a previous school, where the contract was with a hospital and the students were nurses, all women. Apparently, they had specifically asked for a male teacher. Julie's message to me was very clear.

"If we get another one of those, you're doing it."

My next adult lesson was an RE00, the most basic class. Thankfully, there was no need for the PA's to round them up, and they weren't frighteningly excitable when they came in. They were friendly and sociable with each other from the start and, as I got ready to begin the lesson, everything seemed serene and pleasant.

Then Chrissy came in. She was young, taller and bulkier than the average, petite Chinese woman, and quite pretty. She sat in the spare chair and I got started. From pretty much the moment she saw me in full view, I felt uncomfortable.

Chrissy made it clear she had the hots for me. It started with unnaturally long fixed gazes, most of which I noticed out of the corner of my eye. Then, when I handed out material for a task, she would say 'thank you' and smile in a very particular way. Then she just flat out said it with body language, resting her elbows on the desk, cupping her hands together and resting her chin on the palms, fluttering her eyelids and sighing. Even the other students noticed and had a little giggle. It was off-putting for me as I had a job to do, so I just smiled and carried on, hoping her obvious attraction to me meant she endeavoured to be a stellar student.

As it turned out, the lesson was a lot more difficult than I had anticipated. My instructions were too tricky because the tasks I was giving them were too tricky. I had decided to go down the bingo route, despite what I had seen in Tanja's class. I assumed that they would at least grasp the concept, if not already know what it was. How wrong I was. I had the exact same problem Tanja experienced with her kids.

Bingo is a game that has pretty much escaped the Chinese – I don't think you can play it at the Venetian in Macau. I had managed to demo a simple group introduction, including teaching the phrases "What's your name?", "My name is..", "Who's this?" and "This is...." and so had felt confident from the offset. However bingo, for a first lesson, was asking a lot, and it turned out to be a big fail. I carried on with my lesson plan though, unable to quickly come up with any kind of alternative.

I should have known. I had done my CELTA working with upper intermediate and lower intermediate students. Even the worst of them had been able to hold a basic conversation. My RE00 class was completely different. These students could only use a small number of set phrases, so communicating with them on an adult level was impossible. The whole point of the communicative approach is to teach students in a similar way to how we all learn our native tongue as children. Their language was at that level, yet I had, for some dumb reason, hoped for something more grown up.

This is not a criticism of them; it was my own stupid fault for making too many assumptions. For some reason I had thought they would already have a basic grasp – as had so many shop staff I had encountered already. I had made a major blunder; one should always teach for the lowest level student. I don't mean bring everyone down; the next rule is to account for differing degrees of ability and ensure the more able students have challenging tasks too. Also, my assumptions were clearly bullshit from the start. How could I have made any assumptions when I'd never met the class?

I'd now had the full gamut of classes and was firmly entrenched in the school. I'd had a couple of very good lessons, a couple of middling classes and a couple of disasters, all within the first few weeks. I was glad that it had all happened so soon, especially the bad stuff. Now, every dream had been confirmed, every fallacy corrected and every assumption kicked in the teeth. I was now a real teacher, and the rest of the year was ahead of me.

Another week finished, and as I packed up my things on the Sunday evening I was looking forward to an early night with a few beers and maybe some grubby fast food. The teacher's room was dead, only me, Rory and Julie, and as I put my laptop in my bag, Rory suggested I join them for a spot of shrimp pot. I've never been a big seafood eater. Growing up by the sea, I used to see the jars of winkles on sale at the local fairground, and they weren't exactly appealing. I was game though.

We headed to a local restaurant and, to be honest, it seemed to be a normal hotpot joint. The big difference was when the bowl was presented. Instead of a broth with raw ingredients on plates, we were presented with a large bowl of broth, filled with a large pile of pre-cooked shrimps, tinged with the red hue of the chillies that made the hotpot so tasty.

I dipped in, and my God it felt like I was repeatedly slapped in the face with a soft pillow. It was insanely good, and I became greedy. I could see my plate filling up with the dismantled shells of the cooked crustaceans, and my fingers got sticky from the oil and juice. I was in heaven, absolute food heaven. I'd thought hotpot was great, but this was divine.

There were other parts to it too. In the broth there were clumps of rice noodles, tied up like shoe laces still in the packet, and chips too. We also had side dishes of egg fried rice and little bowls of garlic and oil that came to life with the addition of the dark vinegar and soy sauce. It was becoming clear that all my worries about the food in the city were completely unfounded.

The night was young though. A few streets away we entered one of the many buildings with a doorway dazzling with gaudy neon. The sign above the door said 'KTV'. Finally, I would get to see what was on. It was an ornate lobby, with staff smartly dressed and, incongruously, a bland convenience store in one corner. Rory made an arrangement at the reception desk and paid some money, and then we headed into the store to buy some booze and snacks. Then we were taken to our room, and I understood what it was. 'KTV' is Chinese for karaoke.

It was a small room with a big sofa, a massive flat screen TV and a small touch screen terminal. Our food and drink was delivered, and then the fun began. I'm not a public performer in anyway, and I can't think of anything worse than karaoke. I don't mean that from a snobbish point of view – I actually think it's entertaining when other people do it – but it's not for me. Whenever I've been in a pub and there's been a karaoke machine on a podium I've always avoided it, no matter how drunk I was. This was different though. It was in a small, segregated room, where the only people who could watch are one's friends. If you're going to look like a dick, then it's going to be in front of friends, and what are friends for?

As it was with the food in this city, I was in for a penny, in for a pound. I had a few shots of Jack Daniels and cold tea, and a couple of beers, while Julie and Rory belted out a few numbers. It turned out that they had been in a band back home in Missouri, and Julie had an especially good, powerful, diva-esque voice.

Then it was my turn, and I was stuck for ideas. I can't sing, so there's never anything on my mind in that sort of situation, so I decided to nominate the first, truly cheesy song that came into my head. What I thought of was *Hungry Eyes* by Eric Carmen, from the soundtrack to my least favourite film of all time, *Dirty Dancing*. I won't say that I did it justice.

I actually have a soft spot for 80's film soundtracks and some of the crappy, light rock songs that filled them, and *Hungry Eyes* is one of the better ones (my favourite is *Win the End* by Mark Safan, from *Teenwolf*). I was awful, truly awful, with not a single phoneme sung in the key it was meant for. I was drunk as well, so my physical performance was as slick as you can imagine. I tried a few other tunes and consumed far too much booze, and it was one of the most fun night's I'd ever had. Also, Rory recorded it on my phone, forever saved for the historical record.

1. Shrimp pot. 2. KTV. 3. My photo in the school reception. 4. Skyline of Chaotianmen. 5. World Trade Centre. 6-7. Buildings around Hongyadong. 8. The metro.

11 第十一章

The kind of people you meet can make or break any experience, no matter how amazing or horrid it is. Everyone at the school seemed pretty cool, and I was getting along with them all well enough. Some had bigger social circles than others. At the weekend, Rory and Julie had taken part in a tree-planting ceremony/event that had been attended by a number of senior teachers from other schools in the city. They'd met someone there who'd come out with, what ended up becoming, the mantra for EF Paradise Walk.

"We'd done the whole tree planting shit." Julie said. "We'd had to pose with the others and pretend to really want to be there and that we were all best buddies. Then we got taken for dinner where we were sat with a few of the others and there was this one freak."

"He asked us the weirdest question ever." Rory said, taking over. "In the middle of eating chuancai he turned to us and said….'Do y'all like wolves?' I swear to God we had no idea what the fuck was going on. He kept on like 'I like wolves. Wolves are great. D'ya like 'em too?'"

"Oh, and what was your answer?" I asked, feeling as confused as they must have been.

"I just said 'I don't not like wolves!'"

Thanks to Rory, the world now has a reasonable answer to a question that, more likely than not, will never be asked again. But if, by some bizarre miracle of the universe, it is asked, the answer can be found here.

Something momentous happened, making me react in a way I never thought possible. Julie, Rory and I went to the mall's basement for lunch. They took me to a restaurant by the Cbest that did some truly fantastic food, brought out on sizzling hot plates. I chose the sliced beef with onions and almost died with delight.

Once finished, we headed up the escalator, back to the street and, looking up, there it was, misty and glowing through the dust and pollution in the atmosphere. The sun. I had been in Chongqing for a month and, until that moment, it had been completely obscured, 24 hours a day. Now I could see it, even though it was very hazy, but it was unmistakably there. That's how bad the pollution is in Chongqing.

What a strange, primeval feeling, to be so stunned at the sight of a heavenly, celestial body. Maybe I was suffering from a lack of vitamin D, but it did something to me. I felt refreshed and more energetic. I had a lot of work to do and, as if by magic, I had the power to get it done, no matter how tired I felt or how much my head hurt most of the time.

It was still early days but, weirdly, I seemed to be finding things so much easier with the TB's. The teenagers were the hardest working, the most enthusiastic and the easiest to control. The only problem was their shyness, and I felt especially sorry for Henry, the only boy in the group. They seemed to like difficult logic or memory games, and one they responded to well was pelmanism.

It's a very simple task that's also very versatile. Students, normally in groups, are given two sets of cards, face down. They turn over one from each set. If they think the cards match, they put them to one side. If they don't then the cards are replaced, face down, and they try again. It's primarily a memory game, but it also requires students to make connections as well. These can be as simple as two pictures, though they can have complex reasons for being paired. They can be words or a word and a picture, or two parts of a phrase. One can even go nuclear and have three or even four sets of cards

The HF's were quite rowdy, but given the right activities they were okay. There were a few problem kids, but most were fine. Sky seemed to be the worst troublemaker. He seemed to revel in joking around and goading the other kids to join in, and I didn't hide my displeasure, with a few raised pointing fingers and a loud "NO!" or two headed his way. I tried not to be too much of an ogre though, and I wondered if that was the problem. Either I should lose it completely or just ignore him.

They liked Hangman. At the start of one lesson I demonstrated the game by playing it on my own. I drew out the dashes on the whiteboard and called out a letter. It was correct, so I wrote it on the dash. Then I called out a couple of wrong ones and drew the portions of the gallows. The kids easily got the idea of guessing the word, but they were fascinated by the picture I was drawing. I went all the way, and the kids recognised it in an instant. No matter how cute and cuddly they look, kids can be very morbid and take great enjoyment in the macabre. All I had to do was split the class into two teams and make it into a competition, and they were well into it.

Another technique that worked well was finger counting. I was shown it on my CELTA course, and the other teacher's swore by it too. When teaching a formulaic expression it's good to emphasize each word or syllable with the hand, as if counting e.g. "It's a cat" and showing thumb, index and middle fingers, or "It's a pencil" showing thumb, index, middle and ring finger. I'm not sure how it works, but I guess it gave them a visual cue to which sounds were separate and which went together.

Conveying stress was also important, and this could also be done with gesture. This can be done in many ways, but I preferred an open palm for stress and a closed palm for no stress. Writing the words or phrases on the board, I put a dot above the stressed letters.

I did have one issue I had thought about raising with Linda. There were twin girls, not completely identical, but pretty close. Both, like all the other kids, had English names. One was called Annie, the other was called Anna. In my mind, I was exasperated. I was slowly getting used to some of the weird ideas the Chinese had about so many things in the world, and so choosing what were effectively the same names for sisters wasn't something I found so shocking. I mentioned it to Julie and she said it was okay to ask the grandparent's (the girls' guardians) to change the names. I felt bad about that too, so I let it be, for which I'm very glad.

The RE class didn't get off to a great start. I had assumed I would connect best with them, but I was clearly mistaken. The one thing I didn't do was click, not even with Chrissy. She liked me, and made no secret of it, but I wasn't flattered. I had a job to do and wanted to do it without any sort of hassle or distraction. Her fawning was annoying, so I did all I could to ignore it. I think she got the message eventually though, as the smiles rapidly became more courteous than cute.

It was with my SS class that I experienced a momentous event, even more important and more encouraging than the hazy glimpse of the world's energy provider. It was a couple of weeks into the course. I was doing the usual tasks with them, asking them "What's your name?" and getting back "Jerry", "MacQueen" or "Angel". I got to the end of the line and asked the question "What's your name?" and received the reply "I'm Timmy".

It seems like nothing, but at the time it made me stop, just for a second, with shock. I had been trying to get them to say "I'm…." and had been failing each time. It was as if they thought it was part of my name. Not even my gestures of pointing to myself had made any difference. Then, out of the blue, one of them had got it.

It seems like something so minor, so mundane, but to me it was the best thing that had happened to me in a long time, and the best up to that point in China. In no uncertain terms, Timmy had learnt something from me. After that lesson I was so pumped up and couldn't wait to tell the others. Rory was genuinely happy for me; he and Julie were real enthusiasts for teaching, so I think seeing me so delighted was a big blessing for them. At least they knew there was another teacher with the passion they felt.

Another weekend came, and once again the city was shrouded in a thick, polluting, poisonous smog that blotted out the blue sky and the golden sun. I met Tanja at the front of the apartments and we headed down the road for another new experience.

The metro system was in its early stages, with only two lines in operation, but it was already pretty impressive. Because of the topography of the city, they had chosen a monorail system, with sections going underground and then coming out tens of metres above the streets, on massive, stilted tracks, and even passing through sections of the towering apartment blocks. We whizzed through the metropolis, passing through a multitude of residential and commercial districts that were as crowded and as bustling and JieFangBei and JiangBei.

Tanja was quite an interesting person. She was one of the more experienced teachers in the school, having worked in a place called Guiyang and some experience in Korea. In fact, she seemed to have quite a nomadic nature. Despite her name, and her obvious American accent, she preferred to call herself German. She had been born there, to a US military family, and had spent her formative years in the country, before moving to Indiana, where her mother still lived. She'd definitely found her calling as an English teacher and seemed to have found herself some roots in China.

Our destination was Chongqing Zoo, not exactly world-renowned but still not something to be found in every big city. Outside the entrance were a couple of women selling items devoted to the one animal that actually matters in China – the panda. There was also a little child taking a shit on an old newspaper.

If you ever visit China you'll notice that a lot of the toddlers wear romper suits that have a big slit in their crotch, going from front to back, exposing their genitals and arse. When I had first visited China I had assumed it was a health thing, due to the high heat and humidity. Actually it was because nappies at that age just weren't used, so it was easier to let the kids take a dump in the drains whenever they needed it. I guess it saved money and resources on making nappies, but it certainly wasn't done out of any environmental concerns.

The zoo was a collection of contrasts. Through the gate was an open courtyard with a wide path, lined with statues of various animals, not all of them present. Right at the front, in big, spacious enclosures, were the pandas. To be fair on Chongqing Zoo, their enclosures seemed a lot bigger than the ones in Beijing, and they had piles and piles of bamboo to devour, but they were still living in one of the most polluted cities in the world, so it hardly seemed fair on them.

Sadly, that was about as good as it got. The open enclosures for giraffes and elephants seemed reasonable enough (for a zoo) and the hippos seemed to have enough water to bathe in. There were deer, antelope, rhinos, zebras and various other cloven beasts I couldn't identify, all homed in various degrees of space and vegetation, an aviary that was a wooded area covered with a net, glass-fronted enclosures for the big cats, and primates, some tropical birds in big cages and some pools for otters.

A lot of these enclosures seemed quite grubby, especially for the cats, but the bears seemed to have it worse. They were just in big cages and had no vegetation or water to wander round in. Their cages looked the dirtiest of all and, despite me having no knowledge of animal psychology, it seemed obvious that they were in some distress. One even had a leg missing, but that didn't stop him standing up against the fence, sniffing and looking around as if to hunt for a way out.

All the teaching staff gathered for a regular meeting and training session on a mild, Thursday morning in Paradise Walk. Maria, Karen, David and Theo came over from New York New York, along with Dulce. Dulce was another Filipino teacher who had been there a while and had just returned from a visit home. She lived a few floors above me and Dave, so I assumed we'd all be hanging out a lot.

We had our meeting in the Life Club zone, the only room with the necessary interactive whiteboard. There was the usual officialdom and bureaucracy, and then Rory led a training session. I had the feeling that this was more their party than Theo's. I'm not saying that Theo was lazy or didn't give a shit, but he was certainly less officious and strict about practice and procedures. Rory and Julie loved the "science" of education, and were keen to try and get the rest of us involved in their passion. Not many of the others seemed too enthused by it, but that's always the way with such things.

It had been quite the whirlwind month and a bit, and my head was struggling to keep my brain in place at times. Tanja made a suggestion to help; a trip to Chengdu. So, on a Sunday night, I stayed over at her place, getting to meet her adorable ginger tom cat NanGua (Pumpkin) and early on the Monday, we hopped into a taxi and headed to the main train station.

Located in one of the many new districts that have sprung up since the 1990s, the north train station looks more like a modern airport terminal from the outside. We had to fight our way through the chaos of the underground taxi rank and the crowds milling around, as well as having to put our baggage through the only x-ray scanner I had ever seen outside an airport, but eventually we made it onto the train, and were on our way.

The journey was by high-speed rail, and we were whisked through Sichuan province to our destination in two very comfortable, and surprisingly quiet, hours. I'm sure the view outside was of a stunning landscape, full of mountains and plains, but once again the pollution covered everything.

The square outside Chengdu station was even madder than in Chongqing, with thousands of people waiting for the latest arrivals or selling wares to visitors. Tanja wasn't keen on queuing for a taxi, despite the long line moving along steadily and quickly from what I could see. After a hunt that seemed to take longer than the queue, we hopped into an auto tuk-tuk and were whisked to our hostel in pretty good time.

Like Chongqing, the air in Chengdu was mixed up with God only knows what toxins and pollutants. We took a walk along the riverside and then headed south, finding our way to the Wuhou Temple. The temple is part of a preserved historical zone in the city centre, which looks a little too sparkling and well cared for, considering its age. Jinli Street is the main - and very narrow - thoroughfare into the warren of streets that reminded me of CiQiKou, even down to the horrid stench of stinky dofu and the souvenirs that were allegedly handmade by local craftsmen.

The temple itself wasn't exactly grand and impressively dominating, but the ornamental lake did provide an oasis of elegance and beauty, with calm waters, a zigzag bridge and pink blossoms lighting up the dull bricks and stones on the ground.

We took a long walk east, following one of the main roads that made up the city's concentric ring road system. Eventually, we found our way to a place I could have stayed in all day. Bookworm is a coffee shop, bar, bookshop and lending library all in one. It's also one of the most chilled-out places I've ever been in and seemed to be petty popular with the local expat community, guitars and all. Its book collection was mainly fiction, history and biography, and the vast majority of books were in English, and for a monthly fee they could be borrowed for as long as needed. Even better for me was that they stocked my favourite magazine, *Monocle*. It was one of the many things I was missing from home, so it was nice to know that I could get it in China. We had coffee and rested our aching bones for a while before dragging ourselves back out for another trek.

We made it to another of the expat's favourite haunts, Pete's Tex Mex. We were both always up for a bit of local tastes, but we had our limits too, so we feasted on steak and chips, filing our bellies with enough real food to set us up for the rest of the day. We headed back to our hostel and, after some more relaxing, headed along the river to the German bar, where we had a couple of pints of dark Kostritzer. Our route back turned out to be the prime location of local street prostitutes. They seemed to be no different from the ones I'd seen in other places, until Tanja told me what made them special. Let's just say, the Adam's apple never lies.

In the morning we headed north across the river, avoiding the heavy traffic as we traipsed through the central business district. It was a very different environment to Chongqing. Apart from the filthy air, the streets were clean, wide, busy but not jammed, and the high rises were decently spaced out. It was clear that the planning of Chengdu was far superior to that of Chongqing and yet, in my eyes, it was a less desirable place to live. It seemed to lack character and soul, like it was too neat and tidy. It reminded me of Washington DC – nice enough, bit it lacked a certain bite.

We arrived at Tianfu Square, the focal point of the city. Standing on the far side and dominating the space was the statue of Chairman Mao, his pose both heroic and noble with his hand raised in a half wave, half salute. Looking at the old fella in stone made me realize something; I hadn't seen a single statue or grand portrait of the revolutionary leader in Chongqing. Ok, I hadn't been there that long, but I had been to a few of the main gathering places and open civic spaces and his image was conspicuous by its absence.

We continued north, heading past offices, expensive apartments, the main sports stadium and shopping malls, arriving at the Wenshuyuan Monastery. It's the largest Buddhist temple in the city, originating in the Tang dynasty (AD 618 – AD 907, none of this CE and BCE crap) and now houses a large collection of relics and treasures. Its gardens were peaceful and tranquil, but lacked the colourful foliage that a good English garden would have in abundance. It was good enough for a small population of cats though, and one of the lakes had the biggest and blackest frogs (or toads) I had ever seen. Statues of deities, protected by polished glass, were adorned with floral tributes and the courtyards reeked of the scent of burning incense, lit as prayer offerings by the locals hoping to share in the rapidly rising prosperity in their country.

A short taxi ride took us west to the Dufu Cottage. Dufu is one of the greatest and most important poets of Chinese literature. After living an itinerant life after the An Lushan Rebellion in 755, he settled in Chengu, living in a thatched cottage until returning to his home region of Luoyang in 768. It was in this cottage, sat next to the Flower Bathing Stream, that he wrote 240 poems. The grounds are like a mini woodland, containing a pagoda, winding paths, a small canal and courtyards now used to sell souvenirs. It lacked the glorification and dazzling ornamentation of a Buddhist temple, but it still held the same reverence.

My trip was over, but Tanja was staying an extra night (her weekend was Tuesday and Wednesday), so that afternoon I took a taxi back to the main station and, after negotiating the melee of passengers and the unexpected baggage scan, I was back on the fast train and back in the city, ready for another week.

Chongqing Zoo – 1. Panda enclosure. 2. Three-legged bear. 3. Tiger cub on show. 4. Giraffe leaning over the fence. 5. Hippo. Chengdu – 6-7. Wuhou Temple 8. Tianfu Square. 9. Downtown Chengdu. 10. Dufu Cottage.

12 第十二章

It's very easy to think of modern Chinese society as being quite heartless and mean-spirited. From the outside, it's on such a rapid growth spurt that many people are being left behind, and many important considerations are being ignored. The wealth gap is rampant, at levels exceeding even the wildest dreams of the most hardened US Tea Party Conservative nut-jobs, and the environment has been put to one side in favour of infrastructure and industry.

There are the things you see at street level – the beggars, the cripples and the old people selling whatever crap they can to make ends meet. Then, of course, there's the government, with its repressive laws preventing free speech and a fair trial. However, China is also capable of great humanity, the kind that is rarely found in the West.

On 14th April, a magnitude 7.1 earthquake struck Rima village in Yushu County, Qinghai, near the border with Tibet. It spread out to the town of Gyegu, 30km away and in all, 2,698 people lost their lives, 12,135 were injured and 270 were never accounted for. This was a huge disaster, one that dominated the life of the nation's media right across the board.

A few days later, the country went into official mourning. When I got off the bus in the morning I noticed that the usual glitzy, loud and sparkly adverts on the mall's video screen had been replaced by images of the tragedy, and it went on for the whole day. Along with that, only essential businesses were open. It was very touching and moving, and surprising too. I couldn't imagine that happening in Britain, but whether that's because we are heartless or lucky enough not to suffer like that I cannot say.

There was an even bigger crisis in the country though. For some reason that no-one could understand, there was a spate of stabbings in schools, specifically people from outside gaining entry and knifing kids and teachers in classes. There were fatalities, and for a while it seemed that every week there was a new case of a knife-wielding nut-job walking through gates and slicing their way through classrooms. On the bus to work, the TV screens showed the latest news updates, and increasingly they showed schools taking part in evacuation drills with the police, just in case it happened to them.

I was well and truly settling in, and getting my bearings around the city. JiangBei district had a very similar feel to JieFangBei, but it was its own city centre too. It had its mega high rises casting looming shadows over the citizens, but there seemed to be more space between them, making the area feel less oppressive than the main centre. The bus stopped very close to, but not always in, the same place, and often the quickest way to get to school was by passing through "Meat Alley".

"Meat Alley" is where one can experience the real China. It's a short parade of small food stalls, all located in diminutive units underneath one of the many residential and commercial towers in the city. The smells coming out from each of the dispensers were, to be frank, sickening. I know it's all about local tastes and how things are different around the world, but it wasn't very pleasant to my nostrils and yet, it never stopped me walking through. There was something very appealing about the alley, as if it was reminding me just where I was and what I was doing.

It also provided some entertainment, one that I'm sure wasn't technically allowed. There were two big, flat screen TVs – one mounted above the stalls in the middle of the row, and one mounted on a column in a corner. Pretty much every time I walked through, the one above the stalls was showing a Michael Jackson live concert video. The other sometimes showed the same thing, but sometimes showed a feature film, either Chinese or Hollywood. It was quite brazen but, as I would find out over the year, not uncommon.

Beggars are everywhere in big Chinese cities, and Chongqing is no different. These aren't the kind you get in England – a bit grubby but generally healthy, and sometimes faking it. These are the real deal, though some are made disabled as children by gangs who need new recruits. There were a few women who were so deformed that they scooted around on wheeled wooded boards, looking like they had been bundled and dumped like old rope or laundry.

There were other beggars who had not been subjected to a harsh form of recruitment. One was a young guy with some sort of growth defect on one leg i.e. it was twice normal length, twice as thick, had a knee that looked like a fabric joint on a rag doll and feet that looked ready to burst.

The other was even more awful. He always sat against one of the pillars and most of him was normal, except for his left leg. On the shin, almost all of the skin and fatty tissue had gone, probably from some hideous industrial accident. His muscles were visible and, on a small portion, the blackened ruin of his dying shin bone. Clearly, this man had given himself over to China's economic miracle, and all he'd gotten in return was ripped flesh and a life of abject poverty.

Not all were so pathetic though. There was a group of four blind musicians who always sat just outside Meat Alley. They each played the erhu, a two-stringed violin-like instrument that's played upright on the knee with a bow, producing that classic, tiny, grating tone that is so ubiquitous in the minds of us in the West.

Walking through "Meat Alley" away from the school took me to another building, with an underpass lined with shops that undercut the main road and led to the main square on the other side. Here was a welcoming open space, with more big shops on three sides, a park and the Future International Building, another of the city's commercial landmarks. The park was mostly paved, with large flower beds giving foliage for nature to try to thrive. A large fountain with a dancing display stood at one end, and crossing the park eventually led to an artificial lake, where trees provided shade for the hundreds of elderly men and women who gathered to play chess, mah-jong and cards.

It had escalators leading down to another world. Underneath the park was another shopping mall, replete with a few bars, a couple of nightclubs, a snooker hall, a supermarket, a cinema and various small shops. Everywhere in Chongqing, one never seemed to be more than 5 minutes from at least one major shopping area. It seemed crazy, but then again the city was so densely packed that there was plenty of people for it.

David and I went to one of the nightclubs there. It was small and dark, but it had a decent atmosphere and, unlike the ones in JieFangBei, had a proper dance floor. Tanja and I visited a couple of bars there after work a few times too. One felt like a real bar, except for the sound-proof karaoke booth that looked like a recording studio. We got to see the videos of the songs chosen, and they were always really awful, cheesy Mando-pop or Canto-pop songs. Imagine the music of Glen Medeiros, but even more revolting.

There was another bar we visited, where we were often approached by locals for a toast. It was usually a fun place to be, except for the waitresses who had whistles and insisted on blowing them, a lot. There were also women whom I assumed were hostesses. A couple of times they got us drinks and then joined us for a toast, with our drinks. Needless to say, I was pissed off with the liberty, and didn't let them get me a drink again. We even met some Belgian students there, on their own little Chinese adventure.

If we didn't go to the bars underground, then it was often a floor below the school and at the other end of the mall to De Si Bao, the German restaurant. It's kind of bizarre to see something like a beer keller in China, as well as Chinese people dressed in what they must have thought was lederhosen and dirndl. We rarely ate there, but they served some good German ales and, of course, Tanja was especially fond of the place.

Another favourite of ours was the teppanyaki restaurant in the Metro mall in JieFangBei. This is a great bit of Japanese cuisine that absolutely needs to be in the UK. Each table has a large griddle, where a chef cooks the food for the customers, while putting on a bit of a show with their clever-handling skills. We always chose the set menu, a combination of meat, fish and vegetables, and it was always heavenly to devour. Weirdly, just across the aisle, was a full-sized ice rink. I never tried it though.

My timetable was getting up to speed, and I had set myself a routine that I thought made sense. At home I didn't have cable TV, so it was all Chinese channels with no English-language programming. This meant that there were few-to-no distractions other than the Internet, so lazing around at home wasn't tempting. I had a grand plan to get up at about 7am every morning and do some exercise, including a 30 minute run, but that soon became very irregular, and the smog wasn't exactly appealing either.

When I did exercise, I was always amazed by the older people out in the courtyard at that time. Some were on the exercise equipment, some were walking around the empty pool, clapping their hands repeatedly for some odd reason. I assumed they did it for the circulation. Others were doing tai chi, in small groups, sometimes with swords but always with energy and grace. Clearly in China, age is no reason to become infirm.

I would always get to the bus stop for 9, pay my 2 Yuan, and get shuttled to JiangBei in reasonably quick time, getting into school for about 9:30. If I hadn't had breakfast I'd pop into Qin Yuan for a croissant or doughnut, and sometimes a latte. On the Wednesday I would get all my lessons and Life Clubs for then, Thursday and Friday done, so that on Thursday and Friday I could work on everything for the weekend, when there would be very little time to do anything other than teach.

I stuck religiously to the syllabus in the course books, but it quickly became clear that the suggested lesson plans were woefully inadequate. It's not that they were inherently shitty, it was that pretty much every plan could have been completed in half the suggested times. It was still a good starting point though, and at first I copied out these plans into mine and then figured out what I needed to add in to flesh out the time. The only exception was with the SS books, which provided such an insane amount of detail that it was almost pointless doing the plan myself, but I had professional pride.

If I needed any special materials then I would get making them ASAP too. I took lunch after twelve and had a few options. There was the "greasy spoon" place Sandy had taken me to, CSC, the hot plate restaurant next to Cbest, MacDonald's, Starbucks and Cbest itself had an open kitchen where I could get freshly cooked spicy fried rice or noodles with vegetables or pork.

There was also a branch of KFC in the mall, but this was not the option it should have been. The problem is that in China, they don't play by the same rules. They use some sort of spicy, tangy sauce that makes the chicken taste weird. Also, the chicken in the burger looks grey and greasy, just like it does straight off the leg bone, not the puffy, white, juicy heaven. The only thing I could eat were the nuggets and the desserts. I know I shouldn't have been bothered, but it was something familiar that I couldn't enjoy.

Then in the afternoon I would make sure everything I needed for that day's sessions were ready and waiting. It soon became clear that the Ericsson gig wasn't going to be easy; not because they were demanding or tricky to deal with, but because they kept cancelling. I was advised not to put too much effort into it as the stop-start nature of the course had been apparent from the moment it began.

I tried not to be too relentless though; even the most dedicated people need a break. Sometimes I would just pop out for a walk locally, often having a browse around the Xinhua book shop or getting a drink for Qin Yuan, Starbuck's or Frisco's, a café at the opposite end of the mall, where I would read a book, or try to learn some more Chinese at my desk, thanks to a another audio and book course I'd been given.

The weekends were pretty busy and only gave me a very small window to do any kind of planning if needed. I made my classes a priority; if I was struggling with Life Clubs I would just leave them and move on, maybe borrowing something someone else had tried.

I needed all the time in the world. I really envied the others, who seemed to turn up at midday and get their lessons planned in half the time. True, they weren't throwing in anything like as much detail as I was, but I needed it. I couldn't just write *Task: Pelmanism for ten minutes > Mingle for ten minutes*. I had to give details for each, including how I would present each task, even down to including key phrases. I'm not sure if it was because I was a novice, or because I just didn't have that natural flair, but I couldn't just think of a lesson and teach it. I needed all that paperwork and all that text or I would be screwed.

It wasn't long before that schedule proved to be more useful than I could have imagined. Sandra's contract ended, and she decided not to renew. On a Sunday afternoon I gave her a hug and a kiss and she was gone. There was no leaving party, which I found odd at the time, but maybe that was just her personality (or maybe she wasn't that popular). So there was just Julie, Rory, Tanja, Susan and myself. Our timetables were modified to pick up the slack. It was a challenge, but it was going to happen eventually, and I was feeling a lot better about my work.

Then it got bad. It soon turned out that that wasn't the whole story, and out of the blue, Susie resigned. Just like that. She'd gone back home for some family business and it seemed they had persuaded her to return home, for whatever reasons, and so she had decided to just up-sticks and leave. Just like that. Within a week, we were down two teachers, and up shit creek.

The classes and Life Clubs were split between us, mostly Tanja and me, and suddenly I had pretty much a full programme of teaching, and no idea how I was going to do it. Tanja had the biggest load, but we were all put under great stress. Julie and Rory still had their normal admin and managerial duties, as well as the actual teaching, and none of us were particularly thrilled at the thought of the coming weeks. Dulce and Maria would be joining us, but not for a few weeks, so we were set up for a lovely little period of complete and utter mania.

There was no let up. Before, I'd been able to do some planning then have a bit of a break, but that was out of the question now. I had so much more to do that resting between plans was hardly an option. I had a new class on Saturday afternoon, TB1A, and I was given another corporate course. Thankfully, it was also on a Saturday, and the three guys came to the school. It was relatively easy to plan, but it meant that I had even less time to plan anything else. Now, absolutely everything needed to be sorted before my class on Friday, or I would have been screwed.

I always tried to make Wednesday the most stressful day, which wasn't too hard seeing as Ericsson kept cancelling their class at the last minute (after a whole bunch of planning on my part). Eventually, they cancelled all together, after I'd only actually given them three classes, in which no student attended more than once. What a waste of time that was. At least it gave me an extra couple of hours for planning.

Life Clubs weren't nearly as easy to plan as I had hoped. The theme was pretty much a random choice by Rory, and that was all we got. From that theme we had to come up with our own ideas to fill a one hour session which, at times, was pretty straightforward, but often left me looking at my timetable with a gormless and empty expression.

My extant lessons were moving along steadily. HF00 was a good mixture of abilities and required a lot of thought to make sure they all got a good chance of achieving something in class. That's the hardest part of lesson planning; understanding your students and tailoring tasks to fit them all. One technique was to put them in groups, but to choose who the kids sat with. It mixed the abilities, the theory being that the stronger students would support the weaker ones, and that the weaker ones wouldn't be singled-out in their own groups.

That was the nice utopian view, but the reality was much different. Kids always want to team up with their friends or others with a similar ability, so when they are told to sit with a particular student it can breed a certain amount of resentment. The trick was to be firm but friendly, maintaining authority without letting the kids think I was an ogre. In some cases, that was easier said than done.

SS Orange was pretty decent too. They were very young, and so patience with them was the absolute key to getting through a lesson. MacQueen was still the one who misbehaved the most, and Angel often joined in with a gleeful exuberance, but I was able to keep my cool. I managed to not raise my voice much, or have the kind of complete freak out that Rory had had in that fateful lesson I had watched. For me, not getting to that point was a victory.

TB3A was a great bunch of students. I had gotten over the stress of screwing up the first lesson so badly, and they were turning out to be a big surprise. These were not the moody, pubescent horrors I had been worried about though Andy, a late addition, was painfully shy. They were enthusiastic, intelligent, eager to learn and above all, brave. Splitting them into groups of mixed abilities was irrelevant because they were all pretty much the same, and when they were given a writing task they were always keen to push the boundaries of their language.

One thing they were especially keen on doing was coming up with something funny. Humour is actually quite a difficult thing to get to grips with in language. When learning, students are bombarded with formulaic expressions, a set vocabulary and grammatical rules that often have a whole bunch of exceptions to memorize. These examples tend to be pretty bland and to the point, focussing on particular survival functions, but humour is about expression and imagination.

I gave them one task where they had to split into groups and come up with questions about hypothetical scenarios to ask the other group what they would do, practising a combination of future tense and modal verbs. Jenny, Susie, Jennifer and Amy were sat together, and it seemed that Jenny and Susie were the real leaders when it came to being silly. Throughout the preparation time they were giggling to themselves as they tried to come up with the most ridiculous scenarios imaginable.

When it came to asking the questions the other group, led by the dour yet frighteningly intelligent Henry, presented scenarios that were perfectly normal for everyday life; not completing homework, going to the cinema and finding the film they wanted to see was full, and missing the last bus home. Susie and Jenny's group had chosen a different line; alien invasions, monster attacks, waking up in the middle of a desert naked.

Henry's team gave answers equally as silly and amusing as the questions; using Andy as a human shield, crawling across the sand until a tree could be found to use the leaves for clothing, running away like a coward. It was so encouraging to see these kids not only pushing the boundaries of their skills and imaginations, but also doing everything they could to have a laugh. I don't remember my GCSE French lessons being like that. Our textbook, *Tricolore*, wasn't exactly geared towards making French fun.

What surprised me was how hard it was teaching the adults. I knew it wouldn't be like the guys in Poland; here I was, teaching students at the most basic level, and so they had little-to-no skills. However, their basic abilities wasn't the problem. The big rule in the school was "No Chinese". That wasn't just for the teachers; it was for the students too. Getting the kids to follow that was pretty impossible, but the adults should have understood it pretty well. If they did, they clearly didn't care.

At first, it seemed I had made mistakes. I set up a mingle task (where the students had to ask each other questions and record the answers) but they found it very hard to complete, and ended up talking to each other in Chinese. I assumed they were talking about the task, as they didn't have the language to ask me to clarify in detail. They still tried though. There's nothing worse than being given a task you can't do, so I tried to make the lessons a bit simpler, so that they could at least finish.

That didn't seem to work though. In fact, it seemed to get worse. I kept saying "No Chinese" and even intervening to push them along. A common task was to give each student a card with personal details for made-up people, rather than getting them to answer questions about themselves. To get the ball rolling I would join in with my own card, or take the place of two students and demo the task from both sides. It worked for a short while, and then the Chinese would come out again pretty quickly. It was very demoralizing, and I often came out of the lesson feeling a bit depressed. This was not how I'd imagined teaching to be. It wasn't supposed to be relatively straightforward to teach kids but hard to teach adults.

I hit a wall when, trying to do another mingle, the class just flat out didn't bother. Before, they had made an effort. I had managed to get them to stand up and get talking eventually, but this time they wouldn't budge. They each picked the cards with the details they needed to ask about, but they didn't move, and they just talked, looking at the cards and discussing whatever it was that was on their mind. This time I chose not to intervene.

When the time was up I asked them questions about the information they should have gathered, just like I had planned. They didn't seem to feel too bad about not having done anything. I had hardly started teaching, and already I was realizing that the adults were not turning into my favourite group.

They weren't all bad. Chrissy had lost her initial enthusiasm, and Ping was an older woman who just had no ability to pick it up, even though she tried. Cherry gave it a go, but could display childlike frustration if she got something wrong. Rose and Terry were the worst offenders of the No Chinese rule, even though their English wasn't too bad for that level. Audrey was the best student in the group. I think she should have been in a higher level, but we didn't have an RE02 or 03 class, so she had gone in at the bottom. She worked hard though. I just had to hope that things would get better as they learnt more.

1. Meat Alley. 2-10. Square and park in JiangBei.

13 第十三章

It wasn't long before I received a package from mum. It contained a jar of instant coffee, which I kept on my desk, a big handful of tea bags, a packet of chocolate digestives (which I gladly shared with my friends), a double packet of Jaffa Cakes (which I didn't share, because Jaffa Cakes are more important than friendship), a small tub of pick 'n' mix sweets (candy like you get in a cinema) and some other assorted bits that reminded me of home.

It's weird the things you miss. I had plenty of Starbucks, Subway, Pizza Hut and MacDonald's on offer, but already I was getting a craving for Burger King. That fast food outlet had yet to wend its way to Chongqing, and I wondered how long I would have to wait to taste it again. A good curry was needed too, as the local Indian restaurant left a lot to be desired. Other foods I missed were fish and chips, Sunday roast, Cantonese food (what Westerners call Chinese), Tango, Frazzle's, Domino's Pizza, real English ale and salted peanuts. I wasn't going mad though, and could easily have survived without the package, but it was still nice to know that, no matter how far away I was, I still wasn't so far away that I couldn't be reached.

Thankfully, there was Carrefour to service one's Western needs. My local branch was near Chaotianmen, and it was great to be able to get real bread, cola that wasn't Coke, Cadbury's chocolate, a limited selection of pick 'n' mix-type candy and meat that I recognized.

Interestingly, I wasn't missing TV. I watch a lot of it, too much in fact, but I was so busy with lesson planning that my mind was occupied, and the Internet did a good job of distracting me in my free time. Any shows I missed I could just look up on one of the Chinese versions of YouTube, such as Youku or Tudou, neither of which seemed to give much of a toss about copyright infringement. Eventually, my TV stopped working, but I didn't bother getting it fixed.

I think the stress of the extra teaching got to me. The preparation was relentless from Wednesday to Friday, and sometimes I was forcing myself to work in the evenings. I've never liked the idea of doing that, and in my time at Ford I'd largely avoided it, but in China it became pretty important. It didn't always work though. Once the lesson was planned I then often had to make materials, and I didn't always do a good job of estimating how long that would take. So I found myself rushing to get things done at the end of Friday, which often meant leaving the weekend Life Clubs until the last minute, and by that I mean sorting them an hour before starting.

It made me tired, but mostly it gave me big headaches stressing out about the quality of my lesson plans. I was still taking a long time to get them completed, which sometimes made me cut corners to get the plans done, and sometimes it caused me problems. The main one was forgetting what it was I had meant to do. I would write 'Explain verbs with cue cards on the floor', and when I planned it, I knew exactly what I was talking about, but by the time I was in class it had cheekily jumped out of my mind. That left me scratching my head in the class and looking like a bit of a chump, trying to think of what I had thought of before, and then an alternative.

With the HF's, the and easiest get out was to throw the cards on the floor and ask a student "Where is the …..?", then when they pointed at one I would ask another student "Is this the….?". I would then get the student I asked first to ask another student "Where is the……?" and so the cycle continued, going around the class. It was a pretty decent task, and it certainly helped them, but the problem was that without the detailed note in my plan, it became too much of a safety net and too repetitive, so the kids got used to it and knew what to expect. What they needed was variety.

That may have explained their behaviour. It was my biggest class, so it was the biggest challenge for classroom management. It was also on a Saturday evening, so I could imagine some of them were a bit tired and restless. Sky was the most restless of the group, and in one lesson the other students squealed on him. Apparently, while I was checking a student's work, he did the "throat-cutting" action behind my back (the others pointed at him and demonstrated, the grasses). I was in a bad mood, but without seeing it there was nothing I could do about it.

The lesson progressed with problem after problem. They were constantly chatting to each other, fiddling with whatever stuff they had brought into class, acting lethargic and disinterested when I tried to get them to do something and generally just being monumental pains in the arse. As it progressed they got worse and worse, and my headache followed suit.

I was tired and fed up, more than they were on a Saturday evening, and towards the end I just lost it. Taking a tip from Rory's book, I chose the short sharp shock. I slammed my marker pen on the shelf in front of the whiteboard and, in the loudest voice I could muster, shouted "BE QUIET!" I'm sure they didn't actually understand me, but there are universal meanings to certain actions, and they knew exactly what was going down.

Everything stopped; the talking, the playing, the fidgeting. I had been pretty tolerant with them up to that point, but now I had lost it completely. I grabbed the pile of report books and pointed at them. They looked shocked, but they knew exactly what was about to happen. Thankfully, it was right at the end of the lesson, so I took the last few minutes to write a detailed note in each of their books. I was fair. I made sure that it said that everyone in the class was getting a bad report for general bad behaviour. As they filed out, I ticked the frowny face in each book and handed it to them. Some looked quite miserable, others didn't care.

Back in the teacher's room I slumped back in my desk. Julie came to check on how I was. Apparently I could be heard in the reception. That made me feel pretty embarrassed, but she was cool about it. Once again, it was something that happened to every teacher at some point; all part of the learning curve. As per usual, to cheer myself up, I diverted to MacDonald's for grease and starch. I genuinely felt bad about my reaction. I had completely lost control and, even though there was never any danger of me turning nasty and aggressive (or worse), I was still worried about how the kids would react to me after that.

One thing I had been taught on my CELTA, and reinforced at EF, was that if there is a problem in class – either with behaviour or learning – then it was more than likely the fault of the teacher. Either the teaching was bad, the activities were boring and useless or the classroom management was worthless. Whatever the cause, the golden rule for the teacher is to look at themselves before pointing the finger at the students and calling foul.

I had something else to think about, although it wasn't nearly as big a deal as losing my temper. It was about local sensibilities. I had an RE Life Club, and the subject was geography. I was explaining something about another country and, to try and explain it better to them I gave them a comparison.

"It's a bit like the difference between China and Taiwan." I said, thinking nothing of it.

"No, it's not China and Taiwan." Said Rose, a different one from my RE00 student. "It's mainland China and Taiwan. Taiwan is ours."

Oops! I hadn't bargained for it being that big a deal. I corrected myself and moved on. Later, I mentioned it to the others. It turned out that Rose was a fully paid up member of the Communist Party (Comrade Rose), so she was a true believer, although I'm not sure what that really means in China anymore. However, I had no political inclinations in the country, so I made a mental note never to say that again.

At least Julie and Rory recognized how stressed we were. One Monday evening we all met up outside my apartments and we headed up the road to a little place we would refer to as the "barbeque restaurant". There was me, Julie, Rory, Dave, Maria, Dulce and Tanja and, as would happen so often throughout the year, Rory and Julie insisted on paying.

The restaurant was mostly outdoor seating on the street, with tables and chairs covered by flimsy-looking canopies. Food was ordered from a tick sheet that no-one could read, but at least Rory could talk the talk. We called it the barbeque restaurant because of the barbeque outside, where the spicy meat on skewers was cooked, but that wasn't all. A selection of dishes and spectacular egg fried rice were delivered, but the most intriguing for me were the oysters.

On each shell was a lozenge of white meat, with a dash of noodles, herbs and garlic. The advice was to mix it all up and scoop it down in one go. I did, and the taste was an utter sensation. I had never eaten oysters before, but this was special. I felt like I had been missing out on something for most of my life. True, they were cooked completely differently to how they would be in a French restaurant, but that didn't matter to me. These oysters in garlic with noodles were insane, so Rory ordered a couple more rounds and I devoured as many as I could.

The other sensation was just around the corner, but for all the wrong reasons. I needed a piss, so I was directed to the public convenience nearby. Whenever I have to visit a public toilet I've always been prepared for a fair old stench, but nothing in my life had prepared me for the poisonous reek that slapped me across the face. I had been in a hideous smelling latrine in Latvia, which was just a hole in the floor where the turds were clearly visible, but this was on another level. It looked disgusting too, and I came out hoping there would be a sudden downpour, just so that I could feel cleansed of the awfulness before going home.

My mood at this time wasn't helped by the weather. Rain; that's all there seemed to be in Chongqing. Rain, rain, rain, rain, rain. Now, I know what you're thinking: "But you're British, you should be used to it." Ha bloody ha. Actually we don't get as much rain as people think, and certainly not like it was in Chongqing. This was constant drizzle; "The fine rain that gets you soaked through" in the words of comedian Peter Kay. There was never any hard downpour, just a constant, even sprinkling that went on and on and on and on and on. It had two effects. One was to make the city even greyer and deprive me of much needed vitamin D. The other was to make the air clearer, as it washed out all the soot from the air.

However, that soot had to go somewhere, and there was only one place for it; the ground. The streets looked like everyone had just walked through muddy puddles. Every collection of water on the paving stones was a filthy, black mush of the pollutants everyone was sucking into their lungs. It was a nightmare. Walking on the streets felt hazardous enough, especially on the multitude of inclines that dotted the city. More than once I was forced to reach out and grab something for fear of falling on my arse and smashing my laptop in my rucksack.

Amazingly, that wasn't the most hazardous aspect of it. Getting indoors produced a whole new world of problems, especially in the malls. The Chinese loved to build their shopping cathedrals with polished marble floors (or whatever was equivalent). It looks absolutely lovely, when it's dry outside, but when it rains it becomes a death trap. I had more slip ups inside the malls than I did out in the streets. Mall management tried to mitigate this by having staff stand at the main entrances dishing out little plastic bags for umbrellas, but that did nothing to stop the water and mush coming in on people's shoes. British malls may have dull, even grubby-looking floors, but at least they have grip.

If you want to know how the city looked at this time, get on Youtube and, in the search box, type *Ghost in the Shell musical scene*, or something to that effect. It's a three or four minute establishing montage of street scenes in a fictional, futuristic Tokyo, but it was closer to reality than the animators could have ever realized.

Interestingly, it wasn't very windy either. It took me a few weeks to notice, but there was absolutely no wind chill to speak of. There were light breezes at times, but never any strong gusts. It's true that, coming from Britain, I'm used to a lot of blowing, but even deep inland in Poland, the air had a habit of stirring on a regular basis. In Chongqing there was hardly a breath.

Then there was the advertising screen. Our school was not only on the same floor as the big video screen at the front of the mall, but the teachers room was right behind it, and some of our desks were facing its back. These included mine. It was an undoubted distraction, so I was grateful for the music on my laptop, but sometimes I just didn't want to listen to Bach, Faure, Jeff Wayne, Jean-Michel Jarre or Ed Alleyne-Johnson. The adverts were on a rolling schedule, and I was soon able to name the product or service that was up next. The most prominent advert was for the Shanghai Expo.

Two years before, China had hosted the Summer Olympics in Beijing, and it is considered a major event in modern Chinese history, a moment that showed it was seen as more than an Asian dictatorship with a rich imperial history. The Expo was the next step on China's headlong charge into the modern world, a world it was already close to dominating.

The advert was everywhere; on TV, on mega-screens in malls and on the little TVs on the buses. The sound of it was quite pleasant in a way; a woman's voice singing "laaaaaa la laaa la laaa, ah aaaah ah aaaah " and hitting a top C, followed by a voice over that probably espoused the theme of the exhibition – *Better City, Better Life* – over some very nice shot of the site and its pavilions. Interestingly, the big buzz was centred round the design of the UK pavilion, with its long hollow tubes sticking out like spikes, each one holding a single seed.

The other advert was for Chery cars, one of the many national manufacturers that had seen massive growth thanks to partnership deals with Western companies. It was a pretty typical car advert, with a haunting soundtrack, lots of fast moving shots with streak lighting effects and, of course, a very, very, very beautiful woman. The 7UP advert was also typical, with a scene depicting friends together having fun, just like back home. There was even a L'Oreal Men Expert advert starring Daniel Wu, a hugely popular young Chinese actor who really should have made it big in Hollywood by now. Maybe he was too much unlike Jackie Chan for Western prejudices to deal with – he wasn't known for his martial arts and he can actually act.

I was able to relax a lot at the weekends though. I spent most of my time alone, which is something I have always done in my life. It's not that I'm an unfriendly or unsociable person, but I do like my own time and my own space. I liked walking around the city – it fascinated me. I loved the overpowering skyline that shot up along the narrow streets, casting dull shadows over the grubby, soot covered thoroughfares. I loved how an old building was still younger than me, and that big construction was going on all the time to give the city new features to its face.

My favourite place to relax was Starbucks in Monument Square. I would often get lunch in the CSC in the basement, then head upstairs for a latte. It was one big open space, with a long window reaching from one side to the other, overlooking the square and all the people milling about. It was almost perfect, except for the fact that the windowsill was a foot too high to see over comfortably. I hoped they would build a platform to raise the seating, so that some of us could do some hard core people watching. Eventually, later in the year, there were some major renovations, and it certainly changed the people watching experience.

If I wasn't popping into CSC, or having the one Starbucks panini I liked, I would cheat and grab a MacDonald's. It was especially helpful in the mornings, if I didn't have any cereal or milk at home and I needed a good breakfast. When I say "good", I mean "sufficient". I'm not making any claim for its quality. It did the job that it needed to do, but then again, so did a croissant or ring doughnut and latte from Qin Yuan.

In the evenings I would spend a lot of time at home, on line, often talking to Miisa but also to friends and family back home. Even Mum, a real technophobe, got into it, thanks to her more tech-savvy neighbour who helped her use MSN. She call Mum when I popped up online, and Mum would climb the stairs to use what to her was still a form of witchcraft. She appreciated the webcam though, as the instant text would have been strange and impersonal to her.

I hadn't really looked for any bars to hang out in at night, but Ci Ci Park was decent enough, and the clubs didn't charge entry. I also tried out Soho and Babyface, but they were just like Bar 88, only darker and trendier looking.

Maria was popping round a lot too, and it was soon obvious that she and Dave were an item. I took to spending more and more of my time in my room, leaving the lovebirds to watch their DVD's in peace. I wasn't completely ignorant though, especially when Maria made a bucket load of awesome Korean kimchi (ironically, we ended up watching the Korean classic *Oldboy*).

I always had good intentions about the weekend, ones that involved doing some lesson planning ahead of time. I was still conscious of what little time I had and how long it took me to get anything done, so I always had it in mind to get a couple of lessons and clubs sorted on my weekends. As one might expect, my good intentions usually went to waste. Sometimes I got stuff done, but most of the time I found myself wandering the warren of streets, sitting and chilling, or holed up at home, surfing and chatting. My mind was often frazzled by the end of Sunday and it needed a rest.

1-2. The Party zone in JieFangBei. 3-5,8-9. JiangBei in the rain and gloom. 6. JiangBei Cheng. 7. Haibao, the mascot for the Shanghai Expo. 8. Skyscraper in JiangBei with external lift. 9. Future International Building in JiangBei.

14 第十四章

Maria and Dulce finally moved over, and we hired a new Chinese teacher, Grace. I was still only a couple of months into my new profession and I had managed to get through a pretty significant crisis without making any catastrophic mistakes or totally losing my mind. I felt a lot less pressure to work outside of school, so weekends became more fun. I still hadn't explored the city to any great degree, so I decided to do what I should have done from day one. On a smoggy Tuesday morning, I left my apartment and joined the now familiar Huayi Lu. Instead of turning right and heading downhill, I turned left, and climbed into an unknown world.

The street was lined with dirty-looking apartments and restaurants, and as the road levelled off, it wound its way over the hilly ground, where more apartments, offices and malls lined the pavements like I'd seen everywhere else. One side was different though; there was a hill rising from the street, and I soon found the winding access road that took me to the top. By the time I reached the summit, I was sweating hard and my legs ached.

Embarrassingly, the park at the top was full of elderly people, all of whom had made the same climb as me, some even having enough energy to play vigorous games of badminton. It was easily the most stereotypically Chinese place I'd seen in the city, with other groups performing tai chi and all around, little birds in cages hung from tree branches, tweeting and singing in a cacophony of avian melody.

That evening, we had a treat. John, the owner of the local EF franchise, had hired one of the party boats that lined the Jialing and Yangtze rivers around Chaotianmen. The views of the city as the boat chugged along the silted waterway were stunning, despite the hazy air. The towers and streets were brightly illuminated as we wound around the peninsula, tucking into the buffet and necking bottles of 1958. Shockingly though, the bar closed at 10, and we were somehow left high and dry on one of the mightiest rivers in the world.

For all the stress I had gone through in those initial few weeks, it was nothing compared to what Rory and Julie had to deal with. Julie, as the DoS, was responsible for all of the teaching side of the school (Boss Audrey was in charge of the business). She had to arrange the timetables, allocate classes, hire and fire teachers AND teach her own lessons. Rory had a lot of lessons to teach too, as well as organize all the Life Clubs and act as the main support/overseer of the teaching staff and provide teacher training. However, they took this all in their stride, but it was something else that made them want to bash their skulls against the wall. It was called, without any hint of irony, the EF Angels.

One afternoon, after taking a walk, I returned to the school to see a bunch of kids and their parents. It was odd, as some of them were my students but I didn't have their classes that evening. There were no Life Clubs scheduled either, but I did notice a block on the timetable for 'EF Angels'. After a couple of hours, Rory and Julie came back into the teachers' room, looking a little flustered, something that was very unusual for them.

The EF Angels was a choir, made up of students from both schools. The purpose of the choir was to promote EF locally: they would perform at local events as well as EF-specific promotional efforts. I don't know if they volunteered, or if Theo or Audrey had dumped it on them, but they were already looking like they regretted it. They'd had to audition each kid individually, and then they would select the best. That was the easy part though. As the weeks went by, Julie and Rory would have the delightful task of training these kids to sing English songs while performing little dance routines. Whatever stress I was going through with lesson planning was nothing compared to what they had to deal with thanks to the choir.

I'm not a child of the Internet age, but I don't know how people managed to get by without it when they were living abroad. For me, it was a lifeline to stay hooked up with loved ones and events back home. Even my mum, the world's archest Luddite, had gotten online to chat. MSN was one tool, as was Facebook. However, the Chinese government had decided it was far too dangerous for the population to use, and had completely blocked access to it. Thank God for proxies, or I would never have gotten round the 'Great Firewall of China'.

Miisa and I spoke pretty much every night. In fact, I spoke to her more than I did to my family and close friends combined. It felt easy to talk to her, although I preferred typing than using audio. I don't like the sound of my own voice, and I just seem to think of more to say on a keyboard. Eventually though, I moved into the second decade of the 21st century and downloaded Skype, but I still stuck with text.

In May I was gripped by a big event back home: the General Election. We'd had 13 years of a Labour government that had sent us into 4 major armed conflicts and a recession so significant that our banking system nearly collapsed. The Prime Minister, Gordon Brown, had been a failure in his short time in office, and it was clear that they were going to lose, but what wasn't clear was if the Conservatives were going to win.

I was able to watch the whole thing unfold online at a reasonable hour, rather than staying up for 36 hours like I did in 1997. It was a Friday, and after doing a bit of work in the school I took my notes and my laptop and headed down to Frisco's. With a hot latte and their wi-fi, I logged on to the BBC web site and watched the election coverage. It was a little bit patchy and unreliable, thanks to having to use the proxy, but when it worked it was crystal clear.

It's such a typically British thing to be excited by a draw, but that's exactly what happened. There was no clear winner, we were heading towards a coalition, with Labour or the Conservatives having to join up with the Liberal Democrats. I wondered what the Chinese would make of it. Surely, a decisive government with the power to get things done quickly was the best thing for a country. After all, that's exactly what they had, and they were doing ok.

True, they didn't have freedom of speech, freedom of association, fair trials, the right to remove incompetent and corrupt politicians, freedom to protest, free access to information, healthcare free at the point of delivery, oversight and public accountability for ministers and government departments, a social welfare safety net or any other benefits that we in the West claim to have for ourselves, but at least their government got things done. I couldn't really complain though. I hadn't bothered sorting out a postal vote before leaving so my preference was never taken into account.

I was becoming a more and more trusted member of the teaching team. Lessons were being delivered and, so far, no-one was complaining about my quality of work. I'd been there for three months and had dealt with a particularly trying time pretty well, so it was time for me to progress to the next level – the OPT.

The Oral Proficiency Test is given to each new, prospective student to see what their current level of English is, and which class to put them in. We didn't have classes at every level, so a lot of the time it meant putting them on a waiting list until one came up (letting them come to all the various Life Clubs), or shoe-horning them into a current class that was a little bit above or below their abilities, and hope they could catch up or not be left behind.

The test is a list of set questions and subjects (that could be added to as the teacher saw fit), and the students were assessed on their understanding of the questions and the language they produced in response. This was the thing I dreaded the most. Get it wrong and not only would a student be put in the wrong class, but do that enough and it could jeopardize the reputation of the school.

It was also the first time the students would have any contact with the teaching staff, so it was doubly important to put on a smile, even if one was having a really bad day. The process was usually that one of the teachers would be on OPT duty at any one time. If one was needed, a PA would hand that teacher the form and, on occasion, suggest a level based on their own assessment. Sometimes this was annoying, because they would often tell the student what level they chose, and they often chose a level higher than we did. Time and time again we told the PA's not to tell the students, but there was always an element of face-saving involved. As long as the teacher did a good OPT and could justify their decision, then Julie and Rory would always stand by us.

I had a very intriguing encounter with a local. I popped into Starbucks for a latte and sat at an occupied table. The guy there looked in his thirties, and his suit and expensive laptop suggested someone with mighty ambitions. He spoke excellent English, so good that he didn't display the desperate and needy enthusiasm to practice. He asked me about my job and what I used to do before, and after a while he asked if I had ever thought about working in the property market. It had never appealed to me, but I didn't let on. He gave me his number, and suggested I call him if I wanted to earn some good, extra money.

My contract with EF was pretty clear; I worked for EF and that was it. No moonlighting. I told Rory about the meeting, and that I had no interest in it. I hadn't come to China to make my fortune and I had enough stress planning my lessons. Rory revealed something: it was almost certain that that job offer had nothing to do with working and making money from property transactions. It was about that guy having a white face with him.

Apparently, in many parts of China, there is a great deal of kudos in being associated with white people in business. Sometimes, business people would actually hire white people (normally out of work actors) to "be around" looking "businessy" during business meetings. This, Rory said, gave that party an air of success and grandiosity that was supposed to impress their prospective partners/customers/suppliers.

It sounded weird, but then again it wasn't completely out of character from what I'd seen already. Also, wouldn't it be obvious to the other parties? Would they really see these white people and not know they were hired to pretend? Wouldn't they have a round-eye of their own?

Saturday, 15th May was a huge day. It was perfectly normal at school. I did all my tasks as normal, and in the evening I headed home. Usually I would have made some food and lounge on the sofa, surfing the net and chatting to friends and family online, but this evening was different. It was the night of the FA Cup Final, and Pompey were in it.

The season had been a harrowing one for Portsmouth (nicknamed Pompey), my favourite team. It had been such a glowing few years after so many in the doldrums. We were in the Premier League and riding high. In 2007-08 we won the FA Cup for the first time since 1939, and our first major trophy since 1950, and in 2008-09 played in Europe and almost beat AC Milan, but the current season wasn't working out well. An insane ownership debacle had led to the club being put into administration and given a ten point deduction, which pretty much sealed our relegation with barely half the season over. All we had was the Cup.

Rounds three and four were pretty straight forward with wins against Coventry City and Sunderland. The draw for the fifth round had given us a dream tie, a match against Scummers (Southampton FC) at the Shit Mary's (St.

Mary's) Stadium in Scummerhampton (Southampton). As you can tell, Pompey fans hate Scummers and vice versa. On the Sunday before I left I had the pleasure of watching Pompey give Scummers the kind of spanking that they deserved; 4-1 on their own turf.

The quarter final must have been an insane atmosphere at Fratton Park as we beat Birmingham City 2-0, and the draw for the semi-final gave us another dream matchup; Tottenham Hotspur, coached by Harry Redknapp, the man who won us the Cup in '08 and who then jumped ship just before all the crap appeared (he'd also left us once before, to coach Scummers). We won 2-0, and were in the final.

The next day I was beaming and I knew one thing; there was no way I was going to miss the final. The problem was that it would be on a Saturday, and in the evening Chinese time, and I had to teach on a Sunday. I explained the situation to Julie, giving her a brief, and no doubt thoroughly interesting, history of Portsmouth FC and the FA Cup, just so that she would understand how important it was.

"Here's the thing." I said as she looked at me from her desk in her office, politely smiling to hide her disinterest and/or confusion. "I have to watch it. There's no way I can miss it. I will find a bar somewhere that's showing it and I will watch it, and I will have a few beers. I might even go out to a club after. However, I promise I will be in on Sunday, on time, and I will do all my lessons, but I will probably be hungover."

"That's cool." Julie said, her smile showing a warm understanding. "Just as long as you do Sunday it's cool."

My next job was to find a spot. I hopped on line to the CQ Expats web site, where I posted a pleading, begging message for anyone who was planning to watch the match and knew where to go. I soon received a response from someone who suggested the outside bar in JieFangBei or the Harp Irish Bar in Hongyadong. I was in two minds so I decided to go with the easy option and chose Harp, as it was closer and indoors.

That Saturday night I was in Harp for the first time, ordering an ice cold pint of Tiger Lager. I was served by Shang, a pretty Chinese woman who was the co-owner with her American husband Chris. There were a few other expats, and a group of Swedes turned up too, all on business for Volvo Cars from Gothenburg, but they had no interest in the match, choosing to congregate with their Chinese colleagues outside.

From the moment the match kicked off, I was in emotional turmoil. It was bottom of the league versus the champions, Chelsea, and we had it all against us. They had thrashed us in the season and scored 100 goals, so people were half expecting a murder, but it didn't matter to me. 1-0 was the same as 10-0 if we were the 0 team. I won't bore you with the details of the match though. I can barely remember it.

All I remember is how I was. I was going mental. Shouting at the screen, grabbing fistfuls of my hair, swearing, gasping and falling to my knees. I was a mess. We put up a great fight though, frustrating the posh, pampered foreigners and the token fake Cockneys with every attack they tried. Every now and again, one of the Swedes would walk past me and ask if I was okay. Clearly my pain and anguish was bursting through the walls. It was also pointed out that I may well have been the only Pompey fan in the whole of China.

Then, in the 54th minute, we were awarded a penalty, and it seemed that history was beckoning. Kevin-Prince Boateng placed the ball on the spot and took a few steps back. As he stepped up I had a portent that he would miss. He didn't; it was saved. I fell to my knees and curled up into a ball, knowing full well that it was all lost. Four minutes later, Didier Drogba scored with a glorious free kick, forcing me to scream "Drogba you fucking cunt!". 35 minutes later the match was over. We had lost 1-0. Chelsea had done the double and we were back in what I still prefer to call the "Second Division".

From then on, I was able to relax. The match had been a big adrenaline rush and now I was on the come down, finally able to enjoy the beer and the ambience. Harp wasn't the most Irish-looking Irish pub I'd ever been in, but it had a good atmosphere, some big leather chairs and sofas and outdoor seating on the concourse leading to the neighbouring seafood restaurant. Shang had been pretty entertained by the whole spectacle, although Chris seemed unfazed. He must have been around a few sports nuts in his time, or maybe Shang just couldn't see why anyone would get so emotional over any sport other than table tennis, and so thought it was hilarious.

The Swedes were pretty sympathetic to me, and generous enough to buy me a drink or two. I didn't want to get hammered though, but I had started to cross the line where going home seemed like a waste of time. So I joined them, and we headed out to the Cotton Club.

Inside the club, the crowd was already packed in. I avoided the tradition of downing a few vodkas and instead stuck to the bottles of Heineken. The dance floor was rammed, and I joined in, by now losing a certain amount of coordination and visual clarity. I still had it in my mind that I had a day of teaching ahead of me, but I was having a great night out in a place I felt comfortable. It was Saturday night, one of the rare Saturday nights I would be able to enjoy in my time there, and I wasn't going to waste it. It was great to be hanging around with some of the ex-pats who had to work a normal week and, as always, everyone was perfectly friendly.

I spent all night at the bar, drinking Heineken and chatting to random people who seemed friendly enough. I got talking to a local woman called Amy, whom I would eventually come to know as "Crazy Amy". She was only 21, locally born and bred, but with perfect English like she had spent time abroad. She told me she worked for a magazine, writing articles about sex advice, which she seemed a little young for, but maybe she was just very good at it. Eventually

I reminded myself of my job and headed home, at about 4am, downing a bottle of water on the way.

The next morning was a struggle. I hadn't gotten blind drunk, but just enough to know that I hadn't been as stable or as eloquent or as charming as I had thought. Thankfully I didn't have an early start. I woke up at about 11 with a thumping headache and a throat that felt like it had done twelve rounds with a wallpaper scraper. I had a shower, a quick cup of coffee and took a couple of pre-purchased croissants as I headed out the door, my growing hair still wet.

When I arrived at the school I was so glad I hadn't yet had a full timetable. Sunday mornings were for the kiddies, the Small Stars especially, and my God it sounded like it. I was still bleary-eyed as I made it in to the teacher's room, surviving the screaming of the 'Little Emperors'. Rory seemed pretty impressed that I had made it. In this job, people can often take things for granted, like thinking that the rules aren't as strict as they are in the rest of the world. At least Rory and Julie pushed a professional ethic and, even though I showed up clearly the worse for wear through purely self-inflicted means, I still showed up as promised, and was fully prepared.

How wonderful it was that my first class was my TB3As. It wasn't just their intelligence and humour that I liked; it was their immaturity. That sounds like an insult but it really isn't. They were kids, and they still behaved like it. When they talked about their weekends or hobbies they often talked about "playing with their friends". If there's one thing a Western teenager would never say it would be that. They would be "hanging out" or "chilling" or even "partying". These kids reminded me of the teen dramas from when I was young, where teenagers were portrayed as older children who still wanted to muck around down the park or have adventures down the beach.

Now, teen dramas are all about drinking and fucking - pretty soulless and depressing. I've not seen much of these shows, but I can imagine it being pretty miserable being a teenager these days. My TB3As seemed sheltered from this, maybe because they spent all their free time in extra classes or doing homework. They seemed a lot more innocent, and I liked that. There's plenty of time to feel pressure in life, but when you're a teen you should just educate yourself and play with your friends.

After the lesson there was a quick and simple Life Club, and then that was that. My day had actually been pretty easy and the hangover had been manageable, but I really didn't want to stay any longer than I had to. I headed out to MacDonald's, where a Big Mac and fries went some way to soaking up the residual alcohol lurking in my blood stream. Then it was the usual bus ride home, back up the hill and into the flat. A few hours online kept me awake for a while, but soon my bed called and I hit the sack. It had been my first true test of professionalism, and I had passed.

1-4. The park on the hill. 5. A big hole in the ground. 6. A heroic, Socialist Realist statue. 7. City Hall. 8. The Three Gorges Dam Museum. 9. The old in with the new. 10. The city at night.

15 第十五章

A couple of days after the football it was Rory's birthday, and we had a big chuancai meal at a place in JiangBei called Metempsychosis. Once again we engorged on a wide variety of spicy meats and vegetables, washed down with a never-ending supply of the gold label Chongqing beer. It was in the taxi on the way home that Dave told me he was moving out and living with Maria, that night. I was a bit peeved that he hadn't done me the courtesy of telling me before, but then again I preferred living on my own. I'd been a bit frustrated at having to share – I'd been living alone since 2003 in Essex and so was used to having space all to myself.

    At least there was one thing Rory wouldn't have to deal with – Chinese birthday cake. For the most part, they were pretty standard sponges with cream, jams, icing and sprinkles, but what shocked me were the toppings. Normally, one would expect to see strawberries, raspberries, cherries, blackcurrants, Satsuma chunks or even kiwi fruit. Never, in my life, have I ever considered topping a sponge cake with cucumbers or tomatoes. They didn't look hideous, just weird, and don't give me that crap about tomatoes being fruit. If it belongs in a salad then it doesn't deserve to be on a cake.

We had a new edition to the team. Martin was a young guy from Newcastle who would be working at New York New York. He seemed intelligent and nice enough, if perhaps a little nerdy. There was another get together to welcome him to China and then he could get into the swing of things at the school.

    To welcome Grace and Martin into the fold we had a big group outing to KTV. All of the teaching staff showed up and it turned into one, mad party. Rory and Julie dipped into their own pockets to pay for all the booze and food and refused the offers from myself and others to contribute to the kitty. This was where I revealed my perfect karaoke rendition of *Hungry Eyes* to the rest of the guys, though for some reason I did it while straddling and grinding on top of Rory like some sort of lap dancer. It was also the night Julie and I first performed our duet of *Waiting for a Star to Fall* by Boy Meets Girl. Once again, Julie was pitch perfect while I was tuneless and unbearable, but effusive and ebullient (the perfect karaoke performance).

    Lady GaGa was another popular choice. Most of the videos with the songs were really cheesy productions clearly made in the early 90's, showing couples on beaches or cycling in the country or some other fun activity, giving a simple visual stimulus without having to pay for official music videos. However, this was China, so many of the songs came with their actual videos, replete with title credits added by MTV or VH1. To be honest, it was good to watch Lady GaGa.

There was one song that seemed to be particularly popular. *Zombie* by The Cranberries had captured the imagination of the Chinese. I'm not sure if it was recent, or if there was some local nostalgia, but it got chosen a lot on other visits to KTV, always by the Chinese. Interestingly, the video that came with it was always some performance of the song by a Chinese artist, and one that looked quite recent. Even Grace couldn't explain China's fascination with a song about the futility of 'The Troubles' in Northern Ireland. I just hope the band actually got their royalties.

It was also the night I did a very bad thing. 'Dick move' is the common term used these days, but I would say it's inadequate. When Rory took a turn he decided to choose a song by Coldplay. I fucking hate Coldplay, with a passion that verges on the insane. I hate their boring music, their trendy wine bar appeal and, above all, I hate Chris Martin and his smug, self-satisfied pretentiousness and painfully revolting attempts at being a "serious artist" by contorting his body like he's trying to outdo Jim Morrison (a real artist). However, no matter how much I hated the song, it didn't justify what happened next – the only thing that can explain it is the cocktail of beer and Jack.

Throughout Rory's singing I feigned agony, holding my ears and screaming like I was being subjected to some sort of Nazi torture programme. It was all taken in jest, and Rory did make sure he sang to me for a lot of it. Then, when he had finished, I stood up, walked up to him, and slapped him hard round the face. I'm not joking or exaggerating. That's exactly what I did, all because he sang a shitty song.

He was pretty shocked, and even in my drunken state I realized what I'd done, so I did the first thing I could think of and hugged him. He kept asking people "Andy slapped me, right?" He didn't make a big deal of it for the rest of the night, but the booze didn't wipe the incident from my memory. The next time I saw him I was grovelingly apologetic. He said he was okay about it, acknowledging that I was hammered, but I felt pretty fucking terrible, and embarrassed.

Once again, the teaching team expanded. Dani was a young woman from Shrewsbury, Shropshire and, like me, she had her first taste of real China in the chuancai restaurant underneath our apartments. She had been moved in with Martin, so we were getting ourselves a nice little community in the block. It was another typical buffet of interesting and delectable delights, washed down with a few bottles of 1958.

I had already decided that shrimp pot was my favourite dish in the city, and possibly in the world. I can't describe how great it tastes. I'm not a big fan of seafood, despite the fact that I grew up in a coastal port city with a decent sized fishing fleet. The shrimp in shrimp pot were insanely tasty though, and I always felt cheated when I finished a meal, like I hadn't been given nearly enough.

The culinary scene was added to when Harp started doing food. There were standard burgers and fries, and a few Mexican dishes like burritos and enchiladas. I like to think I'm up to speed with American culture, but there was an item listed that I'd never heard of; the Sloppy Joe. To me, this was heaven, a sandwich of minced beef, onions and sauce served in a burger bun. Damn it was good! Sunday evenings often became Sloppy Joe at Harp Night.

It was at this time that I realized I had made another monumental fuck up. This time with the Small Stars. I'd been worried about their behaviour and thought they might have been bored. The lessons seemed quite repetitive, even though I was just using the course book to plan everything. Looking through the sample plan, I had often been surprised by how thin it could be, and how little the kids were expected to progress, but I kept at it, just waiting for the course to move on. The kids were doing well, they just seemed fed up. I put it down to them wanting to be playing with their toys or watching *Pleasant Goat and Big Big Wolf*.

One day it hit me. I wondered how long it would really take to get through the entire book, so I flipped through a few pages and came to a sudden, horrific realization. I had fucked up once again. When planning lessons for a new course, the first thing any teacher should do is browse through the book to get an idea of what the units are about, what they cover and where the teacher needs to be week after week.

I had done that for my HF's, TB's and RE's but, for some reason, I hadn't done that with Small Stars. Each sample lesson plan had each task numbered but, for some reason, I hadn't thought that a contiguous set of numbers made up a single lesson. True, there were a lot, but they weren't separated by unit and lesson number indicators. To cut a long story short, over those initial months, I had effectively given the kids three lessons. I was many weeks behind.

This wasn't a 'schoolboy error', it was the mistake of a complete and utter moron. I had no way of explaining it to myself, let alone to Julie and Rory, so I decided not to. I decided I would catch up. By then I should have been teaching them about animals but I hadn't even covered stationary. It was time to pull out all the stops. I talked to Tanja about 'making the lessons more fun', and she gave me loads if hints about games to get them playing, and I immediately set to work catching up.

The first one I tried was a race. I would take two trays into the class, full of items from the book; pen, pencil, ruler, scissors, paper. I would put the trays at the front of the class, either side of me, and split them into two teams, lined up. I would then call out an item. The kids at the front would run up to their tray, grab an item and run back to their team. I did it as a competition, and there were different ways of scoring. One was to give a point to the first one back to the line with the correct item. The other was to give a point if they had picked the right one, and another point to the one who got back first.

The kids absolutely loved it and would get super hyper. Sometimes they would get over excited and I would have to get a bit strict, but they still had fun. Also, and this is a message to any British teachers out there, they loved the competitive aspect. There has been a growing trend in Britain, which admittedly has sometimes been exaggerated by the tabloid press, where competitive sports have been reduced to a pat on the head for taking part, because having winners and losers is "so harmful" to children. My kids had more fun being competitive than in any other tasks we did. Another reason why countries like China are rapidly taking over the world.

A few weeks after my revelation, Kathleen, my SS PA, told me that the mum of Nina (the oldest in the class) had said that Nina had been bored, that they'd been doing the same thing over and over again. I'm not sure when this had been said, but I wasn't surprised. By then I could genuinely tell Kathleen that I'd "reviewed" my lessons and had felt the same, and that I was making a particular effort already and things were looking better. She seemed happy, and I was relieved that it hadn't been an actual complaint.

The days were warming up pretty quickly. What counted as spring in Chongqing had already passed and summer was ramping up. The days were getting brighter, and long gone were the horrors of the smog-shrouded winter days when the sun fought a losing war against the poisons of human activity. By then, the jeans had been ditched and it was three-quarter length shorts all the way.

Mum seemed to be getting the hang of the Internet, though she still needed help from her neighbour. We tried using audio, but the quality was pretty poor so we just typed and used the webcam. It certainly helped her feel better about me being away. Live video communication for the masses was still pretty new, even for me, so for her it was something she could never take for granted.

Miisa and I still spoke a lot, and even used the webcam on Skype a few times. I don't really like voice chatting, but it was always good to see her and hear her voice. She'd made a momentous decision of her own. She'd decided to sell her flat and most of her big belongings, take a sabbatical from her job and move to Bangkok for six months. There was no great career plan behind it – she just wanted a break. It was amazing, as I would be able to see her again. It was just a case of when.

Tanja and I started paying weekly, Sunday visits to the bars under the park in JiangBei. Our local was the one with the karaoke booth, but we also visited the packed bar with the annoying, whistling waitresses and the hostesses whose price for getting us drinks was taking a shot for herself. It was nice just to chill out with Tanja after work, as we were both adept at having a rant at some of the most troublesome kids we had to deal with.

Crossing the square between the main road and the park, we would often be picking our way through crowds in some official celebration or, more likely, mass formation dancing. This is not tai-chi, but it is a form of exercise, mostly performed by women, and usually in groups of five to twenty. In JiangBei, it was clearly over a hundred, all stepping, turning and gesticulating in incredible precision, uniformity and timing.

The bang-bang seemed even more incredible in the summer heat. For me, just being outside was a struggle, and I wore shorts and t-shirts and only had to carry my laptop with me. They were often dressed in shirts and trousers, and relentlessly carried loads that would have snapped my collar bone under pressure, and they never looked like they broke a sweat. Granted, they were more used to such weather conditions, but I had expected them to suffer some sort of discomfort.

Rory and Julie were having such a wonderful time doing the choreography for the EF Angels choir. Once a week, the large classroom in the middle of the school, next to the Life Club Zone, was full to bursting with kids, mostly Small Stars and High Flyers. Every time I walked past the room at that time I could see the stress written across their faces as they did their best to keep the kids in line, let alone learning the songs and simplistic dance routines. Sometimes Rory would look at me as I passed as if to say "Kill me".

I had another new class, a second SS Orange group. This lot were scheduled for 10am on a Sunday, which meant that the last bit of useful free time I had left for planning on my timetable was gone. Now I had no choice. I had to get everything done during the week or I would be in big, big trouble come the weekend. I thought I had the measure of this level now, but my confidence would be proved unfounded like it was on so many occasions during that year.

On Wednesdays I was given another HF00 class, and this one would prove to be particularly tricky. From the first lesson, I could tell I was going to have particular issues with this class. Jake, a taller than average 8 year old, seemed to have it in for me from the off. He wasn't a particularly sweet looking child, nor did he come across as a cheeky little chap. He liked whispering to his regular neighbour Hans, a fidgety, hyperactive boy who was more adept at bouncing in his chair than sitting still and listening. I kept my patience though. The last thing I wanted was a repeat of my outburst in my other HF group.

The TB's were still great but the RE's were still a struggle. The small adult class was going quite well though. They were reliable and hard-working, and the freedom I had for the lessons gave me scope to experiment with different tasks. I guess part of the reason for this was that they already had a good grasp of English, so it was much more like the classes on my CELTA.

I was also given a one to one student. His name was Steve, he was 17 years old, and he was looking to improve his English so he could get into university in America. It meant I had to teach IELTS, the International English Language Testing System, managed by the British Council, Cambridge English Language Assessment and IDP Education. It's one of the two major English language tests in the world, but it wasn't something anyone in the school was particularly familiar with. Really, all that was needed was to go through the standard course book, so it didn't seem so hard. How wrong I would be.

I don't want to break the golden rule of teaching, but in this case I will make an exception. Steve was a dick. He was always late for his 90 minute session, usually by 15 minutes. He never seemed particularly enthusiastic, despite his desire to go to university. When I asked him what he wanted to study, he had no idea. I asked him what he was interested in and he said 'nothing', which I found ridiculous. Even if you don't know what you want to study at university, you should at least know what subjects you enjoy most. He revealed that he had an older sister studying in America, so I asked about what she was doing. He said he had no idea, because he hadn't spoken to her in three years.

So, Steve had no idea what to study, didn't particularly care about any subject, and didn't give a shit about his sister. He was a bit of a twat, and his attitude didn't exactly improve as the weeks went by. I really feel that I tried my best, but each time I sat down to plan his sessions I felt less and less interested. At one point, Julie had a word with him about his habitual lateness and occasional non-attendance, and eventually he was passed on to someone else. I didn't mind having the extra work to do, but only for something worthwhile, and his sessions just weren't worth it.

More worthy lessons continued apace. My TB's were pushing themselves as much as I was pushing them. After one lesson about travel, I set them homework to write about a memorable holiday they had. Pretty standard stuff. Each one brought back a nicely detailed short essay in impeccable handwriting. At the end of the lesson I went through their essays, just to get them talking more freely. Most of them talked about trips to other cities in China, or nearby countries like Korea or Japan, but one was of particular interest. Sabrina, one of the older kids, wrote about her trip to Oulu in Finland. This was pleasantly shocking. Clearly, Sabrina was one of the lucky ones – a Chinese kid with cosmopolitan parents who want their child to experience as much of the world as early as possible.

I managed to deliver what would turn out to be the most successful Life Club of my time there. It was for RE levels 3-5, and the theme was pronunciation, and when I first saw that, I was clueless about what to do. The key to these themes is to not take them literally; think laterally and be flexible. Rory threw out a few suggestions and one latched into my head immediately; slang. Slang is a universal concept; I don't think there is a single language in the world that doesn't have a lexicon of alternative words based on historical events or regional experiences. Britain, however, has easily the most unique, the most fun and the most bizarre slang of all; Cockney Rhyming Slang.

Planning this Life Club was an absolute delight. The first task was a Life Club wall picture pelmanism. I had twenty pics, in ten pairs. For example; a picture of an ear and a picture of Britney Spears, a picture of a calendar (years) and a picture of donkey's ears, a picture of some apples and pears and a picture of stairs. Obviously, none of the students even came close to choosing the right pairs, and were baffled when I showed them the results, though they understood the rhyme bit. Then there was an explanation of London and what a cockney is and then the nitty-gritty. The end result would be that they had to invent their own rhyming slang using a text I gave them, read it out, and the others would have to guess what was being said.

This club had a number of functions; it taught them about rhyming, it taught them about London and it gave them an insight into some of the weird things they would hear if they ever visited ("getting your Barnet cut", "having a butcher's", "having dinner with the trouble", "piercing your Britneys"). In fact, it was a lot more important for them than they realized. It also taught me something; proper Cockney rhyming slang isn't just about rhyme, it's about rhythm too. Repeat these terms and you'll pick out the stress-unstress-stress pattern: Britney Spears, trouble and strife, plates of meat, donkey's ears.

It was a demonstrable success, although I'm not sure why. Maybe it was because they learnt something about Britain, maybe it was because it was pitched at just the right level for them to understand while needing to make an effort, or maybe it was because they thought it was so ridiculous that it became fun. They did a great job of inventing their own, although most of their work missed out the stress pattern. Life Clubs can often be where students are lazy or not engaged in the subject, but in this case they were positively immersed.

It was also an interesting mix of students, all of them professionals looking to improve their skills and, hopefully, their prospects. Two in particular stuck in the memory. Dana was in her forties, married with kids and a trained lawyer. However, her actual job title was the "Chief Prosecutor of Chongqing". She had been instrumental in dealing with the gangs of the city and had even helped get the then Chief of Police to take the job. The other was Jackie, also in his forties with a wife and kids. He was a brain surgeon, and very well respected in the field. Apparently, he'd actually developed a surgical technique, and was so well regarded that he'd had more than one lucrative job offer to work in America. The only thing stopping him was that his English was at barely intermediate level.

By the way, on a side note, if you ever hear a Brit using the term "donkey's years", feel free to slap them. It's wrong! The slang is "donkey's ears", meaning "years" e.g. "that happened donkey's ears ago", and the contraction is "donkey's" e.g. "that happened donkey's ago". It should NEVER be "that happened donkey's years ago"! Rant over.

Another Life Club that worked well was for RE's and was about music lyrics. I played some randomly chosen music videos, gave the students the lyrics and then we discussed what they said and what they meant. I deliberately chose a lot, just in case the discussions were too quick. There was only 2 students, and one of them was Dana, and they were very interested in some of the classic tracks I had chosen. One that worked well was *Whip It* by Devo. As we talked through the lyrics, I suggested it was all about forgetting the past and moving on with life. Dana disagreed, suggesting it was about overcoming adversity to better oneself. When I looked at the words again I realized she was right. How could I, the native speaker, not have seen that?

A few weeks later, I lead another RE Club entitled "Eurovision", so we did a simple music video review, in which I included at least one Mando-Pop video, and they had to talk about good and bad points and pick a winner. I even included the hideous karaoke video of me for a laugh, which they chose as the best.

Not all Life Clubs were so successful though. Despite doing okay with the lessons, I found HF Life Clubs to be somewhat tricky. Maybe it was down to the scheduling, or maybe I kept going into the planning with an overly inflated confidence, but I often struggled to put together something that even I was happy about. In this situation I, and most of the other teachers, fell back on the same task – colouring. At times it was a perfectly good choice. I'd go through the club, explaining the topic, showing slides and/or videos, getting some sort of active task going on and then give them a blank outline picture related to the task for them to colour.

I never left it at that though. I kept control of the pencils and the kids had to come to me to ask for the colour they wanted. While they were decorating the pictures I would go round and ask them questions about theirs. At the end I would get as many of them up on the stage to present their picture, ask them questions and encourage the others to say something. It was often a lifesaver as it could take up as much as a third of the club, but there was a problem. A lot of that time the kids were talking a lot of Chinese, and that was a big no-no. Julie and Rory made a point of saying that there was too much of it going on and that it as an obvious "get out of jail free" card for our planning. Obviously, there were times when it was useful e.g. teaching colours, but it was being used too much for their liking.

There was also another Life Club that I would remember for a long time. It was about the upcoming World Cup in South Africa. It wasn't that it was a failure – if anything it was a success because the students were really into it – but it revealed something about the Chinese mentality. Americans are often accused of being ignorant of the outside world, but I would argue the Chinese could give them a run for their money.

It was the map that provided the revelation. All they had to do was stick the flags and names on the correct country. I knew there would be plenty they didn't get – I'm sure Honduras is not on the radar of Chinese current affairs – but I expected a few to be pretty easy, such as UK, USA, Japan, North Korea. What I experienced was a level of ignorance that beggared belief. America was stuck on Brazil, Argentina was stuck on South Africa, Japan and North Korea were switched and, most outrageously, the glorious Union Jack was stuck on France!

I was so amazed that I just had to do a test. In the guise of helping them orient themselves I asked a simple question: Where is China? Even this elicited confusion and head scratching, but they managed to get it eventually (after one of them pointed at India). These were not dumb people. One of them was a lawyer, one had her own business and one was a teacher.

I was shocked by the low level of knowledge on the subject, and when I told the other teachers about it, it was Grace who solved the mystery.

"Geography isn't taken so seriously at school." She said, recounting her own experiences. "It's the one lesson where kids are allowed to go to sleep without being punished."

I found it hard to believe that kids were allowed to nap during any lesson, but the message was clear; geography is less important than subjects such as maths or English. I suppose that makes a certain, logical sense, but I still found it incredible. Sure education should be as much about the pleasure to learn as the measurable, practical, physical benefits one can get out of it. Also, geography isn't just about countries and cities, it's also about such things as population, something a country of 1.3 billion people would do well to learn more about.

1-7. The weather getting better and clearer. 8. View along the Jialing, similar to the front cover, without the smog. 9. Formation dancing in JiangBei.

16 第十六章

Joyously, we were given a weekend off. June 14th-16th was the Dragon Boat Festival and, while that was on a Monday-Wednesday, it was clear that no-one had any intention of coming in for class, so the school was closed. On the Friday evening Tanja, Dulce, Martin, Maria, Dave, Dani and I decided to make a night of it.

We popped down to the street for some hotpot, where all the ingredients were on sticks and we could help ourselves from the fridges. The sticks were put in pots in the table, and once done, the staff counted our sticks and charged us accordingly. It was a wonderful piece of logic and common sense that I had found lacking in so many other places in the city.

There were a couple of other hotpot restaurants on the street that I never got round to trying, perhaps for the best. In these, the bowl is brought out with all the ingredients included, but cold, dry and congealed. A block of fat is sat on top and the heat melts the lot. I'm sure its smelle great, but from the window it looked awful.

We headed across the river to Nanbin Lu, the main road running along the mighty Yangtze in Nan'an district. It was a typical evening, with the city illuminated on a backdrop of misty smog in the air above, giving it a spectral halo from every angle. We enjoyed the view with a few beers in one of the plush (and largely empty) riverside bars, and were intrigued by the strange blue glow that was emanating from the middle of the skyline. Was there a festival going on? Had a UFO landed? Had science finally gone too far? When we heard cheering coming from somewhere nearby it clicked.

It was June 11th 2010, the first day of the FIFA World Cup in South Africa. The first match had kicked off between South Africa and Mexico and, despite no-one having any special loyalty to either nation, the locals were getting into it. China isn't known as a footballing nation. They've qualified only once for the World Cup, in 2002, but other than that they've made no impact on the sport, except for one year when Channel 4 in the UK showed weekly highlights of the Chinese Football League for absolutely no bloody reason anyone could think of.

Walking along the main road we passed the two, ugly, golden towers of the Sheraton Hotel and the most vomit-inducing road marking ever – a Zebra crossing with a big heart and the words "I Love You" in the middle.

The next evening, however, was the important one, the one that would bring together the expats from all nations in patriotic passion and neutral pleasure – England vs USA.

There is some deep history to this fixture. In 1950, the plumbers, builders, clerks and other assorted, normal professions from the colonies beat the greatest players in the world of that time (Billy Wright, Tom Finney, Stan

Mortensen, Wilf Mannion and the mighty and indestructible Jimmy Dickinson from the mighty Portsmouth FC) 1-0. It's still regarded as the greatest upset ever.

The veranda outside Harp was packed out when I arrived. It was mostly English, but there were a fair few Septics (Septic Tanks = Yanks), as well as Canadians, Germans and assorted locals. From the kick off, it was hell for us English, as it always is supporting our nation. Joyously, we took an early lead, something we just aren't used to, and all was looking rosy. Then, just before half-time, Clint Dempsey equalized, and the usual story ensued. The Septics started chanting "USA! USA! USA!", so we fought back with (to the tune of *She'll Be Coming Round the Mountain*) "If wasn't for the English you'd be French!"

In the end, it was 1-1, another typical England failure, as most of us expected. The Septics continued with "USA! USA! USA!" and waved their flags, to which we replied (to the same tune as before) "You can stick your fucking flag up your arse!" It was all pretty good natured though, until an English guy, whore bore a ridiculous resemblance to Sideshow Bob, decided to set fire to a small Stars and Stripes. Even the most vocal of us English fans thought he was being a dick and Chris, the owner of Harp, gave him a few pieces of his mind.

The rest of the holiday time was a delightful rest. I spent an afternoon with some locals I had gotten to know at Harp. We bought some nibbles from the underground supermarket in JiangBei, including duck, chopped off the cooked carcass in store, which we ate with pancakes and a few beers in one of their apartments. I'm not a fan of duck, but at least it tasted just the same as in any restaurant in England. After that it was the normal weekend for me. The streets were packed out with people enjoying their own free time, and the bars, cafes and restaurants were doing a roaring trade, just like any bank holiday back home.

One thing I didn't see were any dragon boats. This holiday is a huge deal in Hong Kong, and footage of the boats racing has become quite the cliché when depicting the former colony. For the mainland, it's still pretty new, and there didn't seem to be any great desire for anyone to get down to either riverside to watch anything on the waters. It seemed to be just another public holiday; an excuse to drink on a school night and go shopping.

I took this extended time off to watch the football. I had decided that Harp was going to be my local. It was easily the best drinking hole for expats. True, it was expensive – more expensive than back home for some beers – but they weren't locally made fakes. If you bought a bottle of London Pride, you got one that came from the Fuller's brewery. Import tariffs and shipping costs pumped up the price, but it was worth it. At least the Tiger beer was cheap. I went every night during my time off, keeping myself sober and keeping up with the World Cup matches. It was also a great place to meet locals and expats. As is the way in life, some were cool, and some were worth forgetting.

Ryan worked at the British consulate. He was a lanky English northerner who seemed to think nothing of coming to a rowdy night out dressed in his formal working suit. Rory was another northerner, from Newcastle (Geordie Rory), who was only there for 6 months. John and Sam were business partners in a small tech company and, surprisingly enough, John and Geordie Rory were cousins. Steve was a Londoner who was at the forefront of the on the spot song creation among us Brits. There was also Sam, a British-Chinese whom I'd met in Starbucks. He was working for his dad's design company and, ironically, spoke not a single word of Mandarin. These were among the good guys I got to know.

I was a bit naughty too, popping to the pub to watch late matches on a school night, but it was the World Cup after all, and I didn't have classes until late. I headed out on a Wednesday night to watch Spain's opener against Switzerland, and something momentous happened. Leaving my apartment, I looked up at the night sky. It was dark, which was unusual, as most of the time it was quite pale from the light reflecting off the smog. In the rarely seen blackness of night I saw them; stars. It was the middle of June, and for the first time in my stay there I saw stars. It had been many years since I had been in such awe of the great, celestial bodies, but don't worry. I didn't get all "Goddie".

One other night I was stood at the bar, watching one of the matches on my own. There were a few expats around and I was sociable, getting involved in random conversations in a way I would never have done back home. One guy was Jim, a fellow English teacher from Northern Ireland who worked at a school called Meten. I'd never heard of them, but he assured me they were big. Then he asked me a question that, normally, would be considered rude.

"How much do you earn?"

"Ummm, not a lot." I replied, a little wary.

"I earn 10,000 Yuan a month. Do you earn close to that?"

"Ummm. Not really."

"I've heard that about EF."

He changed the subject, talking about some bullshit conspiracy theory about the Bible and astrology and other religious texts and whatever. I can't remember why he brought up the subject, but he even had a hard copy of an article he'd printed from a web site and just happened to have handy. He suggested I read it as it was "very interesting" and could change how I viewed the world. I was so grateful.

Watching another match showed me how the public, international image of China was very different from the intimate, on the street reality. North Korea were in their first finals since their sensational quarter final performance in 1966, and it looked like they had the chance to shock again, when they only lost 2-1 to Brazil. Like in 1966, they faced Portugal, whom they'd lost to after being 3-0 up. Revenge was on the cards.

I was at Harp, once again, to watch the match, and was expecting the locals to be firmly behind their Asian, Communist brethren against the decadent, flashy Western imperialists. From the off, the large number of locals in the pub seemed to be surprisingly apathetic towards the Korean minnows. There were no reactions to any of their attacks, to any cool skills they displayed, or any fouls committed against them. In fact, the biggest and most positive reactions where to the goals Portugal scored, all seven of them.

The match was a massacre – 7-0 to Portugal – and it was a real shame to see. Like most English fans, I hate Cristiano Ronaldo, but have a soft spot for the Portuguese team as a whole. However, we love the underdog even more, and watching North Korea lose so badly was a real anti-climax, but I was more shocked by the reaction of the locals. They seemed to be quite happy, as if they hated North Korea. I couldn't understand it.

Shang explained that Chinese people had no special affinity to North Korea – that was a government thing – and Chinese football fans were no different to any others. They loved star players, and if their own team failed then they followed their favourite heroes. It made sense. People love to watch the best athletes perform well, even if it's at the expense of their own neighbours, and since when was being a neighbour linked to support? The Scots, Welsh and Irish tend to support England's opponents (despite the English often supporting the Scots, Welsh and Irish), and we certainly don't care for the French. As for "Communist brethren", if I really had thought the populous of China entertained such ideas, then that was completely killed by their cheering for the Portuguese.

In some cases though, I didn't even need to go to Harp to watch the games. Across the river from Hongyadong was a modern science museum and an ultra-modern theatre. I had seen on a couple of nights that the theatre wall was a giant, asymmetrical video screen that would often show loud and gaudy adverts. At Harp one night I popped out to get some fresh air and there, across the river, the match was being broadcast on the wall.

I'm no expert, but I'm going to go ahead and assume that that wasn't strictly allowed. Sure, matches are often show on big screens in public places, but that's usually a public square or a park, and it's normally an organized event where the sponsors get to do their promos. There was nothing like that. There was no open space in front of the theatre – just the river – and there wasn't a huge crowd on Hongyadong being given freebies by Budweiser or MacDonald's. It was almost as if someone had just plugged a TV aerial into the screen, and I'll wager that FIFA hadn't given their express, written permission.

I also met another local. Her name was Amy, and she was a friend of Shang's. We got chatting at Harp one night and it turned out that we lived in the same apartment block (Neighbour Amy). Her English was pretty much perfect, and physically she reminded me of Boss Audrey and Yogi; she was taller than the average Chinese woman, broad, physically more imposing and she didn't show the same, almost excitable reaction to Westerners as others did. She knew a lot of the foreigners in the city because she worked for the company that managed the Somerset building, a city centre apartment block where a lot of them lived. I'll admit it, she was really, really gorgeous, and if Miisa hadn't been on the horizon I'd have definitely used my limitless charms to magic my way into her affections. Instead, we just shared a taxi back home.

The heat had the effect of clearing the air. Finally, we had blue skies all day. Standing on top of Hongyadong I could see right across the Jialing and there, in full view, was a massive city skyline, stretching into the distance along the reinforced river banks. Don't get me wrong, I'm not saying it was a beautiful view, not even by high rise standards, but when you've spent so many months living in a shroud of dull, poisonous and choking clouds then any sight has a certain picturesque quality when the sun is out and the sky is clear. The air still smelt as bad though, maybe even worse, but that natural vitamin D production was doing a good job of improving my mood.

This time provided something extra for the view. There had been heavy rains in neighbouring Sichuan province, and the deluges caused a lot of flooding. It wasn't devastating like the earthquake, but it didn't help much either. The water cascaded down the Jialing and came to the city and, every day, the waters rose a little bit more. Opposite Hongyadong was a massive cylinder, tens of metres across, drilled into the river bed, with a crane inside. It was the genesis of a new road bridge, but at that time it was the marker for the rising river. Every day there was less and less of its walls on show until finally, its height was defeated, and silted river water flooded in.

The flood affected Hongyadong, but not as much as some very stupid locals who used it. The building had a car park that was below the level of the river side highway. I think you can guess where this is going. According to Shang, there were constant warnings to people about leaving their cars overnight, and every night people ignored them. It might have been forgivable if these people had shitty, Chinese-brand cars, but these motors were Mercs and Beemers. Eventually, the flooding got to the parking levels, and a few very, very, very expensive cars had to be written off.

Tanja and I took the opportunity to try out the Belgian restaurant. That's right, there was a Belgian restaurant in Chongqing, called Waffei. I've never even seen one of them in London, and the ones in Belgium didn't exactly wave the flag. It looked more like a canteen, one that wasn't exactly popular with the locals. We were the only customers, and the only other people were the Chinese women who worked there. I had a cheeseburger with fries, and to be honest it was good, but nothing special. At least it tasted like a burger though. When I go to a bar or restaurant that associates itself with a nation, I expect to feel some sort of connection to that place. Harp may not have been stereotypically Irish, but it wasn't far off either. Waffei felt like a local Chinese restaurant that just happened to dish another country's food.

In the evening I decided to try the outside bar, in a small plaza opposite the plethora of nightclubs. It was a balmy night, and the lights on the buildings were shining a multi-coloured glow down on the tented bar and the ornate tables and chairs set out on the paving stones. I was sat on my own, but a couple of ex-pats waved me over to join them, and we shared a few jars that night. One was Joel, and Australian teaching English at a school called Web International. Once again, the subject of pay came up, and his was a couple of thousand Yuan more than mine, although he, unlike me, had to pay his own rent.

We were then joined by Graham, a middle-aged British man who was already pissed by the time he sat down. We got talking about our backgrounds, and I talked about my time at Ford. For some reason, that seemed to annoy him, and he started accusing me of not knowing anything about cars. I didn't understand the aggression, although he was correct. I'd worked in IT, mostly for the finance division, and hardly ever came into contact with the production process. I told him that, but he continued, getting really riled up. He then revealed that he had been very high up in the product design or engineering division of Rover Cars, and that was why he was better than me.

Now, I openly admit that I know nothing about cars, but I will never take any criticism of my car knowledge from anyone who worked for Rover, the last bastion of large-scale British-owned motor manufacturing that collapsed because it couldn't sell enough cars in its own country. In their last few years they made some utter shit, and yet this guy was boasting about how much better he was than me because of his role in helping create the cars that fucked up a once mighty British icon. It was almost as bad as one of the candidates on *The Apprentice*, who tried to assert her authority and superiority as project manager by telling her team that she used to be the UK sales manager for, you guessed it, Rover – the car company that failed to sell enough cars in its home market i.e. her market.

He really was pissing me off, to the point that I was getting uncharacteristically wound up and confrontational. I tried to calm him down, but it didn't work, and my blood was beginning to boil. I actually told him I was getting fucking angry, but it didn't seem to register in his beer-addled brain. In the end, Joel had to intervene to get Graham to stop being such a twat. The old guy tried to drunkenly apologize to me, but I just ignored him, and made a mental note to avoid him in the future.

1-5. Nan'an riverfront. 6. What it's like to support England. 7-10. Blue skies over the city.

17 第十七章

Living in a country like China, which is massively different from home in so many ways, means that one encounters many odd sights and alien practices that would be considered bizarre or even downright unacceptable anywhere else. One of those things is the sale of live animals. There are two types of live animal sales; pets and food.

You'd think that pets would be sold in pet shops, and this is true, somewhat. One problem is that in China, there is no great push to get pets neutered, and so it's very common, when owning a female, that it will have offspring. These need to be offloaded somehow, but as far as I could tell at the time, there was no equivalent of the RSPCA, and pet shops aren't exactly booming. So people did the only thing they could do short of dumping kittens in a river or leaving puppies on a park bench or sticking bunnies in a pot – they sold them on the street.

That's right, people in China have a tendency to impulse-buy pets, or at least I think they do. I suppose it's likely that they decide they want a pet and know that the best people to get them are from the ones who show up randomly in the shopping streets with boxes or baskets of young, trying to offload them as quickly as possible. If you're an animal lover then it can be a distressing sight. In China, the government hasn't exactly made any great effort to promote neutering, and it required such campaigns to persuade us to do it in the West. This is the best, and most humane, option.

And then there's food. I'm a true human: I'm an omnivore. I eat fruit, vegetables and meat. I don't buy the moral arguments for vegetarianism, and I'm not convinced by the health claims either. However, I do accept that there is a certain amount of hypocrisy on my side. I've never killed an animal for food and I probably never will (like the vast majority of people in the West since the 19th century, I assume). In China, you can buy the animals live.

It's not just fish in the supermarkets. Small shops also sell live poultry; chickens and ducks are the most popular. You can walk down a street and see the owners sat on a bench, plucking the feathers out of a recently slaughtered bird, while just behind them are more stock, still alive, their wings and feet tied to keep them from escaping their inevitable fate. To be honest, I think killing an animal, preparing it, cooking it and eating it would be a lot like making bread from scratch. I think it would make the meal taste even better, knowing that I had done the whole process from start to finish, and I know it would be better quality than the stuff you buy in the shops, all pumped up with water and whatever else they add to make it look better.

One Saturday afternoon, after having another lunch of spicy egg fried rice with pork, I started preparing for my TB1A class. As normal, the noise of the parents and the kids rumbled through the walls into the teacher's room and mingled with the thumping from the latest, high definition product placement on the big screen outside. In the teacher's room I was getting my last bits together, when Julie came in.

"Someone's left a chicken behind reception." She said, with a straight face.

"Oh, is it in a plastic bag?" I asked, trying to be helpful. "It could defrost pretty quickly in this heat."

"No, not a frozen chicken, a live one."

Naturally, my confusion needed sorting out, so I headed out there and, lo and behold, behind the reception desk was a live chicken, its wings and feet secured to keep it in place. I asked the PA's where it had come from, but they had no idea. It was normal for the parents to dump bags behind reception for the PA's to look after. Sometimes it was the kid's satchels while they played on the PC's, but often it was the parent's shopping, so they could go off for a wander while their little darlings were in class.

At some point that morning, somebody had dumped their shopping behind the desk and, seeing as it was so normal, the PA's had paid little attention. When their kids were done, they'd picked up their bags and walked out, forgetting that big, fleshy, live purchase. I thought it was hilarious and, in my Western mind, I had assumed it would be just as funny to my students as it was to me. I entered the classroom to tell them the great news.

"Have you seen outside?" I said, enthusiastically building up to the punchline. "Someone has left a live chicken at reception."

There was no reaction from any of them. I tried again, assuming my language was too difficult, but there was still no reaction. Either they didn't understand, or they thought it was pretty unremarkable. It was Helen who put me in my place.

"It's a hen." She said, practically telling me off for not knowing the difference.

It was another lesson learned. Buying live animals in China is a perfectly normal thing to do, and that goes for pretty much the whole of the social strata. I had assumed that, despite live animals being readily available for consumption, it would still resonate as something noteworthy. These kids failed to react to the news of the live hen because, most likely, their parents had done exactly the same thing once or twice. How many times have you left a big bag of shopping on the bus, or a heavy item at the supermarket that should have been obvious due to the lack of weight on your arms? The hen wasn't a live animal to that parent; it was shopping, groceries, no different to a baguette or a crate of beer.

So what happened to the hen? Well, we teachers had no freaking clue what to do, so we left it to the PA's to sort out. Yogi took it under her wing (duh dum tssshhhh!). The next morning, when we arrived, it was gone. Apparently, when closing up the school, she had just left it outside the door, still in the mall. We have no idea what happened to it, but logic would dictate that either the mall's night security or one of the cleaners swiped it for a free dinner. Good for them, not for the hen.

The restaurants have an odd tradition too. I mentioned before about the cult-like gathering of restaurant staff near Meat Alley. Well, it wasn't just that one establishment. Every time I passed a restaurant in the morning I would see all the staff lined up like a battalion of paratroopers on parade. Sometimes a supervisor (I assumed) would read out some announcement or whatever, but other times it looked like they were giving a pep talk. One time, I saw a young guy, pacing up and down, trying to be quietly menacing, sometimes pointing at one of them like they needed special treatment.

It wasn't just the restaurants. Once or twice I saw the entire support staff of a mall, fifty or a hundred, lined up in the precinct, standing patiently while their boss gave then what seemed to be a call to arms, before crying out three times, arms punching the air, then heading back to their jobs as waiters, cooks, cleaners, security guards and assistants.

There was also the "FaPiao", which is basically a receipt that's used by the authorities to gather tax. It's also a scratch card for the customer. Clever Chinese, they had figured out a way to get customers to force shops and restaurants to pay their taxes – by making the receipts a lottery.

It wasn't just limited to food. The Chinese have a really bizarre fashion, one I had seen nowhere else on my travels. A lot of people, mostly women it seems, wear forearm covers. Now you might be thinking "Sleeves dickhead!" but you'd be wrong. These items are cylindrical, with two elasticated holes at each end that they slip over whatever they are wearing. They're made of a similar material to waterproof jackets, only a lot thinner. They aren't boring either, being available in a range of patterns, including the logo of the Oakland Raiders (permission for which I'm sure was never sought). I guessed it was just a fashion thing, because they seemed to serve no purpose. Karen wore them a few times in school, even when teaching, although she said it was due to hygiene. Personally, if I'm that worried about hygiene, I'm going to wear gloves.

Other fashions can be noticeably different from back home. For the men it's pretty generic, as one would expect, but the women like to dress up. For young women, short skirts or short shorts and knee-length, high heeled boots are the norm. They really did like showing off their legs, and they loved dressing during the day like most women back home would reserve for a Saturday night.

It was a consequence of the rapid rise in wealth and the increasing affluence young people were enjoying and, I assumed, more social freedom for the young women. They especially love bright, garish colours and patterns, just like the horrid dresses in the wedding shop in New York New York. There were some women who, at first glance, dressed like they were "drumming up business". However, they were as likely to dress like that in the day as on a night out, and their favourite place to hang around was in Starbucks.

There was another fashion which I think wasn't actually a fashion. For some reason, parents would tuck little towels into the backs of the collars of their very little kids. It seemed to be limited to kids up to the age of four, so my SS Orange students sometimes had them, but generally it was the younger ones who carried this mini cape. I never actually fount out why, because if the towels were ever needed it was mum or dad who used it. The kids still needed their noses wiping for them.

There was also a trend for wearing night clothes in public. Going out and about in pyjamas has been a bit controversial in the UK, with at least one supermarket banning some people (almost always women) from entering their local branches in such attire. In Chongqing it seemed to be okay, with women and men often out and about in the city centre wearing a warmed, padded type of tunics and trousers, usually wearing slippers too. No-one seemed to bat an eyelid.

And then there are some of the annoying habits. Something that drove me nuts was clapping. I'd first noticed it when exercising in the courtyard of my apartments. Elderly women would be walking around the empty pool, clapping their hands in front of them. In fact, they did this pretty much anywhere they could walk. It was almost impossible to walk around the city without hearing the 'clap clap clap clap…..' of these women, going about their business while making this grating, irritating, incessant noise. I never found out why, but older Chinese people do like to stay in shape, so I assumed they thought it helped with their circulation. It certainly didn't help with my mood.

Spitting isn't frowned upon, no matter how loudly and violently they hawk up mucous from the bowels of their guts and empty onto the streets. People even spat it out on the bus. Nobody seemed to react to it though. It was a struggle to avoid the mess out and about. No wonder they either left their shoes outside their front doors or wore plastic coverings indoors. It's a wonder I was hardly ever sick.

Talking of cleanliness, the city authority liked to have the streets sparkling. The soot in the air laid on the ground, leaving a dusty film, so the municipal government employed an army of street washers. A truck with a huge water tank would crawl through the streets, spraying water on the pavements and a team of cleaners would scrub the ground with long-handled brushes.

To be fair, the streets did need it, but then again they wouldn't if the air wasn't so bad. Also, it was a hell of a lot of water to use, in a country that wasn't shy about using natural resources. To make matters worse, there had been severe dust storms and droughts in the spring, affecting the southeast region, including Chongqing. I wondered if the people who actually suffered during the drought knew that an affluent city was using precious water to wash the paving stones.

On the buses, people seemed to prefer the aisle seat, so when someone hopped on and needed to sit, they would have to squeeze past the occupant, and I mean squeeze. The occupant wouldn't stand up to let them in, but just shift their legs to the side a little. There were times when I had to just stare at the person in the most condescending manner to get them to actually shift out of the way. Even at my leanest I was still considerably bigger than the average Chinese guy.

Eating can be quite a noisy affair too, but I think that's quite normal everywhere around the world, especially when eating rice with chopsticks, which requires a scooping/shovelling method with the bowl right up to the mouth.

As for drinking, they really loved their tea, so much so that many people kept some with them everywhere they went. In the UK, and most of the West I presume, it's common for people to have bottled water with them, or a hot drink in a travel mug. In China, they favoured tea, and I mean fresh tea. They would take whole tea leaves and just stuff them in their travel mugs, usually transparent ones, and fill them with hot water repeatedly during the day. For China, the fresher the food and drink, the better.

They can be a very friendly people, especially if they know some English and want to practice. There were numerous times on buses when a local just came over and said hi, and proceeded to go through the conversational motions. I did my best to be polite, and patient, but sometimes the teaching just wore me out and I could barely muster even the simplest courtesy. Sometimes, if we had a good conversation, they would ask for my number, so I'd make one up, though I once saw Rory just flat out refuse.

Relaxing is something they do in their own way. Squatting is the most well-known. Remember how I described how I couldn't use a squat toilet? That squatting position is a common relaxation method, and it's something you will see out on the street (just relaxing, not taking a shit). They also love napping, and it was something I saw everywhere. Starbucks, CSC, Subway, KFC, the bus stop, park bench, school reception area, they seemed to love grabbing themselves forty winks. They had an especial habit of slumping forward, resting their heads on a table with their arms wrapped around. People back home generally only nap publicly on public transport or while sunbathing, not in a fast food joint.

Another practice that I could never get used to was the customer service in department stores. Whenever I visited one to look for something like a new iron, a memory stick, stationary etc. I found that I had the attention of what I thought, at first, was an inquisitive local. Actually they were always staff, but not really bad store detectives. They were assistants, and they were looking to help, but their idea of helping seemed to be following me slavishly wherever I was. It was so annoying, and I know they were just trying to be helpful, but I really didn't want to have a diminutive shadow while I looked at appliances or a new phone. I tried not to let it get to me, but sometimes I had to communicate as best I could to get them to stop.

Customer service, in general, was problematic. I'd already had to suffer the so-called "assistance" at a supermarket, but it wasn't just there. Restaurants could take a long time to get food sorted, even if it was a simple thing. One time, Rory and Julie were left waiting for an hour, the excuse given that the kitchen was cooking more rice. Rice doesn't take an hour to cook, and it's such a staple that it's pretty much impossible to run out. There were times when I would point to an item in my *Dorling Kindersley Visual Dictionary*, only to be faced with a shake of the head, and then to actually find the damned thing by accident. There were even times when I stood at a counter to be served, only to be ignored until I had to loudly call for their attention. That was, of course, if somebody hadn't pushed in front of me.

Their habit of saving face could be frustrating too, trying to avoid holding their hands up when they'd made a mistake. Most of the time it was minor – usually a shop assistant making a mistake and then not even trying to acknowledge it. Sometimes it got big, and weird. I read in the *China Daily* that, during the previous census, it had been found that a character had not been included in the standard Chinese dictionary. It had been spotted because most people in one village had it as their surname. Rather than adding it, and asking the likes of Microsoft to create a software patch, the government had decided that everyone in the village would have to change their name.

It wasn't all bad though. The big international brands were operated to the expected standards (good and bad), and there were many local businesses that bent over backwards to help, sometimes sycophantically so. Coffee was a lovely little café, and CSC was just as good as any American fast food chain. Qi Qi Hotpot always delivered the goods, and the barbeque restaurant never failed us. It just showed that China is a country of extremes; very polite and really rude, helpful and obstructive, quick and inefficient, welcoming and bigoted. It all balanced out, and never even came close to ruining the experience of being there.

And then there's the dental hygiene. Americans always like to take the piss out of us Brits for having bad teeth, but that's mainly because we tend to let ours form naturally, rather than brace them straight as kids, or whiten them. Americans must have heart attacks when then see Chinese teeth. In some cases, the problem is down to smoking, though I've known many heavy smokers whose teeth aren't dark grey. That's assuming that they have teeth though; many older people have large, rotten gaps in their mouths. Even some kids have issues. Jerry, in my SS Orange class, looked like he had fangs, as if they were rotting from the sides. I'm sure he had a problem, but he never seemed in pain.

For me though, the worst thing was something they didn't do – queue. When I first visited China I was amazed at how the locals just didn't feel like waiting their turn. When I was in Shanghai I had to get a train ticket, and at the station I stood in the queue at the "English-speaking" kiosk. "Bundle" would be a better description, and as I got closer to the front I found myself being jostled by locals who clearly thought their ticket was more important than mine.

Thankfully, the clerk signalled to me to let me push through. The taxi rank at Beijing train station had an armed guard who made sure people didn't push in, and on the Shanghai metro, when the train doors opened, it was war to get off through the mass of people pushing on. Chongqing wasn't as bad, but there were still problems of locals pushing in. Sometimes I just had to grit my teeth and remind myself that I wasn't in Kansas anymore.

I also had another issue to deal with, one that worried me almost as much as where I could take a shit. Just before leaving England I had made sure I got myself a good haircut: not a crew cut, but short enough to last a few months. It was getting a bit long though, with the fringe tickling eyes, and the increasing heat and humidity was making it uncomfortable on top. I needed to get it clipped.

The problem was that there are some goods and services you can purchase without knowing the language, and some you can't. Groceries can be done with pictures in a book, but a haircut needs a description. My Chinese was still super basic, so there was no way I could manage it. I had help though. Student Audrey, from my RE00, helped me out. One Monday we met up outside Paradise Walk and we walked down the underpass, across the other paved precinct, under the main road leading to the bridge my bus crossed every day, and to a little salon, almost hidden under grubby scaffolding.

It wasn't a barber shop as such, more like a men's styling salon. The pictures on the walls, and the staff themselves, were the perfect adverts for the craziness of the styles young Chinese men were favouring. They were spikey all over, with a bit of length at the back but NOT a mullet. They were quite feminine looking, though they were clearly inspired by the styles on some of the craziest characters in Japanese anime.

It was a weird experience. I've always been conservative with my hair, so I've never had much more than grade three back and sides and a tidy up on top. I sat in the chair and Audrey passed on my instructions to the stylist. It took a while, as I needed to explain it multiple times to her, but she eventually understood. My hair was washed and then I was back in front of the mirror, where the stylist began applying a cream to my follicles. I was immediately suspicious. All I wanted was a simple cut, so I asked Audrey to ask what it was for. It seemed that the guy was so dedicated to styling that he had just decided he would style my hair, just a little bit.

Not a chance! Audrey passed the message on and my hair was re-washed and the cut began. It wasn't so much that styling was a bit more expensive than a basic cut, it was the principle of the matter. What a bloody cheek he had to just decide that I should have a style. He could have suggested an alternative style and I would genuinely have appreciated it, but he didn't even explain to Audrey what he was going to do. However, he did a good job of the simple cut, and I was happy to go back later in the year, with the help of Audrey. I was certain they wouldn't forget me.

1. Cable car to JiangBei Cheng. 2. Looking back to JieFangBei. 3-9. Hongyadong.

18 第十八章

When I was a kid, there were all sorts of activities laid on by the local council and various organizations for us during the summer. A regular one was the Holiday Club, run by the local church and held at the nursery school where my mother worked, but as a teenager I often attended week-long sports courses, mainly athletics.

At EF, we prepared for the Summer Course, a series of extra lessons that would take place during the long school break. On the face of it, it sounded like a horrid, long slog that would put my normal lesson planning at risk. We would all have to work an extra day, and we'd each have at least one extra class running in the weekday mornings, as well as occasional Life Clubs.

The prep for it started a month or so before. The first relief was when we saw that, rather than having to invent a whole new bunch of lessons, EF had created a complete syllabus that we had to follow strictly, complete with basic plans and a whole bunch of materials. The more I saw of it, the less scary it became. In fact, it had the potential to help, as I would have to be in school at a normal time, and be around for most of the day, which meant more impetus to plan lessons way ahead of time. The only hassle would be at home, where I wouldn't have two free days to get things like laundry sorted. That wasn't so bad though. It was summer, so the clothes would dry in minutes.

I was given a HF00 class, which was cool because I had plenty of experience already. The course material was pretty straightforward and explanatory, and it didn't require any great effort to create anything new and whizzy. The new classes were going to be simple to the point of being planned for us, and the extra time at school forced us to work on more planning ahead of time.

From the moment my first class started, I knew it was going to be a long summer. It was all down to one little "angel", Wayne. I assumed that was his English name, although he could have said his name was Win. Whatever it was, he was a little shit. Well, that's what I thought of him at the time, but I shouldn't be harsh. He was only 6 and probably not very interested in learning English. His parents would have paid for the course primarily to give them a rest for a couple of hours a day during the summer school break, and the last thing any kid anywhere in the world wants to do in summer is learn stuff. They want to be at home playing with their toys, or out and about with their friends. However, at the time, I couldn't stand the little sod.

He was quite hyperactive and disruptive, easily the biggest problem child I'd had to deal with to that point. He didn't want to sit still, and he didn't want to stay quiet. What a shame he didn't want to be noisy in English. It was just him though. None of the other kids were like him, and at times they got annoyed too. One of the others was Rick, and he was a shock to the system.

Before the first lesson, I stood in the reception area, and Linda gathered the new class together to line up in front of me. One was a teenager, and quite tall – close to 5ft 6in I thought. He smiled at me and said "Hello teacher" and, confused, I asked him how old he was. He had a basic grasp already and he answered "10". I assumed he'd gotten his numbers wrong, so I asked Linda. She confirmed his age. This giant of a kid, the same height as the average Caucasian woman or teenage boy, had only recently crossed into the realm of age in double figures. He was also bulky too. If he had been in a fight with any of my TB3A boys he'd have had a chance of crushing them. He was a freak of nature, but he was also the nicest kid in my class, a real gentle giant.

The other classes continued as normal. My planning was getting a lot faster and a lot easier, and I was feeling a lot less stressed by the whole process. Small Stars were the easiest to plan, as the classes were shorter and there was a bit more scope for repetition. I found I could plan a lesson in about fifteen minutes. HF's were also reasonably simple, but there was a need for more complex activities to keep them interested. My TB classes were harder, but I enjoyed working on them the most. TB1A was harder work than 3A, but they still put the effort in, which gave me boundless encouragement. The RE's were the hardest. I genuinely tried to think of ways to get them enthused, but it never seemed to work. Professionally, I should have asked for a lesson observation, but I never did. Perhaps I was in the Chinese mind set of not losing face, or maybe I just wasn't bothered. Either way, I should have asked for help.

My first HF00's and SS Oranges were ticking over nicely, approaching the end of their courses, and they seemed to have learnt a decent amount. The second classes of each were still problematic, mainly due to classroom management issues. I really found it hard to deal with Jake and Hans in HF, and Hero in SS. There was also Jason, in my second HF class, who just seemed to be slow. At first I thought he was just a lazy kid, and I mentioned it to Julie. She told me that the other kids had told Linda that he was slow in Chinese, so maybe there was something else.

In one lesson I noticed he was struggling to walk. It wasn't so bad at first, but as the tasks progressed it seemed to get worse. The tasks were quite physical, but he didn't seem to show any discomfort, yet he was walking on his right foot like it was twisted. At the end of the lesson, his mum got him from the class, and he was limping like he had done some serious damage – he couldn't plant his foot flat, like he'd broken his ankle. I got Linda to point it out to his mum, but his mum smiled and nodded. Apparently she already knew, and it didn't seem to bother her that her son was walking like he had a cheap prosthetic.

Like every year, 2010 was momentous in so many ways. There were the earthquakes in Haiti, China, Indonesia and Chile, revolution in Kyrgyzstan, the Deepwater Horizon explosion, the world record sale of a piece of art by Picasso, the sequencing of the Neanderthal genome, Wikileaks publishing 340,000 top secret US government reports, the release of Aung San Suu Kyi, the first trapping of antimatter, the start of the Arab Spring and the death of President Lech Kaczyński of Poland. For many though, the one thing that represents 2010 is something genuinely dark and horrendous – the vuvuzela.

This may well be the single worst and most pointless thing ever invented, even worse and more pointless than the slimming pill (stop eating cakes and go for a walk!), Southampton football club, salad, Ashton Kutcher's career and all hipsters. This stupid horn is what people remember about the 2010 FIFA World Cup, probably more so than the actual matches and the long-overdue success of Spain. It was a hateful thing, and managed to pervade most countries including, sadly, China.

One night in Harp, watching one of the matches, some dicks from America were getting boozed up. They didn't seem to be too interested in the game, but they certainly loved their vuvuzela, and were especially proud of how they could blow it properly, making that oh-so delightful noise that had captivated the world. I'm usually quite tolerant, but it was wearing thin. They were inside, and Harp was pretty tiny, and it wasn't like it was raining outside. The local girls they were with seemed impressed though. Shang asked them to stop and they gave it a rest, for a few minutes. Eventually they started up again, and so Shang tried to reason with them. They stopped for a short while, and then went right back to it.

These guys were arseholes, and not just for being so fucking noisy. If they had been back home in America, or anywhere else in the Western world, they would never have behaved like that. If any bar staff had asked them to stop, those pussies would have done as they were told, knowing that if they shitted on their one chance they'd be out on their ears.

This was China though, and Chinese women, to a large extent, still have an upbringing akin to Western women from the 1930s. They can lack a certain assertiveness and those guys knew it, so they took the piss. If they had done that in an English pub, the landlady would have rammed the vuvuzela down their throats, waited for them to shit it out, and then made them eat it again, and then thrown them out.

Don't get me wrong, I'm not saying all Chinese women are timid, meek, passive and supplicant (Shang definitely wasn't, she was just very polite). There are plenty of Wendy Deng-types, but when you spend enough time in the country you can tell they are fewer and further between than elsewhere. I had talked to some guys who'd married local women, and a few of them had admitted that was why they gone for an Asian woman (from Asia, that is). No doubt that'll change very quickly over the coming years so guys, if you're looking for such a woman, get in there quickly.

A new teacher started. His name was Jayson, he was from America, and for many of the students he was an exotic revelation: he was black. He wasn't the only black person in Chongqing. There was a community of people from West Africa, mostly Cameroon but a few other countries too, but as far as I knew, none of them were teachers. He was the latest edition to Paradise Walk and, as expected, there was immediate interest in him, especially from the younger kids.

His first week was just like everyone else's; easy. He observed a few lessons and got to dash home early, his home being in an apartment complex just across the road, while the rest of us had to slog away as usual. As the week ended, we all decided to have a random blow out, and shrimp pot followed by KTV was the perfect party.

I, however, had a bigger fish to fry. The knockout stages of the World Cup had started, and on that Sunday was the big match: England vs Germany. England had been miserable, drawing against the USA (WTF!), drawing against Algeria (WTFF!) and just about beating Slovenia (yeah, whatever!), while the Germans had been awesome once again.

I persuaded Jayson to tag along for a good laugh, so he met me at my apartment and we headed to Hongyadong, where the veranda had been laid out once again with the projector, screen and plenty of seats. The seats were occupied mostly by the English, with a few Americans and a small contingent of Germans. As expected, the Germans took the lead, and then doubled it. Their fans were loving it and taking every opportunity to rub our noses in their superiority on the pitch.

As the half neared its end we pulled one back, thanks to Matthew Upson (that's how bad our strikers were) and then, two minutes later, the mighty (!) Frank Lampard whacked the ball, it hit the cross bar, bounced inside the goal and then out again. It was 2-2 and we were dancing round our Teutonic neighbours, reminding them of our Dunkirk spirit.

Something was wrong though, the England team were crowding round the referee and remonstrating with the linesman. There was a lot of head shaking and face-palming, but it was clear. No goal. The Germans started cheering again and, when the replay's showed the ball had clearly crossed the line, they laughed their tits off while us English fans hurled the most vicious abuse at the official who had made the decision. Mauricio Espinosa will forever be known as "The Uruguayan Linesman."

The second half turned to shit as the mighty Germans scored another two, and their loyal supporters made every effort to remind us just how pathetic we were. It ended 4-1, and Jayson seemed pretty entertained. We didn't leave in a huff though. In actual fact it had been great fun, and we hung out with the German guys for a while. At one point I started singing "I wish that I was

German" just because we were all having a good time. One person objected strongly. It was Sideshow Bob, the English nonce who had decided to burn the American flag right in front of Harp's American owner. He came at me pretty hard, giving me front and demanding I show patriotism. He didn't get close though; Ryan from the consulate pushed him back and told him to calm down. The guy was a total prick, and when I told Jayson, he laughed. His assessment was "You'd have killed that scrawny motherfucker."

We hopped in a taxi and headed back to Paradise Walk, going up the hill for another mile or so to one of the newer retail and entertainment blocks. By the time we got to our room in the KTV, the party was already in full swing. It was mayhem in there, just as it always should be. I think a couple of bottles of Jack Daniels had already been consumed, along with God only knows how many beers and jugs of cold tea. Cigarette smoke filled the air too, as did the sound of Rory singing a Beach Boys classic. Our arrival meant that the room was pretty crowded, so Rory negotiated with the staff to move us, and our booze, into a bigger room.

We needed more supplies, so Rory and I headed to the shop, where I finally managed to persuade him to let me pay for some of the food and booze, rather than him and Julie paying for it all once again. It was on this shopping spree that we witnessed something that was utterly unbelievable, even by Chinese standards.

We had our eyes on a bottle of Jack, stood on a shelf a few feet above our reach. Rory got the attention of an assistant, who glided over to us on a colourful pair of flashy roller blades. Rory told him what we wanted and the guy grabbed a little plastic stool and placed it in front of the shelves. To our abject horror, he proceeded to place one, rollerblade-encased foot on the flimsy platform. Rory and I both yelled out in panic and fright, and the assistant stepped down, looking at us with a mixture of amusement and confusion. Then, incredibly, he did it again. We responded exactly the same, though this time we actually grabbed him and Rory composed himself to remember the appropriate Chinese. Another assistant came over, wearing proper shoes, and we got our Jack, without having collective heart attacks.

We returned, and our supplies were brought in soon after. Almost immediately I was handed the mic and the song was loaded up on the screen. *Hungry Eyes* was butchered once again to everyone's delight. I swear, if Eric Carmen (the original singer) had seen me, he would have either slashed his wrists or slit my throat. It got even messier as the hours ticked by. Julie and I did our rendition of *Waiting for a Star to Fall* and Jayson performed a bit of Dr Dre while most of the others just watched the entertainment and poured the drinks down their throats.

We drank, we smoked (Chinese brands, literally cancer sticks), we ate, we sang, we danced. Dulce got particularly hammered and, at one point, was on a little table, crouched down with her eyes closed screaming "MARTIN!".

She and Martin had gotten very close, although there was no sexual attraction involved. She was off her head and in no fit state to continue, so Martin helped her home.

By the time we left it was nearly 4am. As we were walking down the street we were followed by some of the staff, who kept shouting at us. Rory had to concentrate on what they were saying, and it turned out they claimed we hadn't paid. The fact was Rory and Julie had, but because we'd moved to a bigger room, they wanted more money, something they hadn't mentioned at the time. We carried on walking – as far as we were concerned, they should have made that clear when they had the chance – but they followed us. One of the guys put his hand on Rory's shoulder, and I nearly lost it.

I'm not an aggressive person. The only punch-up I have ever been involved in as an adult was when playing rugby league for Sheffield University in a match against Sheffield Hallam. One of those twats dropped on my head when I had already been tackled, so I started swinging punches at the first Hallam player I could half see. I got ten minutes in the sin bin for that. However, this guy (along with the drink), pushed me over the edge. I got between him and Rory and screamed in his face "FUCK OFF! FUCK OFF!". They got the message. We headed off down the road and to a late night barbeque food kiosk for some simple, spicy grub, and then I was home. Suffice to say, we never went back to that KTV again.

It was a bit weird when I woke up. My head was fuzzy, but not too bad. I was on the sofa, and I noticed my laptop was on. I slowly eased myself up and remembered a dream about being sick. In the wet room I saw the shower head on the floor, and what looked like a residual lump or two of what was almost certainly the former contents of my stomach. I'd been so drunk that I was violently sick, but had the presence of mind to clean up after myself (but not get into bed), and what the hell had I planned to do online?

I showered, dressed and headed into JieFangBei. In Starbucks I sat by the window with a latte and watched an old TV documentary online. That was when things started to go bad. My head got fuzzier and fuzzier as time passed, and I needed a refill of my drink. After about four hours watching TV and drinking coffee I decided to leave. It took me another hour to actually muster enough energy to get out of that comfy armchair and make a move. I was in a terrible state, and by the time I got home I was feeling ill, worse than I had ever felt post-partying in my life. I thought that all I needed was a very long sleep and I would be fine.

I went to bed super early that evening, and woke up decently late. I'd had about 15 hours sleep, but when I dragged myself out from under the covers, I felt almost as bad as before. The big difference was that I didn't have the same shitty feelings in my stomach and bowels, or the nasty after taste of booze and fags, but my head was in a terrible state and I was a little short of breath. The day was another washout; I was tired, hungry, dizzy, sick and aching all over. I decided that another early night was on the cards.

The next day it was back to work, and I still felt pretty bad. I wasn't overly surprised – my student days are long gone – but this felt unusual. Normally I would feel like I needed another early night and a long sleep, but this felt worse. It felt like I was still hungover. I taught my HF lesson and, thankfully, the kids weren't such a pain in the arse, and I partook in another bit of gorging on fast food before grabbing another early night. Thursday wasn't much better, especially as it was the RE's, and I still had a raging headache on the Friday with the SS's. The weekend was a struggle and, incredibly, I was still feeling ill. My head hurt, my stomach felt twisted and my muscles felt like lead. I'm no doctor, and I don't have even a rudimentary understand of toxicology or diagnosis, but I'm sure I had alcohol poisoning of some sort. It just wasn't normal to feel that bad for that long.

The kids seemed particularly stressful this time. No doubt they were just their normal selves, but I was a lot less tolerant. The week couldn't end quickly enough, and on my weekend I didn't touch a single drop of alcohol. By the time the new week started I felt just about recovered, but it served as a cautionary tale of age, biology and booze, one that I quickly forgot.

Not long after that though, I had another bad, bad hangover, but for completely different reasons. After another hard slog of a week at school I headed to Harp for a couple of jars. I wasn't in the mood for drinking a lot, so after a pint or two I headed home, feeling quite sober. Near my apartment, I got thirsty again, so in the little, grubby shop in the back street opposite the complex's courtyard, I bought a couple of bottles of Shangcheng beer. They cost me the equivalent of 27p each, and they lived up to the price tag.

It tasted like an industrial solvent, and the next day I felt like I had been necking vodkas all night. I'm sure there was some sort of poisoning going on, though it could have been that the beer was ruined due to the shops habitually switching off their fridges at night. The heat must have destroyed what little integrity a 27p, 500ml bottle of beer had. I didn't feel well for a couple of days after, and I made a mental note: only buy beers from the supermarkets. At least they could afford to keep the fridges switched on, I hoped.

1-9. Various shots from around the city.

19 第十九章

Steve, the arrogant and unreliable teenage one to one student was given to someone else, and the three student corporate course finished. I was given a new one to one. Her name was Petal, and her OPT rated her as RE18. This is near enough fluent (the top being RE21), so one would wonder why she needed lessons. Very simply, she just needed to keep her skills up, as Chongqing was not known for its extensive Western contacts.

From the very first lesson, I knew I would have a tough job on my hands. I had to give a 90 minute session, but that wasn't easy when the student was pretty much fluent, more intelligent than me and had a better understanding of the rules of grammar. As luck would have it, she did have some noticeable issues with writing, so we were able to work on that.

I always found it interesting how there is a definite disconnect between speaking and writing. No matter how well you speak any language, writing it down is another matter. You can be so verbally eloquent, but when it comes to putting pen to paper, the words can get stuck and the mind freezes. Whatever is in one's head can fail miserably to come out on the page.

The Summer Course was leaving me in two minds. On the one hand it was no big deal. Coming in on Tuesday morning to teach one class and maybe a Life club was no problem, even if there were two Clubs to deal with. Yes, it actually meant planning 4 extra sessions a week, but they weren't two hours long, and most of the planning was standardized from EF, so the only real stress was getting that first lesson of the week sorted. It didn't impinge on my other lessons, and the extra time in school was pretty helpful.

On the other hand it was still an extra full day of work, a day when I wasn't lying in bed until mid-morning, and then getting chores done like laundry, ironing and cleaning the flat. Also, Wayne was a nightmare. He didn't like sitting still at all, and he loved being the centre of attention. The other kids were really cool, but he was their polar opposite combined. I had no idea how to handle him, so at times I moved his chair into the corner of the class and hoped he would calm down.

Yes, I know some of you will be shocked. Some of you will think that's an outrageous way to deal with a 6 year old who doesn't yet know how to behave appropriately and is still learning many basic social norms. In response, I would agree. I probably did handle him all wrong. I'm sure there were better ways to sort him out, but this was my first teaching job, and I had to do something so that I could give the other kids the teaching they deserved. They were able to behave well, so why couldn't he?

All my classes had settled down into a certain normality, although my HF's were still a bit of trouble at times. Jake in my second group was still the biggest problem, and Jackson often made things worse, but I was calm about it. Hero and Jan in my second SS group were still a pain in the arse, but I was getting the hang of them too, and slowly getting them on my side.

TB1A was given to another teacher, but TB3A were still the tops, and kept surprising me. In one lesson, about school, we talked about favourite subjects. Christine, one of the shyest in the class, revealed that she also spoke French and Japanese, and that English was the weaker of her languages. None of the other kids batted an eyelid at the news. My jaw dropped.

One time we did a doughnut drill to practice using modals for advice. Half sat in a circle of chairs, facing outwards, while the others went from one to the next, getting advice for some problem. They were all innocuous; "I eat too much candy, what should I do?" or "I want to improve my English, what could I do to get better?". At one point, Susie asked Andy "I play too many video games, what should I do?" Before Andy could respond, Henry turned round and said "You should grow up.". We lost a couple of minutes laughing and recovering.

The RE's were getting better too, but I still struggled with them. One task that worked well, as well as for the TB's, was the grid game. It's like pelmanism, but instead of cards, a grid is drawn on the board, with each square numbered. Students picked two and I would write into the squares what I had on my paper. If they thought there was a match, then they would explain it. If it was correct, I left it up. If not, I rubbed them off and rewrote the numbers. Another simple memory and logic problem that the older students really engaged with, and I ended up using a lot. I tried it with my HF's, but they weren't so entertained.

Backup tasks were still an issue, but I was making more of an effort to include them, now that I was getting more adept at planning stuff. However, as Sod's Law would have it, if I planned a backup then I didn't need it, but if I didn't plan one, then I ended up with a hole in my class and needed to think fast.

I was finally running out of the deodorant stash I had brought with me. It was summer, and the last thing I wanted was to be caught short in the hideously hot and humid summer it was turning out to be. I headed to CBest, with my *Dorling Kindersley Chinese Visual Dictionary* in hand to avoid any confusion.

I hadn't looked too closely before, but I had noticed that all the deodorants and antiperspirants were roll-ons. I've never liked these – I've always found them to be sticky and cause more armpit stains than actual sweat, so I needed a spray. Clearly my eyes weren't working that day. I looked through the section a couple of times and saw nothing, so I asked an assistant "Do you have any of these?", and pointed to the picture in the dictionary. It was a great help. It had a photo, with the name in Chinese script, the Latin pinyin form, and English. I couldn't fail to be understood.

She looked at the picture a little longer than was necessary, then took me to an aisle, not in with the personal hygiene products. It was with the household cleaners and, opposite shelves full of bottles of bleach and toilet cleaner, pointed to the sprays. I was looking at air fresheners. I looked at her, looked at the sprays, looked at her, looked at the sprays, looked at her, looked at the book, looked at the sprays and looked at her again. I showed her the picture again and she nodded, pointing to the goods. I shook my head, and mimicked the action of applying said spray to my armpits. Without any notion of realization and revelation, she took me back to the deodorants I'd been looking at before and to a small can of spray, sat all on its own, right where I'd been looking before. And then she walked off. Talk about saving face.

I was working on branching my social circle beyond the guys at EF. I attended a meeting of the photography club, organized by Joel, an American who was an English teacher with Web International. American Joel's passion was the camera, and his goal was to work in fashion. That evening I was the only one who could stay all night, so we did some shots down on the highway below, which involved parking ourselves in the triangle where the road split to send traffic along the river and back into the city. We also worked on tidying up my pics on his PC, which he claimed was the most powerful in the city. It was believable. In his tiny apartment he'd created a mini studio, and built his own PC to the highest spec his salary could afford. It would not have surprised me if he had gone without food to pay for it.

The next meeting we had was a night trip. A group of us headed to JiangBei Cheng, the spot right across the Jialing from Hongyadong, to get some night shots of the city centre. Along with us came Joel's girlfriend, a Chinese woman who spoke no English, and her friend, who was fluent and was acting as model for the night. The friend drove some of us to the spot, heading across the bridge on what was essentially a motorway. She missed the junction but, instead of going to the next one, she stopped in the road and simply reversed, making other drivers avoid her and beep their horns. I was in the back with a French guy, and we did our best not to look like we were shitting ourselves. Somehow, it worked. She reversed the car, got onto the junction she wanted, and we were off, all without any incident. Oh, and she was driving a freaking Mercedes!

This is something that is very apparent in China; the driving. To get an idea of what it's like, imagine an average Italian city centre, then widen the roads by 6 lanes, multiply the traffic ten times and then remove from the drivers any consideration for human life. There's a lot of cutting up, and no-one wants to give way. As for pedestrians, well they just need to get the fuck out of the way, even at a pedestrian crossing. And yet, it works. Everyone knows the score and they just get on with it. I never saw any big accidents, and only the occasional minor prang, but no more than back home. It seemed chaotic and nightmarish, but was also perfectly safe, though I would never want to drive in it myself.

Enjoying the nightlife was always a fun experience, especially now that the evenings were so warm. Dress code was no issue, so going out in shorts and sandals caused no problems. If I wasn't out with Tanja in JiangBei then I was at Harp on Sunday nights, drinking Tiger and mixing with the local expats. The British Consulate guys were often there, and Ryan was usually the life of their party. He was generous to a fault too; a couple of times he drunkenly paid for my beer and food even though I'd only said "hi" to him and sat at the bar alone.

There were teachers from other schools, mostly Web International and Meten. I didn't worry too much about hanging out with them as they were their own crowds, and seemed to share certain characteristics. The Web International teachers seemed to be loud and heavy drinkers, while the Meten teachers seemed to like asking other people about their salaries, and looked positively tee-totalled. Us EF teachers liked a good few jars and had no interest in other people's salaries.

Then I'd often head out to JieFangBei to one of the nightclubs. Unlike the UK, there was no policy of no entry after a certain time, so I could often turn up pretty late, or go home, change my mind and go out again. Even on a Monday, the Chinese clubs like Bar 88 were packed out and lively. The Cotton Club was still the best bet for drinking though.

If there was a group of us though, we'd end up in Bar 88, drinking whiskey and tea and toasting with the locals. Jayson and Dani were big partiers, and Jayson certainly knew how to handle his Jack. It wasn't uncommon for me to help Dani home though. She didn't have a problem – she was a young woman enjoying a new experience and taking every advantage of it. Thankfully, we lived a few floors apart.

Dave and Maria weren't coming out as much, but they were nicely loved up. Dulce was usually up for a party too, dragging Martin along even if he clearly didn't feel like it. It wasn't a surprise – he couldn't handle any booze. Tanja didn't come out so much though. She lived in JiangBei and it was a pain in the arse for her to get a taxi back every time, especially when the rest of us could walk home for nothing.

Sometimes we'd go for a hotpot or barbeque before drinks, and here was where I was shamed. I'd not been very good at learning the language, but Dani had been blazing a trail with it. By then she was able to conduct better than basic conversations with the staff, and we always got what we wanted. Dave and Maria were way ahead of everyone (other than Rory and Julie), but Dani had shot off too, leaving me a trailing failure. I had to buck my ideas up.

The summer was insanely hot and humid. For a couple of weeks in July and August it never actually went below 30 Celsius at night, and during the day it regularly hit over 40. That was bad enough, but I had experienced hotter. In 2008 I'd gone to Casablanca and Marrakech, and in the latter city it had gone above 50. That had been a stifling day and yet, weirdly, I had hardly sweated a drop – it was dry heat. Chongqing was completely different.

My evenings were often very late, thanks to the stickiness at night. It meant I had a lot more time to chat to Mum, Miisa, Big Sister Cazzie, or friends like Rick, Dave and Jamie. Miisa and I talked a lot about after the summer. I'd booked my time off at the end of September and we were planning a trip. The plan was for her to come to Chongqing, and after a few days we'd go to Chengdu. After that, our trip would really take off, with visits to Kuala Lumpur and Bangkok, which would also soon be her home.

We weren't the only ones planning a big trip. In Harp one night Neighbour Amy talked about her plan to visit Barcelona before the year's end. It may not seem like much, but to me it was pretty impressive. Chongqing to Barcelona is long haul, in-direct and not cheap. Even I would have to think hard about shelling out for that sort of ticket.

And yet, Amy was very nonchalant about it. She didn't talk about it like she was fulfilling a dream or achieving something she had worked hard for over years, it just seemed like another experience to her. So far in my life, most of the Chinese people I've met in the UK have either worked in restaurants or been students, but here was a young, affluent, ambitious individual who was looking to experience the world just like any of her counterparts in the developed world. Another sign of just how far the country has come in barely a generation.

The humidity was very high, and the heat made the air feel thick and a struggle to take in. I still needed fresh air though, so every once in a while I would pop out for a walk, but it didn't exactly feel fresh walking through Meat Alley, through the underpass and to the precinct on the other side of the main road. The sun was always beating down, and the few minutes it took to get to the park were a struggle and a half.

The park itself always looked pretty empty. When I had first started in Paradise Walk the park had been full of people, sitting around, chatting with friends, playing with their kids or getting together for chess or card games. In the summer heat, the park was mostly empty, of non-card playing old people at least. They congregated in the mall underground, where the air conditioning was in overdrive keeping the shoppers fresh and sweat-free.

Sometimes I would pop into the new doughnut shop that had opened just around the corner from the mall. It was small and hidden away in a corner, but the doughnuts were excellent. Sure they made some with odd ingredients, such as shaved pork, but they made the standards too, with fillings such as cream or chocolate sauce (no jam though). Each visit was usually topped off with a takeaway box or two for the guys at school.

Air-con was the most important thing in my life at the time, though I was a complete novice with it. Being British means that I hardly ever have any use for it. Yes, I've worked in big offices, but the air-con was always controlled by someone else, and at home it wasn't hot often enough to be worthwhile. Now I needed to figure it out for myself, and I wasn't very good at it. The heater/air-con in my bedroom was like the cryptex from *The Da Vinci Code*, so I spent every night sleeping on the sofa, right next to the fridge-freezer sized unit that had fewer buttons to remember.

It was on the buses where I was most worried. These machines were old, rickety and grubby. Some of them had extra fuel stored in plastic tanks squeezed in behind the back seats, and they were bloody cold in the winter. I hate being sticky and sweaty indoors, and a small space like a bus is one of my worst nightmares. Thankfully though, these shitty old coaches were fully equipped with a continuous blast of cold air. You don't get that on the sleek, clean, brand spanking new buses in Britain. Get on a bus in summer in England and the best you get are a few open windows and hope that the bus moves for long enough to create a draft.

There was more excitement to come. John, our franchise owner, had secured an event that he hoped would massively improve the school's profile, both in the company and the city. EF had been hosting regional sales consultant competitions, where the sales staff competed to bring in the most new students. Pretty simple stuff, but John had won us the right to host the national final in Paradise Walk. So, for a whole weekend, all lessons were to be cancelled as the school played host to sales staff from across the country, looking to be crowned national sales champion. There was also going to be a large promo stage outside the mall, with games, prizes and performances to entice the unconvinced locals to part with their hard earned cash.

The PA's were an interesting group. They weren't just classroom assistants; they were also salespeople, so they had a lot of responsibility on their petite shoulders. If they weren't running round getting kids together for class or dealing with parent's, they were trying to sell the school to prospective students. No wonder there was such a high turnover. Linda and Kathleen were assigned to all my classes, and they lasted the whole year, but others only managed a few months before they had to jump ship. Maybe it was because of the pressure of selling and assisting, and Yogi would often push them very hard. Sometimes she and Julie clashed, and their strong wills and personalities could butt heads like stags in mating season.

It wasn't a weekend off for us teachers though. We still had lessons to plan, but not the usual kind. Not only did the sales staff have to sign up new customers through consultations, but they also had to get potential students to come in to have a look around and, if enough showed up, us teachers would give a demo lesson. So we had to plan a few examples across the levels, all for the kids, and then be around, ready to deliver.

It started on a Friday, but it didn't start well. The morning was pretty dead and the consultants spent most of their time sat in their rooms, scratching their heads or checking their phones. A few people popped in and pitches were delivered, but there was no great hive of activity. It was pretty good for us teachers, but not for John, who was a combination of stressed and pissed off.

It soon picked up though. After lunch the parents started coming in with their kids to have a look around and a chat. It was a hot day, but we were all energetic and ready to give our lesson demos. We just needed the numbers to make it worth our while. Jayson spent most of the time making a piñata in the shape of a ladybird (which he kept calling a 'ladybug', wrongly!).

Every now and again we popped out to the promo stage to see what was going on, and the sales staff were doing a pretty good job of attracting a crowd. Every now and again they drew everyone's attention to whichever teacher was standing on the side lines, and we gave everyone a smile and a wave. It often felt like being a foreigner in China gave me a certain, special status and that it would help sell the school. In reality, it was the local staff who were pulling in the students. We were just giving them what they paid for (and not always successfully).

The second day was a lot more hectic. Every one of us teachers had to give a demo lesson or Life Club, and the school was pretty crowded with kids and their parents. John was a lot happier, but we almost had a disaster. I was sat at my desk, listening to music and working, and Grace was at hers behind me. I happened to look around and saw her sat, bent over, like she was thinking or catching her breath. I went back to my work, but a few seconds later I heard Julie calling out to me. When I turned I saw Grace lying on the floor, eyes closed and a few people around her. I'd done a first aid course years before and, even though my knowledge was a bit sketchy, I had enough of an idea.

I managed to get the crowd to back off and checked her breathing. She was fine, and she was able to respond, and even opened her eyes. Just before passing out she'd been sick, but hadn't been feeling ill that day and had thought she'd had eaten enough. She needed a doctor though, so I picked her up and carried her all the way downstairs and out in the street. For a small Chinese girl she was bloody heavy. Carl, a giant of a salesman, took over, hailing a taxi and getting in with her to take her to hospital. Thankfully, it turned out not to be so serious.

The Sunday was quieter than the Saturday, but we still managed a decent trade. Jayson brought his piñata into a demo Life Club, and it became one of the highlights of the weekend as the kids went nuts trying to smash it while blindfolded. The competition didn't quite hit its sales targets, but it certainly increased the school's profile, and we got a lot more customers signing up. Its end was a relief, and John had laid on a party for us.

Being China, it was held at a local KTV, where he had hired a room so big that it could have been partitioned off and still been a decent sized house (by UK standards). It was mainly for the sales staff, but a few of us teachers tagged along later after they'd consumed piles and piles of junk food. There was plenty to drink though, both on the ground floor and on the gallery upstairs (it was that big a room). Naturally, being a KTV, I just had to entertain them with my rendition of *Hungry Eyes*, and Rory embellished it with his improvised interpretive dance routine behind me.

It was weird to think how much I had changed in just the space of barely six months. Performing anything in front of a crowd has always been something I'm loathe to do, even terrified of, but a few months in a city thousands of miles from my comfort zone had changed everything. I think it was the feeling of being a minority, and wanting to "stick together" that pushed me to fit in more than I would have back home.

It wasn't just singing in a private room with friends. That evening I was in front of tens of strangers singing a song with the worst possible tone-deafness imaginable. I hadn't needed to be pushed or bribed. In fact, I think it was me who suggested it. Whatever it was that was happening to me, I liked it, a lot.

1-7. Various shots from around the city.

20 第二十章

Thankfully, the Summer Course was almost over. As the morning sessions came to an end, Wayne seemed to calm down a lot. I had eventually resigned myself to the fact that nothing harsh was ever going to work.

I could raise my voice to him as much as I liked, send him to the corner as many times as I could get away with, and slam my hand on his desk so hard that the floor shook, but it didn't matter. He was still going to dick about as much as he wanted and I really had no authority over him.

I came to the conclusion that it really didn't matter. He was only there for a few weeks, and then he'd be gone. All I had to do was tolerate him. I gave up the discipline and went for the gentle touch. I just pretended he didn't annoy me and that he wasn't a little sod and, weirdly, he seemed to get better. When he misbehaved I didn't worry too much, even if he got out of his chair and ran around, or tried to interfere with his neighbour's work. I tried to be firm but persuasive, keeping my vocal volume to a minimum and my hands far away from any hard surface if I was getting stressed out.

He got a lot better. Maybe it was just attention seeking, or a desire to provoke a reaction from me, but I wasn't biting, and gradually he stopped offering the bait. Lesson by lesson he chilled out, but not too much. His natural tendencies still poked out once in a while, but they eventually became the exception rather than the rule.

His one lapse was when we ventured out of the school and around the mall, doing some class work about shopping. Scarlett, one of the PA's, came along to help, but she wasn't really needed. I spent most of the time trying to keep Wayne in check and not letting him run away, while the others were perfectly behaved.

I was feeling tired though, thanks to only having one lie-in per week. It was pretty draining, especially in the sticky summer, and relaxing was hard. All my chores got done on a Monday, or Sunday night if I was really stressed. There were very few visits to Harp or the underground mall, but more and more I needed cold beers and a long sit down, with a long sleep the following morning.

It had been mentally draining. Even though the extra workload hadn't been that great, it had just been a pain in the arse knowing that we had to be in school, as normal, for six days a week. On the one hand, it meant that chores at home were a bit rushed, but on the other it actually helped my planning. So there were swings and roundabouts, but we were all pretty relieved when the final summer week was over and we could all go back to normal.

We had a treat waiting for us though. John wanted to thank everyone at the school for all our hard work, so he organized a day trip, all expenses paid.

We were taken far out of the city, shooting down gleaming new motorways and then turning off onto not so gleaming connecting main roads through a few small towns and villages. Eventually, we arrived at a leisure complex that didn't look like much fun, but it wasn't the amenities we were after. We walked through the main building, past the leisure pool and pool with a few boats moored and arrived at a large lake, dotted with little islands and framed by a mountainous backdrop shrouded in the smog that blighted our city.

We were in Dazu County, famous for the Dazu Rock Carvings UNESCO World Heritage site. These are a collection of around 50,000 statues from the Buddhist, Confucian and Taoist religions that date from the 7th century, and are among China's greatest historical sites. We weren't there though, we were at Longshui Lake, 80km east of Chongqing. It's actually a reservoir, dug out in the 1950's and holding rainwater over an area of 16.5 square kilometres. It's dotted with 108 small islands and, being the source of two rivers, gave plenty of opportunities for fishing. Rory said he was going to hire a rod and pull out the biggest fish in the water.

We hopped on a sightseeing boat, and it took us on a tour of the lake. It was pretty, but I couldn't help but notice the dead fish, floating on their sides with their mouths and eyes wide open. After a circuit of the lake, we stopped off at an island for lunch. It was a secluded, wooded area, with a wooden hut where we feasted on a cornucopia of culinary delights, and a games room, where mahjong was the game of choice.

These tables were crazy. At the press of a button four slots on the table top open, one on each side, and the tiles are raised to the top, face down and sorted. The game is played and at the end, a disk in the middle raises, the tiles are shoved down the hole and sorted, ready for the next game. Only in China.

The food was chuancai, but it tasted even weirder than the stuff in the city. There was plenty of it though, far too much for even the Chinese guys to clear, and they know how to eat. Once grub was done we were free to wander. I popped into the toilets outside and was nearly sick. They were squatters of course, but laid out more like urinals with short walls separating each unit and no doors, so everyone was exposed to everyone else. They were filthy too, and had the unwashed public toilet smell, only much worse. Oh, and I quickly realized that I had walked into the ladies. Thank God it was empty.

A few of us hopped on the boat and headed back to the dock. Rory, Jayson and Jimmy (one of the local sales guys) hired fishing rods and set to work on who could hook the biggest catch. Rory was adamant he knew the tricks of the trade and would soon be holding up a catch that would make Jesus look like a kid's party magician. We were there for a few hours, and Jimmy managed to catch himself a few little ones, while Jayson pulled out one that would have done nicely, covered in batter and laid out with chips and mushy peas. It made me homesick and Rory jealous. Rory caught nothing.

While Theo, Grace and a few others messed about in the pleasure pool, the boat brought back the rest from the island. There was an impromptu basketball match, where Jayson ran rings around everyone and I looked like a clueless four year-old with less strength in my wrists than Abu Hamza. It had been a lovely day out, and a very generous present from John for all our hard work. That kind of ethos is something fast disappearing from business ethics the world over, to everyone's detriment.

And so everything began to go back to normal. We were back to five days a week, Wednesday to Sunday, easy in the week and super busy at the weekend. All the lesson and Life Club planning from Wednesday to Friday and back to a relaxing "weekend".

My classes were progressing nicely, and moving along through the levels. Both SS Orange classes became SS Reds, but that was because the kids got older. Both HF00's became HF1A's, although Slow Jason in my second class was put back into a new 00 group. TB3A became TB3B, and RE00 became RE01. Some classes had double sessions too, so the timetable was full to bursting. There were no formal exams though – the courses just finished and the students moved to the next level.

One Monday I decided to pay a visit to ShapingBa district. There was nothing special about it, although I'm sure the expats who lived there would defend it to the hilt. It was the usual conglomeration of multi-storey malls, pedestrianized shopping precinct, high rise offices and high rise apartments, heavy traffic, pollution and people everywhere, milling about and getting from shop to shop, street to street.

It wasn't quite same old. In the middle of the precinct was a small, landscaped canal, with a scale model of the Three Gorges Dam at one end. Around it were a few statues of the mighty bang-bang men, one of what looked like mariners pulling a ship out of water, and a carved mural of what I think was a scene from Chinese mythology. All I know is that part of it showed a warrior holding his own, decapitated head.

There was also a public park nearby, with a small lake and green spaces covered in thick, drooping foliage. What was interesting was the decorations. Some genius had decided to dot the park with scale models of famous landmarks from around the world. There was Notre Dame de Paris, the Taj Mahal, the Sydney Opera House, the Statue of Liberty and Mount Rushmore, as well as cartoonish sculptures of animals important in Chinese culture. Sadly, these well thought out and pleasurable statues were in a sorry state, being left unattended and uncared for to the point of rotting. At least the statue of the three sea lions near the bus stop was still gleaming bright.

Later that evening there was another celebration. Rory and Julie put on a party in their apartment in JiangBei, which almost turned into a disaster. Martin and Dulce arrived together, with a large bottle filled with a thin, red liquid. It was cranberry juice, with a hefty dose of baijiu. I still hadn't had the 'white spirit', and too be honest I wasn't that bothered either. I'd heard that it tastes like old, stinky feet. I like cranberry juice though, and we all took a shot of Martin's spirited concoction. It actually tasted nice, but I had no intention of indulging myself. We had a lot of beer to get through and I was thirsty.

The Wii had been brought out, and when we weren't toasting ourselves with beer and JD, we were mucking around on *Mario Kart*. It was pretty clear from early on that I was shit at it. I've never been much good at games though. I've only ever liked sports or strategy games, so shoot 'em ups, driving and role playing games have never really appealed to me. It was a good laugh though, but the graphics didn't exactly do my eyesight much good.

We drank and played and drank and played and drank and played, and soon it began to take its toll on some people. Unbeknownst to us, Martin had finished off most of his special drink, and soon he was slumping on the sofa, becoming limp and barely conscious. I didn't like the look of him, especially when he started falling off the seat, so I dragged him to the bathroom and left him there, almost asleep, just in case he got ill.

He was ill. In fact, when someone popped in to check on him they found the walls and floor dashed with a nasty, bright red liquid that could only have come from deep inside his gut. It was only then that I realized that I had left him on his back. Thank Christ he'd still had presence of mind to turn over.

He wasn't the only one. Dani had wandered into the spare room and flopped on the bed, fast asleep. When she woke up she found she'd left a little mess on the floor and, feeling guilty, drunkenly tried to clean it up, but Rory persuaded her it was fine and he'd do it. I took her home, once again, and she was pretty pissed by the time we got to her flat. The other times she'd been hammered I had left her in the lift to get there herself, but this time I thought it best to make sure she was ok. I took her in, took her to her room, got her on her bed, took her shoes off and stayed with her for a short while, until I felt she was ok.

The next morning I received a strange text. It was from Dani and it read 'Did you undress me last night?'. Believe it or not, I have never been asked that question in my life, but it wasn't a difficult one either. I replied 'No, why?', and then she called me. She'd had a significant black out. When she'd woken up she was in bed, naked, but the duvet cover was missing. In fact, it was in the washing machine, stained with sick. Just like my shower cleaning scenario, she'd puked on her bed, sorted the messed up duvet cover, got undressed and then passed out completely, wiping the events out of her shaken and damaged brain. At least it wasn't just me.

I had a near disaster, the kind I had never experienced in my life despite all my travelling experience. I did my Wednesday HF1A lesson as normal. I'd had a perfectly normal breakfast and lunch and my usual cups of coffee and tea thanks to the latest relief box sent by mum. There was nothing remotely special.

I got home, had a bowl of instant noodles and went online for an hour or so. My stomach felt a bit tight, so I relieved myself and that was that, or so I thought. Sitting in bed, on the laptop, my stomach soon rumbled again, and again, and again, and each time I relieved myself with a bowel movement that should have left me with a rippling six pack. My belly hurt and I knew one thing, I was in trouble. I stayed up until about 2am and I seemed ok, so I got my head down.

I was due in school at 10am for a teacher training session, but when I got up at half 7, my guts went on the offensive. In half an hour I had three big, juicy and slightly scary movements that told me one thing; there was no way I could risk getting on a bus. I called Julie to let her know the wonderful news and she said she would send Sarah, the new account assistant from JieFangBei, to see how I was and if I needed anything. So it was just a matter of waiting. My guts eased off a little bit, but not much. Once every half an hour I was in the toilet, emptying myself in a way I had never thought possible.

I'm not sure how I got it. The tap water is undrinkable, so I was studious to only use it for washing or boiling for cooking. Drinking water came from a water cooler in the living room. It was a pain in the arse having to get a new one, but they were sold by a dry cleaners out the back and they delivered too. I'm a bit of a nail biter, so maybe a few germs crossed from fingers to mouth, but I'm sure I would have been sick more often. I guessed it was just one of those things.

Eventually, in the late morning, she arrived, with Sherry in tow. It didn't require two of them, but I think Sherry wanted to see where I lived (and anything else she could nose). How typical that I hadn't washed up for a couple of days. Thankfully my phrasebook had the word for 'diarrhoea', and as there was a pharmacy in the street below, I was expecting a quick turnaround. I let Julie know the good news and then waited.

I waited, and waited and waited, but there was no sign of them. The trots were still well and truly with me but there was no sign of Sarah and Sherry. I assumed they had popped in to the city centre, but it wasn't that far away. I had a class that evening and I really needed to get cleared up, and it wasn't like I was feeling sick either. Over an hour passed so I called Julie again, trying to find out where they had disappeared to. Half an hour later they were back. Sarah had the medicine, a typical mixture of manufactured pharmaceuticals and traditional Chinese concoctions. Sherry, however, was holding what looked like a big, yellow, bowling ball.

"We've bought this for you." Sarah said, the two of them beaming with smiles. "We want you to feel so much better."

I took it with a genuinely gracious smile. It was a fruit of some kind, and it was heavy, not quite the same as a decent-sized bowling ball, but close. I think I must have been assimilating into Chinese ways because I failed to do one, simple thing; ask them what it was or what I was supposed to do with it i.e. I tried to save face. They left me in peace and I took the medicines as instructed. The next two times I emptied my bowels it came out in two stages; one runny, almost like water and the other as thick as tar. I guessed that meant it was working. I gave it a little more time and, feeling confident, headed to the school.

It was early afternoon when I arrived. I had already missed a couple of hours work so I started to get a little bit stressed. I had already planned a few of the easier, weekend lessons so it was mainly TB3A, a few Life Clubs and the lesson for that evening, the dreaded RE00. As the day progressed I was spared the indignity of needing to repeatedly dash out to the toilet. I was paranoid about that. Sometimes the one seated toilet was blocked up – probably because people didn't think they needed to flush – and it was still my only shitting option. I kept myself hydrated and avoided any kind of spice, and my stomach felt good.

The rest of me didn't though. As the time passed I grew increasingly more tired and lightheaded. My head was buzzing, my bones ached and my muscles didn't seem to want to flex. This was going to be hell. When the lesson started I made it very clear that I was not well but I could still teach. I had no choice; whatever happened I just had to get on with it. I played a Marco Polo video, and as the students watched and tried to follow the basic language, I felt myself slumping in my chair. Cherry and Student Audrey asked me if I was okay a few times.

What actually happened that evening was the best lesson I ever had with them. They were cooperative, considerate, eager, attentive, enthusiastic, engaging and hard-working. I was genuinely surprised by the outcome and incredibly grateful. Had the trots arrived before any of the other lessons I'd had with them, I may well have lost the plot. Instead, the lesson was excellent and I came out of it feeling a lot better.

It also helped that Chrissy had left by then, and so I didn't need to deal with her annoying behaviour making me uncomfortable. Another of them had left too. Terry was the one male in the group and he was doing okay, learning about as well as anyone else. In one lesson we took a break, and when I came back, he was gone. The others said, as best they could, that he had just decided he couldn't continue. Apparently he had a small kid, and he was struggling to keep up with work, learning English and being a dad, so midway through the lesson he'd decided to leave. Fair enough I suppose.

I didn't bother finding out what the hell that fruit was they had given me. I could have checked online, but initially it was never in my mind to try. I could have cut it open, but I was worried it would have one of those freaky stenches, like the durian. It very quickly became an ornament, sat in the middle of the dining table like a pot plant, and I kind of liked it.

I have since looked into it, and as far as I can tell, the best candidate for it is the pomelo (citrus maxima, also called the shaddock or lusho fruit). It is the largest citrus fruit in the world, measuring up to 25cm in diameter, weighing up to 2kg and is usually green. However, the Guanxi Honey Pomelo variety can weigh in at 4.5kg, and I'm pretty sure there aren't that many fruits the same size (if any are even close).

It should have been a sad shock to hear that Waffei had closed down, but it was neither a shock nor particularly sad. It had never been a particularly appealing restaurant, and so I had never bothered going back after my one trip. The unit was boarded up and it looked like nothing was going to happen to it for the foreseeable future. I popped into Harp for a couple of jars, and sat out on the veranda, Chris told me about his plans.

"We're gonna open a Mexican restaurant there." He told me excitedly.

"Interesting? Like a Mexican themed place?"

"No, nothing like that. More like here but with big sofas, and maybe an open fire, and a big bar, and a pool table. I know Mexican food like the back of my hand so I can teach the cooks how to do it properly."

Mexican food isn't a big deal in the UK. There are a few Mexican restaurants out there, and there's even one big chain of them, Chiquitas, but we've well and truly taken on Indian food as our source for hot spices, so Mexican is a case of gilding the lily for us. I'd had it before though, and always liked it, so it was going to be interesting to see what Chris could offer. It was certainly going to be different.

1-6. Our day out on Longshui Lake. 7-10. Shapingba.

21 第二十一章

Summer still felt like it was in full swing. The temperatures were dropping a bit but it was still pretty hot and humid. Dairy Queen, on the floor above the school, was doing a roaring trade from us, though it wound me up how, every time they handed the cup over, they had to do that nonsense of tipping it upside down. I know what it's for, but it pisses me off. Just because it doesn't pour out of the cup doesn't mean it's good quality ice cream.

It was now holiday season, and Tanja was the first to take two weeks. Her mum was flying over to visit, so after a week showing her round they were going to take off for a little national tour. I took on her TB class on Saturday mornings, but I also had to look after cute little NanGua. On the Saturday I popped into her flat, just across the road from the school. The cat was hiding under the duvet as normal, so I put his food out and sorted his litter tray. There was a hissing noise, and when I investigated, I found a leaking pipe in the kitchen and a big puddle of water.

I'm not a very practical guy, so the most obvious option didn't enter my head at first. I headed to the school, hoping Boss Audrey would be there to call a plumber. She wasn't, but Julie and Rory turned up. Julie said she'd get on the case, and so I started to set up for the class. Then it dawned on me; the fucking stopcock. I dashed back across the road, found the pesky valve and stopped the water gushing. By the time the class started, I was sweating like a pig. It was nearly 30 Celsius and it wasn't even 10am. That day was a long, long day, and Sunday wasn't much better. By the time I was done I was craving Tiger, but my bed was stronger.

I actually managed to have a bad experience with the TB3B's. It was a pretty empty class, with only Sabrina and Andy showing up, but a new kid was there too. His name was Alan, and from the get-go he pissed me off. He was clearly confident and good at English, but he was way over the top.

I kicked off the lesson, but he had other ideas. First, tried to formally introduce himself, right as I was starting, which was a bit annoying, but I got him to sit down. Then, as I was introducing the topic, he tried to suggest alternative tasks we could be doing. This was a bit insulting, but I just asked him to pay attention and stick with me. Then he asked me to explain my qualifications and background i.e. justify my position as teacher. He had crossed a line, so I told him I didn't have to justify myself and that he should focus on the tasks.

Then he really crossed the big line. He finally got into the exercises with the others, and we got into some conversations about the topic. I can't remember exactly how it happened but he said "It seems that they are not very good at English", pointing to Sabrina and Andy. That was the last straw –

passing judgement on other students like he was some sort of higher authority. I was very fond of them, so I took it to heart.

To be honest, it was another HF00 moment. Looking back, my reaction was way over the top. I wasn't teaching in a public school, so I should have been more tolerant, discreet and tactful, but at that moment I lost it. I told him, with a raised voice and in no uncertain terms, that he had no damned right to judge other students and that I was sick of him already. I sent him out of the class for the rest of the lesson, letting Julie know in the break what had happened.

At the end we both sat with him and had a chat, along with Kathleen who had been keeping him company. I was genuinely embarrassed because, despite how much of a twat he'd been, he was still just a kid. He seemed embarrassed too, so I did my best to be as chilled out and reasonable as I hadn't been in class. He wasn't back the following week, having transferred to a class in New York New York.

Once again, the team expanded. On a Saturday evening, after another hectic Saturday that felt like it wouldn't stop, a bunch of us climbed into a minibus taxi and headed out to the airport, carrying a supply of cold, cheap, local beers. We didn't have to wait long, and soon our latest teacher was lugging his baggage out of arrivals and into his new home.

His name was Greg. He was a short African-American, with a bit of a Bohemian look about him thanks to his short dreadlocks, beard and grungy dress sense. He was quite the antithesis of Jayson, but one hoped it would just be in style that they clashed, as they were sharing a flat. We headed through the night, drinking welcoming beers and lugging his stuff up to the flat. It was the first time I had gone to meet a new teacher, and it actually felt pretty good to be part of the welcoming party, seeing the look of shock, bemusement and relief I must have shown when I arrived.

I also got to see another familiar look on his face, one I must have displayed once or twice. After the usual week and a bit of late mornings, short days and lesson observations he was finally given a class. From a veteran's perspective, he was given a pretty easy one – SS Green – but when I walked passed the door and caught a glimpse of him through the window, I was reminded just how lucky I had been. His face was a mixture of confusion and total fear, his hands in the air trying desperately to calm the screaming kids down, or maybe to just surrender.

On the Sunday evening I headed out to the nightclubs and bumped into Australian Joel in the Cotton Club. One of the guys he was with was Gordy, one of the Cameroonian guys, and after beers we headed out to the food stalls.

A woman came to our table, selling cigarettes, and spoke to one of the others. As Joel was talking to me he suddenly stopped and turned to face the woman, looking shocked, as did everyone else. Gordy called her over, said something angrily, grabbed a bunch of her packets and threw them across the street. Smiling, she meekly walked away to retrieve her produce.

Joel explained. She'd been trying to sell them to one of the guys and had suggested Gordy might like some. The guy didn't know and she'd said "Are you sure? He looks burnt.".

I'd been told that the Chinese could be quite openly racist, and I'd had the odd experience or two myself, but nothing that I couldn't just brush off and not worry about. I don't think they are any more racist than Brits or Americans, but they could probably do with a bit more of a filter and not be so open. I don't think the woman was racist – she just didn't realize what she said was offensive.

We all tried to be more imaginative and more ambitious, spending more time to come up with some sort of whizzy games or complex exercises. We all made extra cue cards to go with the standard supply, and I put together a generic board game, with a variety of coloured squares and counters. I also made more cue cards for things such as pelmanism.

The tool that made it possible was our glorious laminator. It took a while to get the hang of it, but it meant we weren't just cutting out bits of paper and sticking them on the shelves, where they would get crumpled up and ripped within days. Making the cue cards was a pain in the arse though, as it meant having to cut them out of paper pretty carefully, place them on the laminate sheet with enough space between them to both seal and cut, and have enough cards so that we didn't waste any of the expensive clear plastic. It also meant we were pretty much guaranteed to use that task again, just to get the benefits out of all that effort.

I also spent a lot of free time hunting materials online. There were plenty of web sites with free games, colouring activities and intricate practice activities, but I also did my own searching for various images. If I taught a subject e.g. jobs, I would look for multiple images of those in the course book to augment my lesson, then I'd randomly pick a few more and do the same. Sometimes I'd include these in the lesson, sometimes I'd just keep them in store, ready for the future.

On a rainy Tuesday I headed to the cable car, and crossed the Jialing to JiangBei Cheng. I had seen this brand spanking new district so often, but only visited it once, at night, and only in a small area around by the theatre. I had been told that, just a few years ago, the area was a crumbling, heavily populated district, home to tens of thousands of people with apartments, houses, schools, shops, temples and a couple of churches.

Like so much in the city, the area had been completely cleared, landscaped and rebooted, with the big theatre and science museum replacing the slums and tenements. The only things left of the original settlement were, surprisingly, the two churches, but they had been moved from their original plots. It was a bland and empty area, some would say a metaphor for the true nature of development in the country as a whole.

The following weekend was another one of exploration, and of discovery. Despite being a city of winding streets and big inclines, it wasn't really such a hilly place. It was clear that there were a lot of sheer drops on the land, so crossing short distances could involve a long, tiring walk. I did the familiar climb through the stepped housing estate and took a detour, looking for the other side of the multi-storey car park built into the land opposite my apartment block.

In the middle of this warren of streets and footpaths was, amazingly, another church. Actually, despite the two pristine churches in JiangBei Cheng, this was the Cathedral of St Joseph, centre of the Archdiocese of Chongqing. It was covered in ivy, and its crammed-in location had robbed it of its ecclesiastical grandeur.

I found myself on the main road, heading blindly uphill with no purpose other than to discover. Soon, I found a side street that had a surprising site – my apartment building. It was just tens of metres away, yet I had walked for at least half an hour. It was right there, at the end of the road, but that was no surprise either. As I said, the topography of the city allowed for such incongruity, and it also lead to a genuine discovery.

Just off this side street was a genuine, bona fide slum. It looked like an old district, something one sees in those medieval/fantasy Chinese films that got popular thanks to *Crouching Tiger, Hidden Dragon*. It looked like it was in a pit, and I don't just mean the state of it. It was much lower than the streets around it, but it was in a very sorry state too.

I took a walk through it, making a myriad of turns and climbs, stepping on cracked paving and passing crumbling, one-roomed homes and shops that had been abandoned years ago. It smelt bad too, thanks to the refuse and open sewerage, and its continued existence seemed to be anathema in a city that had no problems destroying and building anew. I did encounter a few residents, but they weren't exactly packed in.

I carried on up the hill, eventually finding another rare piece of history. The city walls were built in the Ming Dynasty, circling for 8km and protecting JieFangBei, and now all that remains are two of the 17 gates, the DongShui Men and the restored Tongyuan Men. The latter was where I ended, and it was a delightful, open museum piece.

This was no passively restored ancient artefact that had been kept for public display. This was a piece of education, with more than an explanatory plaque. It was dotted with active and aggressive-looking statues of soldiers, firing arrows and throwing rocks on the invading army of bronze warriors below. It was a great touch, showing that the gate was more than just an old stack of bricks built hundreds of years ago. It had been a living, breathing organ of the city, one whose success was a matter of life and death for the citizens within.

The following weekend I decided that the city's big, underappreciated landmark, needed tackling. The Chaotianmen Bridge is another of the myriad of mega-engineering projects that are dotting the country but, because it's in an unfashionable city, it hasn't garnered the international attention of the Discovery or National Geographic channels. It's a single span arch bridge across the Yangtze River, connecting JiangBei to the northern end of Nan'an and, when it opened in 2009, its 552m span made it the longest bridge of its kind in the world.

It was a hot day when I decided to walk across it, and it took bloody ages, but the views of the city skyline were pretty spectacular, with the sun glowing down through the light haze of poisonous gases. After passing a few streets with old, crumbling buildings that were closer to rubble than abodes, I arrived at what must have been a quaint little parade of shops by Chinese standards. It was an open-air mall, full of small units like the shops you get in new housing estates in England, only with a hundred of them. There was nothing really going on in the area, and after failing to find the bus stop I walked back across that mighty span of steel and tarmac.

The following weekend I ticked off another district on the Chongqing list. A long bus trip took me south, over the Jialing River, to Nan'an district, somewhere I'd only seen briefly, at night. It was nothing special to be honest. It had residential and commercial high rises galore, many centred round a pedestrianized precinct. There was nothing unique about the place, except for a small ornamental moat with three ships in the middle being pulled by creepily faceless human statues.

I took a walk back, passing the massive convention centre I had passed earlier in the year when going to Foreign Street, the Ferris wheel of the closed fairground on the little hill overlooking the river, and across the Changjiang Bridge, both ends guarded on either side by typically Socialist-style heroic statues that looked positively religious in their form.

Back in Yuzhong I passed by a small, old district of shops and houses that that been better looked after than the one near the city gate. Sadly, I think it had been earmarked for demolition, to be replaced by another modern, high rise complex. As much as I like high rise architecture, I don't particularly like to see old districts wiped out so easily. That's history gone that can never be replaced. If memory serves be correctly though, all the residents and owners had accepted the money happily, but still, it's about more than a fair price. It's about a country's soul.

Julie and Rory had a great little trip planned for themselves. Qingdao is a city of nine million people, located in Shangdong Province in Eastern China. It's one of China's best kept secrets, and for one good reason – beer. Does the name seem familiar now? That's because it is the home of the Tsingtao Brewery, one of the few good things left by colonial expansion in the 19th century. In this instance it was the Germans who sailed their ships and used their military might to capture a small part of the Orient. Despite its more infamous recent history of aggressive expansionism, it was a pretty pathetic colonial power, with a few short lived colonies in Africa and the Pacific. Qingdao was their Hong Kong and, being German, they brought their beer.

The Tsingtao Brewery was set up in 1903, and in recent years has enjoyed a growing reputation around the world as a worthy alternative to the usual, international suspects. Since 1991, the Qingdao International Beer City has hosted the Qingdao International Beer Festival, sometimes billed as the largest Oktoberfest in the world outside Munich. That's where they were going, and they made a bold claim.

"We know that when we are there, we will never have to pay for a drink," was Rory's boast. "The Chinese will see us and just hand us beers all the time, just to hang out with us."

There was something that had to be sorted though. With a DoS and a Senior Teacher out at the same time, they needed to choose someone to take over the school while they were away. Their choice was me. For a whole week, Paradise Walk was to be my own, personal Reich. It wouldn't be such an onerous task – Julie would have the timetables sorted and Rory would have all the Life Clubs planned, so my job would be to make sure it all got done and that the other teachers didn't have any major issues.

My week in charge was pretty easy, as I thought it would be. I took over Julie's office and it felt pretty nice planning everything in some decent space. There were no major issues. The PA's did their jobs as well as ever and the other teachers got on with their work without any hassle or theatrics. A few times I was asked advice on OPTs, and I had to remind the PA's about an open door that week, but other than that it was a pretty simple, straightforward and stress-free week. I had to take an hour out of one day for an online meeting about the new RE course material, but Theo was on the line too, so it was really more his thing. For me, that week was important for other reasons. I had a big trip of my own coming up, and a very important visitor.

Talking of Oktoberfest, that was the theme of an adult Life Club I had at the end of the month. I got Tanja to come in on it, and it was easily the best attended of any of my clubs. This was probably because it involved popping out to the German restaurant for a few beers and a bite to eat. It was the easiest one to plan, as it involved a slideshow about Germany and German drinking culture, especially lederhosen, dirndl and beer festivals. Tanja, being German, took the lead, so I hardly did a thing other than introduce the topic and drink a couple of glasses of the dark stuff. And best of all, not a single word of Chinese was spoken.

Sadly, teaching hadn't worked out for everyone. I hadn't really gotten to know Martin that well, but it seemed he hadn't quite taken to the job. I don't know the details because he worked at New York New York. He certainly hadn't done anything really horrendous as he wasn't given his marching orders and had his visa cancelled, giving him 48 hours to leave. He worked a short notice period before heading off, and a few of us headed out for a bit of hotpot, Harp and Bar 88 to give him a send-off.

It was a massive, heavy night, where we drank and drank and drank. At some point Martin disappeared without saying goodbye, though I'm sure it wasn't out of depression at the thought of leaving. Jayson was a bad influence on me, Greg and Dani, getting us to double our shots. Somehow I managed to control myself though but Dani, being young, still had that sense of invincibility that youth clings on to. By the end of the evening she was more than wobbly, and seeing as she was my neighbour, it was incumbent on me to get her home once again.

Outside it was raining, but she was hungry, so we popped into one of the big tents that served as the Chinese equivalent of a burger van. We each got a bowl of rice, eggs and tomatoes, and I happily tucked into mine, while Dani swayed and wobbled, struggling to get through her portion. Eventually, she decided to give up, hardly touching her food but wanting it for breakfast. We left, me getting her bowl put in a little bag for her to take home. When I came out of the tent she was gone, completely, nowhere to be seen. Drunk and aimless, she had vanished in the few seconds it had taken me to sort out a doggy bag. Where was she? How did she disappear so easily and quickly? Was she safe? Was she conscious?

It didn't take long to find her. I saw a table with two Chinese guys smoking and laughing, looking at something in the street, out of my sight. I headed that way and there Dani was, sat on the cold, soaking wet ground and doing her damnedest to get back on her unsteady feet. I got her in a taxi and we headed home, but as we got close to the apartments she started complaining about her guts and that she was right on the verge of emptying them. I quickly got the driver to stop, shoved her out onto the street and paid. She was okay though, and sat on a small wall to suck in what could ironically be called "fresh air". She also made a strange, whining noise and grabbed my leg, for comfort I suppose. I got her home though, and this time there was no strange text message about mysterious nudity the next day.

1-2. Theatre and church in JiangBei Cheng. 3. Old, district. 4. Tongyuan Men. 5. Chaotianmen Bridge. 6. Nan'an shops. 7. Nan'an skyline. 8. Convention Centre. 9. Statue on the Changjiang Bridge. Another old district.

22 第二十二章

It was finally time for my two weeks holiday. I had been looking forward to it for months and now it had arrived. I had completed a spring clean of the apartment and it was spotless, ready for the arrival of Miisa. That morning I hopped in a taxi and headed to the airport. It was another typically smog-filled day, where the blue sky and sun were obscured by the dust and pollution of endless construction and mass heavy industry.

When she came out of the baggage claim area I was waiting, cold bottle of water in one hand and a big hug in another. It was her first trip to China, and she was a little worried about it. Due to a wheat allergy and health-conscious attitude to food she was quite a fussy eater, and this part of China wasn't exactly famous for its chow mein or sweet and sour pork.

We got a taxi back to my apartment and then headed straight out to JieFangBei, showing her the delights of the central business district, including Food Street, where she made a brave decision and sampled some spicy lamb on a stick. There was no partying for us that night though, not after the epic journey she'd endured.

The next day we started our tour of the city. We headed down to the bus stop and hopped on the rickety old vehicle as it wended its way through the traffic and the smog that I had become so accustomed to. It brought us to CiQiKou ancient village. Tanja was already there and we headed in to this oasis of tradition and quaintness.

By now I had wised up to a few things. On my first visit I had thought it was a mecca for traditional Chinese crafts but, in the subsequent months, I had seen far too many of the pendants, bracelets, rings, broaches and other ornaments in far too many shops to be fooled. These traditional souvenirs were mass-produced, just like everything else in the country, and I wondered just how ancient the village actually was.

It was still a lovable and entertaining destination. We had excellently brewed but expensive coffee and then a browse through the shops selling musical instruments, jewellery and Mao's Little Red Books. The noodle makers were there, as was the hideous stench of stinky dofu, and we even had a browse through the shop devoted to all things panda. Tanja had to head off early, so after taking in the "stunning" view of Chongqing's beach, we headed to a dumpling restaurant, where Miisa was pleasantly surprised by the tastiness of the meat and veg wrapped in the rice-based pockets of delight.

Then it was back to JieFangBei, checking out the streets and shops and heading down to Chaotianmen to enjoy the views of the river. Then we headed to the Yangtze side, where we crossed in the not-so-safe looking cable car. I took Miisa to see the "I Love You" Zebra crossing and she thought it was cute.

Tanja texted me. She had gone out to some big event with her friend but there had been a mix up, and Tanja was at a local hotel on her own, looking for an alternative. We were on the same side of the river, so we picked her up in a taxi and headed back to JFB, where we stuffed our faces with a glorious tepanyaki before heading home. It had been my birthday, and one of the best ever.

The next morning we headed to JiangBei, where I showed her the school and the delights of Paradise Walk, even letting her play a few games on the IWB. As we left we passed Sherry, the accounts administrator. She smiled at me as usual, but her look turned to one of stony suspicion when she realized the petite, pretty, blonde white woman was holding my hand. It was the proverbial "look that kills" or "death stare". We then hopped on the ultra-modern system. It was something I hadn't had much need to use up to then, and I wondered if it would ever truly replace the buses and cars for people to get around.

We took a trip to the zoo, which I was in two minds about. She loved seeing the pandas, but I was still thinking about the conditions of some of the other animals, especially the other bears. For the most part, the animals were ok, and the pandas were especially well taken care of. When we were done we headed into another one of the many shopping malls in the city for lunch at a branch of CSC. I persuaded Miisa to have the steak with egg and chips and, once again, she surprisingly liked it (well, she thought it was okay).

That evening a few of us had dinner at a Korean barbeque place, where we feasted on delightful yak, then headed into the city centre, where we holed up in Harp. It was my birthday get together, but I had no intention of getting hammered. After a few beers and a lot of lounging on the sofas we decided to have a bit of fun local style.

We headed to Bar88, which was almost as full as if it was a weekend. On one of the podiums was a young white lad, taking the opportunity to enjoy the delights of the local beauties. They took him for a walk, and as they passed he said hi. It turned out he was a Finn, from Helsinki, and so he and Miisa had a conflab before the girlies dragged him off for themselves. I expect the last thing either of them had expected to do in Chongqing was to speak Finnish.

Jayson and Greg were enjoying their Jack neat, and Jayson's one to one student, Cherry, had a shot or two. By the time we left, she was crouching down, her arms wrapped around her knees and her face buried. Another 18 year old who could imagine consuming more than she could actually manage.

The next day our trip took us on the high-speed train to Chengdu, where we would eventually meet up with Tanja for a night out. Our arrival was nearly a disaster as I had forgotten to print full details of our hotel, but we managed to get a taxi and get there in the end. It was early evening by the time we'd sorted ourselves out and freshened up, so a quick walk around the centre to get some grub was all we bothered with before heading to bed.

Our only full day there was hectic. Unlike Chongqing, the sky was almost perfectly blue, and Tianfu Square actually felt like a colourful delight, much unlike its smog-shrouded state on my previous visit. Even the statue of Mao was looking bright this time. We wandered all over the city, visiting the stunning Wengshu Temple and heading to the TV Tower for a view and a bite to eat, only to find it was closed. Our lunch consisted of some fruit and cold drinks from a supermarket, consumed on a bench on the riverside.

We followed the course of the river to the Anshun Bridge, a traditional river crossing with a restaurant along its short length. We eventually ended up at Bookworm, lounging around for a couple of hours, pretending to read the books and forcing ourselves to leave the comfort of the armchairs. At People's Park we hired a boat and took a little row around its pretty little lake, while others hired little motorboats that were powered by the charge from their mobile phones. That evening we cheated and had a gut-stuffing dinner at Pete's Tex-Mex before having a few drinks with Tanja at the German bar and, for me personally, it was such a relief to have real beer for a change.

Our next day turned into one of the most stressful of my travelling life. We should have woken up earlier, or at the very least I should have done a bit more research ahead of time. We headed to the local bus station and bought tickets for Leshan. It was about 11 o'clock when we set off, and two and a half hours later we were there.

We hopped on a bus to the world famous Giant Buddha and soon found ourselves in the middle of a crush of passengers that would have killed us had there been any kind of shunt. It took over an hour to squeeze through the traffic, leaving us with very little time to enjoy the amazing site. The last bus to Chengdu left at 5:50pm; we would be cutting it fine. We rushed through the park as quickly as we could without missing out on the hundreds of statues dotted throughout. It was an endless uphill climb too, on a warm and humid day, and by the time we got to the top I was downing mouthfuls of water to avoid shrivelling up.

The Giant Buddha of Leshan is one of the most stunning feats of human creation; a mega-statue carved straight out of the rocks. We had wanted to climb down the steps to the bottom, but our travelling had coincided with a Chinese national holiday, so the locals were out in force and the queues were unimaginably long. We took in the magnificent sight for a few minutes then rushed back to the bus stop, grabbing small bowls of spicy cold noodles for a late lunch. The bus eventually arrived, and that's when the panic started.

One thing I had never experienced until coming to China was the looping bus route. Every bus I had ever taken took a simple route; out along certain streets, then turn around and head right back along the same ones (with a few minor adjustments). I had never been on a bus that drove around a ring, and now we were in for a shock.

I knew what we were in from the moment the bus turned left instead of right, and as the minutes ticked by my panic started growing inside. We could only catch that one bus to Chengdu, and that was assuming there were any seats available. We cut it fine, arriving at the bus station a mere ten minutes before departure, and I rushed in, joined the queue and thankfully got us two tickets back. We couldn't be stranded in Leshan after all.

That evening back in Chengdu we had a very disappointing dinner at what the Chinese like to call a "steakhouse". I'd been to a similar place in Chongqing, and it was clear that all they did was microwave some precooked packaged slab of something that may or may not have come from some part of an animal. To cheer ourselves up, and wash away the horrid aftertaste of whatever it was we had eaten, we splashed out on a bit of Haagen-Daaz. Then we joined Tanja at her hostel for a couple of drinks, before heading back for much-needed showers and a rest, ready for the next stage of our trip.

We arrived in Kuala Lumpur in the evening, but it was still pretty damned hot, and when we got to our hotel we were in for a shock. It was easily the nicest, most upmarket hotel I had ever stayed in and even Miisa, a veteran of good quality establishments, was surprised. Our first problem; how much to tip?

I frantically looked through my guidebook, and thankfully there was a suggestion, so when the porter had taken our bags to the room we were confident we'd rewarded him well. At the very least, all the porters were nice to us during our stay. We then spent the night in the lounge, with cold drinks and one of those lightweight lounge bar bands who can barely fake an ounce of enthusiasm.

Job one for the next day was for me to buy a pair of shorts. I had left mine in the flat and it was hot and humid, so there was no way I was going to stay in my jeans. Just walking around the few streets nearby for a couple of hours was enough to make me dizzy with dehydration, but eventually we found a place that didn't assume you worked for Goldman Sachs.

Kuala Lumpur is one of those cities that oozes the legacy of the British Empire, and is now one of the most fashionable and liveable in Southeast Asia. From the viewing deck on the Menara KL (the TV tower) we could see that it wasn't nearly as high-rise as people think. There were many skyscrapers but, unlike Chongqing, they were nicely spaced out between blocks of low-rise tradition and simplicity. There was a decent amount of parkland and open spaces too, although the so-called river left a lot to be desired.

Two spots dominated the view. The Petronas Towers were, for a number of years, the tallest building in the world and are still the symbol of this thriving tiger economy. Less well-known are the Batu Caves, a 400 million year-old limestone mound 13km north of the city that is still held as one of the most important Hindu sites outside of India.

Our tour took us to the Jalan Petaling market street, a mecca for cheap and imitation goods, and then the Sri Mahamariamman Temple, the oldest Hindu temple in Malaysia still in use. Eventually we arrived at the Central Market, an indoor shopping bazaar that, on the surface at least, has eschewed the knock-off nature of its nearest rival. This was where I did something brave for me and had one of those little flesh-eating foot massages. I hate my feet being touched with a passion, and needless to say, the experience was horrible, but it was kind of fun too. I also finally managed to buy a piece of jewellery I'd wanted for years. On two occasions girlfriends had bought me a spinner ring; a double ring where one can be spun over the other, if you're the kind of person who likes fiddling with their ring (fnarr fnarr!). On both occasions they had been too big for my thin, girly fingers but this time I got one that was just right. If you want a job done well......

That evening we headed a few minutes from our hotel to Bukit Bintang, one of the major centres for the city's nightlife and a popular haunt for expats. We ate at Bijan, where I had a sumptuous Malaysian curry and we were treated to a session of traditional folk dancing that had been arranged for a corporate group. We did a bit of bar hopping, eventually spending the evening in Havana. It seemed to be the only one that didn't have a bunch of local women hanging around in party dress but not drinking. They were either prostitutes or just looking for a free night with a Westerner. Either way, we didn't feel like staying in those places.

The next morning we headed to the top place in the city. KLCC (Kuala Lumpur City Centre) is a city within a city, a collection of offices, residences, a mega shopping mall, leisure spots and a large public park, all centred around the Petronas Towers. This is what high-rise development should all be about; mixed use with plenty of open spaces. Don't get me wrong, I love Hong Kong and New York, but they made a lot of mistakes. We visited the magnificent KL Aquarium which, much to Miisa's consternation, contained a huge collection of giant, hairy spiders. The highlight of the tour was feeding time, when divers got into the tank and put on a display to show off the sea life inside. One did feel for the poor, lonely-looking turtle in the melee of fish.

After a late lunch we headed to the icon of Malaysia. The Petronas Towers are the HQ of the national petroleum company and were the brainchild of Prime Minister Mahatir bin Mohammed and architect César Pelli. Reaching a height of 451.9m they were the tallest building in the world from 1998 to 2004, when surpassed by Taipei 101. Our visit took us on to the Sky Bridge, the connecting walkway between the twins that crosses at a height greater than the peak of the Spinnaker Tower in Portsmouth. Sadly, the views weren't so great, but we were still there and happy, especially as the afternoon rain had poured down and drenched the streets below. After the rain cleared a little we spent some time by the hotel pool. Despite the rain and clouds it was still warm and muggy, and I was just glad there was no chance of me getting sunburned.

The next morning we hopped on the monorail to the Masjid Jamek Kuala Lumpur, one of the city's many expansive mosques. According to a stone plaque, it was built at the confluence of the Sungal Gombak and the Sungal Kelang. I assumed this referred to the "river" running alongside it and through the city. Kuala Lumpur has many great things, both old and new, but what it doesn't have is a might river. This stream running through it looked more like a big storm drain; the water was brown and the banks of it were lined with filthy concrete and large pipelines. Surely this has to be the next big project. For the mosque, we had to wear large blue gowns that clearly weren't designed by people who lived in high humidity. I'm not sure what material they were made of, but they certainly weren't 100% cotton, as the sweat on our backs testified.

A little way down the road we were in a district that still screamed "EMPIRE!". The Royal Selangor Club was the absolute place to be on the social scene of Malaysia, back in the days when Britain was the dominant world super power. It was where the rich Brits and their rich guests used to hang out in colonial splendour, so it seems apt that it was in the neighbouring Merdeka Square where the Union Jack was lowered and the flag of Malaya was finally hoisted, declaring the colony's new independence.

Opposite is the opulent Sultan Abdul Samad Building, and just down the road is the original Kuala Lumpur Railway Station and City Point, the first true skyscraper the city ever had. Most important is the National Mosque of Malaysia, a decidedly understated building considering Malaysia's penchant for big statements. It was here that we were approached by a TV crew to do an interview. They asked me what I knew about halal, and I actually learnt a fair bit from them when they explained it wasn't just about meat. They even asked me to do an ident, where I had to say "Al-Hajirah, the best" with a thumbs up and a big smile. That was the name of their TV channel. To this day though, I haven't been able to find that clip online. I just hope it wasn't some sort of Al-Qaeda mouthpiece.

We headed back to our hotel. On the way we stopped off at one of the largest buildings in the world by floor space; Times Square. After a quick coffee we took a tour of the seemingly endless number of floors of shopping. Thankfully, there were hardly any international brands hogging the good spots, and I was especially happy to find a magazine shop that specialized in back issues. I was able to get a few editions of *Monocle* that I'd missed. There was also a clothing shop that sold t-shirts displaying the Nazi flag.

I know what some of you will be thinking: *The swastika is actually a Buddhist symbol so don't judge*. Well I am judging, because this wasn't just a Buddhist symbol, it was the flag with the red background, white disk and black swastika slap bang in the middle. This was not a Buddhist t-shirt, although I will concede that in that part of the world, the actions of Japan are more significant than those of Germany. Incredibly, the building housed a fully operational fun fair, with a genuinely exciting-looking rollercoaster. Skegness Council, if you're reading this, think about it.

That evening we headed back to the Petronas Towers to enjoy our favourite building in all its illuminated glory. We had a look at some of the restaurants nearby, but none of them took our fancy, and the best looking bar seemed to be a meat market for local women and Western men. We headed back to Bukit Bintang where we had a pub meal and then a few more drinks back in Havana.

Our journey to Bangkok had been a delight for me. Our Air Jordan flight was only connecting there, on its way to Amman and so, being long haul, it had all the entertainment facilities. The in-flight cut of *The A-Team* was timed perfectly, it was just a shame that the quality was all wrong too (and I don't just mean the picture). This was a bit of a training visit for Miisa, as she had done all the complicated stuff for her sabbatical. In fact, she would be back in about six weeks, in time for Christmas and New Year.

Our hotel was just outside the main tourism centre, and after breakfast on the riverside, we hopped on the hotel's river taxi and headed to Thonburi, the historic centre of the city. The Chao Praya River is lined with a mixture of poor and rotting shacks, grand colonial palaces (despite Thailand never being a Western colony) and modern upmarket high rises.

Our first sight set the scene for our entire trip; a gilded and bejewelled temple with bright colours, row upon row of dazzling statues of the Buddha and a lovingly maintained picture of King Rama taking as much prominence as the religious iconography. Outside, the streets were a chaotic mess of cars, cats, cables and consumers. The market stalls were packed in closely and the smells of the local curries made us salivate.

At the heart of Thonburi is the Grand Palace, former home of the much beloved royal family. If you think the Brits are a bit over the top when it comes to royalty then I suggest you visit Thailand to experience true regal adoration. There are pictures of the King bloody everywhere, and any negative comment about him is a punishable offence. Outside the main entrance was a sign giving the opening times and the best warning ever: *Do Not Trust Wily Strangers*. I suggest they should also warn against vagabonds, ruffians, rapscallions and toe-rags.

As expected, the temples and pagodas are the most elaborately decorated you can imagine, but there is no, single, grand building in the centre from which all others feed off. This is a complex of buildings squeezed tightly in a walled enclosure, its opulence in unsurprisingly stark contrast to the world outside. In between temples and kingly rooms was a large scale model of Angkor Wat, and past the strikingly beautiful murals was the temple of the Emerald Buddha, one of Buddhism's holiest pilgrimage sites. The palace was also home to one of the ugliest buildings I'd ever seen, the Phra Thinang Chakri Maha Prasat, a European-style Neo-Classical palace that so shocked local sensibilities that a traditional Thai-style roof was plonked on top.

Across the river we visited Wat Arun, a beautifully tiled stone pillar with the steepest set of steps we'd ever climbed. They were so steep that the only safe way to descend was backwards, i.e. facing the steps. Then we headed back across the water, looking for the Giant Swing outside the Wat Suthat Temple. By the time we got to the nearby Democracy Monument, the afternoon clouds had descended, and we were forced to take cover as the heaven's opened. It didn't look like it would stop soon, so we managed to hail a taxi and headed back to our hotel.

That evening, we headed into Patpong, but not for its sexual delights. We dined at Le Bouchon, a French restaurant that served us chicken that made me want to weep with joy that it wasn't cooked with any weird spices. The area wasn't what I expected though. I had assumed it would be seedy and grubby, full of go-go bars, prostitutes and local women looking for a free night. They were all there, but the main street was filled from side to side with a market. Most of the tourists there were actually looking at the cheap knock-offs on sale (consumer goods, I mean). If anything made the area seedy, it was the stalls selling cheap, imitation crap.

The next morning started hot and humid with a vengeance. A taxi took us to Wat Ratchanadda, another one of the city's many Buddhist temple sites. Within it is the Loha Prasat, a wedding cake of tiers covered in 37 metal spires that has a dark, Gothic feel to it, much at odds with the brightly coloured and preciously adorned temples elsewhere. There were good views from the top, but we had to be careful of the worshippers and monks in their little corners, praying at the shrines that dotted the interior.

As we left we were shocked by the convoy of motorcycles that shot down the main road, every one of the riders wearing a red shirt. For years, Thailand has been in the grip of political turmoil, all based around one man, Thaksin Shinawatra, and the money he allegedly made as Prime Minister from the sale of national assets. It seemed crazy and illogical that a country's political stability was so intrinsically linked to the fortunes of one person, but that's where Thailand seems to be stuck.

He headed to Wat Saket, the Golden Mound. For me, this was the most beautiful temple in the city. It's built on an artificial hill, with winding paths leading to the summit, like stairways to heaven, lined with bells and golden statues of the Buddha himself. The views from the top look across a surprisingly low rise plain, with the skyscrapers shooting up in the distance. Despite my love of high rise, I really hope it never reaches that part of the city. Let the golden domes and spires of the temples take precedence in that area.

We took a tuk-tuk to Chinatown, which didn't seem very Chinese to me. It was very packed in, a bit grubby, and a with few streets stifled by market stalls, a few temples and some Chinese restaurants and shops, but there was nothing about the place that would separate it from the rest of the city. That seems to be the way with these places though. Other than a few eateries and the odd gateway there's nothing especially Chinese about Chinatowns.

A taxi took us to the reclining Buddha at Wat Pho. The statue is 15 metres high and 43 metres long; the feet alone are 3 metres high by 4.5 metres. The soles are inlaid with the most exquisite mother-of-pearl panels, displaying auspicious symbols such as dancers and elephants. Around the statues are 108 bronze bowls, into which people drop coins to bring themselves good fortune. It's a magnificent sight, clad in gold and surrounded by beautifully painted murals. Yes, I know, that's a lot of wealth and expense for a statue, but we can't exactly judge with our Gothic cathedrals and golden altarpieces.

That evening we headed to the rundown-looking Rajadamnern Stadium, the cathedral of Muay Thai boxing. Inside it felt like being in an 80's martial arts film, especially one of the early Jean-Claude van Damme flicks. The bookies were taking bets as loudly as possible, and it was standing room only on the terraces. All the tourists had taken ringside seats and, as the fighters did the best they could to smack each other's faces off, a traditional band played traditional Thai music throughout, with drums beating and horns oozing out that almost scratching, ear-piercing tone that is so associated with Asia. This was Miisa's thing; I would have gone for sure, but I'm not that interested in the sport, whereas she was a keen kickboxer.

For dinner, a tuk-tuk took us to Kao San Road, the other popular haunt for tourists that is devoid of go-go bars, but still has a certain seediness thanks to the street prostitutes and the short-stay establishments. There were market stalls everywhere, and even a few kids going from bar to bar trying to sell flowers to foreigners. A few did the pretend crying if we said no, which was actually quite entertaining, but there was one who was particularly clever.

She challenged me to a few games of Rock-Paper-Scissors, and promptly whooped my arse almost every time, so I was happy to buy a rose from her for Miisa (I'm so romantic). What was even more impressive was that she was barely 10 years old, from a poor family and could speak decent English.

Our final day in Bangkok was as lazy as we could make it. After Miisa had done a very bloke thing by insisting on watching Muay Thai, I insisted on a very girly thing; shopping. Actually it wasn't about shopping. The *Marco Polo* videos at school featured the Siam Paragon shopping mall, and I wanted to check it out. It was big and gaudy, just like one would expect, so it was nothing special, other than being the most upmarket in the city.

We had a wander round the shops, checking out the bookshops and the 3D TV in the Sony store, and then grabbed a bite to eat in one of the multitude of restaurants on the ground floor. We wandered the streets in the area, eventually heading down to the splendid oasis of nature that is Lumphini Park before hopping into a taxi and heading back to the hotel, where we treated ourselves to a night of room service, before heading our separate ways in the morning.

Chengdu – 1. Anshun Bridge. Leshan – 2. Giant Buddha. Kuala Lumpur – 3-6. Skyline, fish foot massage, t-shirt shop and indoor amusement park in Times Square. Bangkok – 7-10. Funny sign, Loha Prasat, Democracy Monument and Wat Pho.

23 第二十三章

My holiday was over and, with summer gone too, I felt like I was on a big countdown to the end. There was still a few months to go, but I was over halfway done, and most of the hard work was behind us all.

I got back into my regular routine; in at 9:30, check emails, plan as many lessons as possible, get some lunch from the little greasy spoon, Cbest, the restaurant next to Cbest or CSC, plan some more lessons and Life Clubs, make some materials, give the lessons, observe other lessons if needed and then, when the last session was done on Sunday, head home or to Harp for a few relaxing beers before chilling out on Monday and Tuesday.

We had another new addition to the school. For a good while, Julie had been telling us about her twin sister Jamie, and in October she finally joined us in JiangBei. They weren't identical, but there was no mistaking them for strangers either. Tall with long, jet-black curly hair, a Bohemian style and that rare trait of being an American who can do sarcasm, it was only their faces that really differentiated them.

We had a welcome meal, as per usual, and of course Julie and Rory were especially super excited about having Jamie there. They had suggested I give her an extra-special welcoming gift, and I was more than happy to oblige. After a hearty and jinjiu-infused shrimp pot meal, we headed to a local KTV. More drink entered our bodies and, while all were in a happy state of inebriation, Jamie was ready to receive her present.

Rory dragged one of the soft, leather stools in front for the big TV screen, sat Jamie on it, handed me the mic, and pressed start on the controller. On the screen, the titles came up and the now familiar drum beat kicked in. *Hungry Eyes*, the Andrew Snape special. I didn't just sing it to her, I performed it with an energy and intensity that even Mr. Carmen himself could never have mustered. It wasn't a serenade by any means. Straddling her lap and grinding my arse and groin into her wasn't exactly sensuous, romantic or classy, but everyone was entertained, and she did grab my butt cheeks at the most opportune moments. She was now, well and truly, one of us.

Jamie wasn't the only new addition. Phil was a young guy, about university graduate age from England, who had decided that he needed a big adventure while he was still young.

In JiangBei, we had the pleasure of another branch of Subway almost on our doorstep. Actually is was on the other side of the park with the underground mall, but it was close enough. It was in a unit in a two-towered complex that was still being built, which seemed like a bit of a health and safety nightmare, but I'd heard of that practice in Dubai. Get parts of a building complete enough to fill the space and generate revenue while the rest of the building goes up. It makes economic sense, but it was unnerving.

I took a wander round the shop units, which included another MacDonald's and another Dairy Queen, but there were also a lot of independent shops selling clothes, jewellery, shoes, mobile phones and household wares. I scaled the floors and found myself in a courtyard, open to the elements with the shells of the towers looming above. There were more shops and, thankfully, another coffee shop.

It was called Coffee for Two, and was owned by a local woman called Echo who, like Boss Audrey, Yogi and Neighbour Amy, had the noticeably greater physical presence than her peers, coupled with superior English language skills. It was a small place, and there wasn't much passing footfall for people watching, but it was a good escape from the school for lesson planning when I needed a change of scenery.

It was on one of my chill out days that I had an encounter that would set me on an unusual course for the end of the year. I was in Starbucks when I overheard a conversation between a British guy and a Chinese woman with impeccable English. They were talking about charity fundraising among the expats and how the guys were doing something called "Movember". I'd never heard of it, so I interrupted them.

It turned out there was a growing trend for guys to grow facial hair in November to raise money for charity. Some of the expats where going to do it for a local care facility for mentally disabled people, so I took some contact details from them.

The next day at work I told Rory, Julie and Boss Audrey about this, and they were immediately interested; it was a great cause and it would certainly raise the profile of EF in the local community. The only question was, how were we going to raise the money? How could we get the parents and adult students to donate yuan? Just growing beards didn't seem like a good enough incentive to get people to give. I had already given that some thought though. My plan was, if I may say so myself, freaking genius.

At the entrance there would be a podium with pots for donations, each one assigned to a participating teacher. With each pot would be an up-to-date photo of said teacher, sporting their current beard design. Students and their parents would then be encouraged to put money into the pot of the teacher whose beard looked the best. So, as the month progressed we would not only be encouraging people to donate, we would also be giving them a reason to donate more than once. It seemed like a good plan, and when we told the others they agreed too. So, it would be me, Rory, Greg and Jayson to beard up for November, although Greg was already well ahead of us.

Sadly it wouldn't be everyone. Julie put the idea to Theo, but he was against it. It wasn't that he was uncharitable or hated people with mental disabilities, it was because he didn't want his teachers to have facial hair in the school: clean shaven was the only acceptable thing for him. So David and Phil were out, although that was probably no big deal, seeing as they weren't exactly blessed with 5 o'clock shadows. It was likely that they would never have been able to grow anything significant in a year, let alone thirty days.

I've mentioned before how driving can be one hell of an experience, what with all drivers having a distinct lack of any sense of a highway code. Quite often though, the traffic was so crowded that vehicles never really got up to speed for there to be any real problems, and the whole system worked, as everyone was thinking the same thing and were able to make accommodations for each other. Sometimes though, their lack of any road sense could cause issues that are just unimaginable anywhere else in the world.

I was on the bus to work when a driver in an expensive Beemer or Merc tried to cut in front of the bus, while the bus tried to cut across three lanes of traffic to get to the stop just a few metres away. There was a collision, and by 'collision' I mean an obviously minor prang that could not have done any kind of serious damage to anyone or anything.

Elsewhere in the world it would be very simple; both vehicles would pull over to the side of the road, drivers would check each other's vehicle for damage, insurance details would be exchanged and that would be that. There might be a tiny bit of disruption for other motorists, but it would sort itself out pretty quickly. Not in China.

The car stopped where it had been hit. The bus stopped too, diagonally across two lanes of traffic. That left one lane free, for all the other cars on the road, in rush hour, in a city where traffic is normally as crowded as the worst excesses of Paris, New York, London or Tokyo. The two drivers got out and, for some reason, had a discussion that lasted at least ten minutes. Ten minutes, over a minor bump that actually did no damage to either vehicle. I know this because I popped my head out and it was clear that the expensive car was just fine. Also, the driver wasn't completely losing his mind, so I couldn't figure out what the hell they were talking about.

When I looked out of the back window I saw a horror show. The tailback was biblical. I may not know anything about the science of traffic management, but I knew something about the roads of Chongqing. In those few minutes, while the two drivers were having their pointless chinwag, a jam had been created that I just knew was already building up for a few miles, into and across the city centre. It was catastrophic, a genuine situation of gridlock as the cars at the front tried to jostle their way into the one lane that was open. The two drivers were utterly oblivious, or they saw it but didn't give a fuck. Eventually they parted company and we drove off, with no personal details exchanged and seemingly nothing resolved, if anything actually needed resolution.

Also, this was a bus. Why was the driver so disinterested in his job? In Britain, buses have a schedule, and the drivers generally make an effort to stick to it. If there is a reason to make an unscheduled stop they try to resolve it as soon as possible and get going, or inform the passengers that they need to transfer to the next bus. I'd noticed that the bus drivers in Chongqing acted more like taxi drivers. There was no fixed timetable, but they were supposed to arrive at each stop about every ten minutes. However, if two buses on the same route ended up close to each other, it was as if the drivers were competing to get ahead or get more bums on seats, like their livelihoods depended on it.

Best of all? On the bus that day, while the two drivers were babbling to each other for no useful reason, the other passengers on the bus had almost no reaction. It was as if what was happening was par for the course, like something they experienced all the time, like it was perfectly normal.

That wasn't the only annoying thing I experienced. Some Chinese people are genuinely fascinated by Westerners. Usually, this is manifested by them asking to have a photo taken with them. It happened to me a few times in Beijing and Nanjing on my 2007 trip, and it was kind of cute. Sometimes though, it was annoying and intrusive.

After another week a few of us hit a local shrimp pot restaurant and had our usual batch of spicy crustaceans, local beer and powerful jinjiu. The staff were rushing about as normal, but we noticed them chatting to each other and looking our way a lot. It was a bit rude, but normal, so we ignored it. As we were leaving Rory noticed a couple of the waitresses took photos of us. We were all a bit shocked and annoyed, but most of us decided to leave it. Rory decided 'hell no', and for the next ten minutes was engaged in a heated discussion with the staff and their manager. He refused to leave until they had proved they'd deleted the pics.

To be fair, the only reason we didn't join in was because we couldn't speak Chinese like Rory and Julie could. It was seriously rude of the staff to take our photos without asking, although we'd have just said no anyway. I'm not sure why they thought that was okay, but maybe it was linked to other common aspects of the Chinese psyche, like not queuing or spitting on the street and on buses. They have a different mind-set, and it probably never occurred to them that there would be a problem. One would hope they'd learnt a valuable lesson.

The days and weeks ticked on, but it wasn't all plain sailing though. I saw some issues with my first HF1A class and I had Dulce sit in to see what I was doing. I wasn't doing anything wrong, just a bit unimaginative and repetitive so the kids were getting bored and uninspired. Dulce was one of the experts at this level and she suggested a few games and reading tasks to kick-start the class again.

I had an HF Life Club entitled "Inspector Gadget", which I had hoped would have been a great way to inspire the kids' imaginations by showing them an episode of the awesome cartoon, and getting them to draw and describe a supercop character. Sadly, it was mostly blank faces, apart from eliciting a few basic descriptions of clothes, body parts and colours.

I had no such problems in an RE Life Club about jobs and personalities. Jamie was observing and I struggled to explain the world "aggressive", so I demonstrated by shouting at her and grabbing her shoulders, shaking her violently. Let it never be said that I gave half measures in class.

I had a moment in my TB3B class that could lead one to describe me as a limp-wristed pinko pussy liberal coward, but I think I was justified in my reaction. We started a new chapter titled 'The Far East'. As I began the class my memory suddenly brought back the nationalistic view of Comrade Rose. The chapter title suddenly seemed inappropriate. It immediately looked like a small-minded Western-oriented tool of ignorance, and I felt duty bound to explain it.

The term 'Far East' is very colonial, and only exists in the West. The local name for China, *Zhong Guo*, means 'middle kingdom', but 'Far East' makes it seem like China, Japan, India and their neighbours are all dislocated and far removed from the real and important events in the world. This is clearly horseshit, and becoming more so as China steadily becomes the largest economy in the world.

I wasn't overly surprised though. The material is developed in Europe and it's very easy for researchers and authors to slip into comfortable patterns of thought. China isn't their only market either, and I'm sure it was done with the best of intentions. However, China is EF's biggest market, and the Chinese are well known to be both nationalistic and sensitive to patronising Western views about them. It would have been better to choose a different term, like 'The Orient' or 'Asia'. Anyway, the kids didn't seem remotely bothered by it, so maybe I overreacted.

I also had an open door class with them, but at the time this felt like a disaster. Linda did her job as normal; she gave the parents the information about the schedule well in advance and contacted them again to remind them. I planned my half a lesson and, when the kids showed up, I double-checked with her that the parents were coming. She said she'd contacted them the week before and they were all expected to be there.

I did the first half then, during the ten minute break, I set up the room for the thirty minute demo, ready to dazzle the adults who had paid for my time. The kids came back, but there were no adults. Usually they'd have been waiting in the foyer, but there was no-one; it was like a ghost town out there. I asked Linda to find out where they were and she got straight on the phone. I assumed there was some sort of Chongqing traffic delay, so I chose filler instead of the plan in case the parents showed up.

Thank God for *Marco Polo*. I gave the guys a choice of subject, I put the video on and then we went through it. I don't know how many times those videos saved my bacon in class, but I genuinely loved them. They had chosen '*Kuala Lumpur – Food*' and we talked about all the crazy things they had eaten (including dog), some of the things I had tried there, food around the world and recipes. It was a great way to get them talking spontaneously using language they hadn't worked on that day and, as per usual, they were dazzling in their ability.

So the lesson ended and I was stressed out. Why hadn't the parents shown up? Why didn't they want to see me? What had I done that was so bad? How much trouble was I in? Was I too chummy with the kids? Had I made them complacent? It felt like a disaster of epic proportions. I trudged back to the teacher's room and told Julie the worrying news. She headed out to speak to Linda while I sat at my laptop, thinking about the HF Life Club I had to prepare for. Julie came back, smiling.

"Nothing to worry about." She said, patting me on the shoulder. "Apparently the parent's didn't see the point. They have no concerns about your teaching?"

"No concerns?" I asked, surprised.

"Nope. None whatsoever. They're very happy with you and how they're kids are doing, so they didn't feel the need to question you. Good job."

Another pat on the shoulder and she headed back to her office. My head was full of WOW! This was a new one on me. It was a great feeling knowing that the parents thought so highly of me, but I still wished they had called ahead to let us know. I could have given their kids a real lesson.

It helped me relax, as I felt even more confident than before. That, along with their excellent abilities, made me feel I could make parts of the lessons a lot less formal, almost like a Life Club. Some of my work earlier in the year paid off too. I'd created a blank board game, with a snaking route and a selection of squares in one of four colours, with some left blank.

We were on the chapter about animals, and the game seemed to be perfect. Blank squares were nothing squares, but each of the coloured ones involved a task. One was "miss a turn", another was "go back to the start", pretty standard forfeits in a game. The other two involved picking one of the animal cards I'd created. One colour meant that they had to do an impression of the animal, either making the noise or performing an action. The other meant they had to describe the animal, but on the card was a list of words they were not allowed to use. The latter was the most useful for language as it forced them to dig deep into their vocabulary, whereas the former was just for a laugh.

They certainly had a good laugh about it. Even reserved Henry and shy Andy had a good time pretending to be a tiger or a panda. The girls were certainly more up for the performance. They even pushed themselves more than I had asked them to do. When one of them was describing the animal the others would often ask questions. I hadn't suggested they do that – they just did it of their own volition. That was one of the best things about teaching them – I didn't have to tell them everything they needed to, or could, do. They just did the tasks and pushed themselves as much as they felt they could. I hardly needed to encourage them.

I decided to try something new, something Julie had been working with and was eagerly trying to promote to the rest of us. It's called phonics, and I had only heard about it on the news, usually presented as a revolutionary educational technique that traditionalists hated. It's a method that makes students "phonemic aware", which just means that they learn by phonemes rather than looking at the alphabet and whole words. The theory is that students will recognize the sounds with their spelling, and learn to blend them and, eventually, be able to read and write better.

After some guidance from Julie, I decided to try it out on my HF's, as they were the biggest classes and needed the most imagination. There were already some materials prepared, so I set aside half an hour each lesson for this new-fangled hocus pocus. They were learning the course material well enough, so I didn't see any risk.

The tasks were pretty simplistic. There were PowerPoint presentations that would flash up phonemes for the kids to repeat. I would go from student to student, making sure each one got a chance to interpret the two letters on the screen. Thankfully, the kids didn't find it easy from the get go. I'd have hated it if I had pinned my hopes of pushing the kids on a task they just sailed through. The likes of Lucy, Charlotte and Susie found it pretty easy, but Annie, Anna and Hans often struggled, but I persisted, and they improved. Sadly, I had chosen it too late in my time there, so I wouldn't get the chance to see if it really worked.

Life in Chongqing changed irreversibly near the end of the month. Just across the precinct, for the whole year, another tower had been under construction relentlessly. As it took shape it was clear that the upper floors would be apartments or offices, while the lower floors would be another bloody mall, called Starlight 68 Plaza, and home to brands such as Gucci, Armani and Cartier. The mall part opened first and, on a brief scout, I found that the basement level also had another chuffing MacDonald's.

It was on another visit that this umpteenth, and seemingly pointless, new mall became a revelation. A new unit had opened, just opposite MacDonald's, called Le Grenier á Pain. It looked like a French bakery, but this was China, so that didn't mean shit. I entered, was greeted by polite local staff, and to my amazement I saw what looked like genuine, Western-style baked products; crusty baguettes, croissants, big slices of thin crust pizza and cakes without tomatoes.

I caught a glimpse of the kitchen and it was mostly Chinese staff, but directing operations was a bald, thin white guy, looking exceedingly French. I knew this must be something special. We'd had the sandwiches from Frisco's and they were good, but only compared to everything else on offer. In reality they were horrible, but we had enjoyed them anyway. Now we had a real bakery, and everything changed.

Now I know what you're thinking: RACIST! Well hear me out. When it comes to food we all exhibit a certain amount of prejudice. You want authentic curry – look for an Indian chef. Real chow mein – find a Chinese cook. Soul food – always bet on black. It's the same thing. The bakeries in Chongqing were crap, so having an expert in the kitchen could only be a good thing.

I bought a croissant, slice of pizza and a coffee and nearly died of bliss. I'm not saying it was the best bakery ever, but after all those months with barely a sniff of real bread, it was to die for. When I told the others in the school, they were stunned – not just at the thought of a real bakery, but at it being so close. This was too good to be true, and over the coming days every one of them came back to the teacher's room with a delightful selection of breads and pastries like it was an early Christmas.

It was also in this building that I had another new food experience, but one that was arguably a bigger antithesis to China that a Big Mac. Tanja took me to the sushi restaurant and explained the concept. Weirdly, this felt like a bigger and braver leap for me than trying hot pot or shrimp pot. It was interesting that, despite there being huge political issues between Japan and China (stemming from the perceived lack of acknowledgement by Japan of atrocities committed in World War II), the Chinese really did like Japanese culture, whether it be their films, their pop music or their food. I actually liked sushi, and we went back there a few times before I left.

1. Drum in the Jialing, the beginnings of a new bridge. 2. View from Hongyadong. 3-4. Main road to JieFangBei. 5-8. Various other shots.

24 第二十四章

1st November was the night of the Movember launch party. A large contingent of ex-pats congregated at Harp for the usual gallons of beer, but this time it came with a free barber, who expertly applied a cut-throat razor to our faces for the single closest shaved I'd ever had in my entire life. I'm amazed that I was able to grow anything after that, as it felt like three layers of skin had been scraped off.

And so it was that the competition began. On the Wednesday I arrived at the school to see the stand with the four pots ready for the donations. Thanks to Audrey, the school had gone to town, getting a banner professionally printed detailing exactly what was going on.

The first few days started well, as donations came in based on the loyalties of our students. It was close at first, but Rory and I took an early lead that first week as our facial hair gradually crept through and we crafted it into our chosen designs. I had chosen the "SAS", which was sometimes mistaken for the "gay biker".

I quite liked the formal lesson observations, although I was always a bit uncomfortable with raising issues if I saw any problems. I try my best not to be self-righteous and unjustifiably judgemental in life, but I'm certainly not perfect. When I did an observation I tried to make it as positive as possible. Rather than saying 'that was bad' I would say 'I see what you were thinking, but maybe this alternative would be better'. When I said something was good, I would go one better, and say it was something I would try in my own lessons, even if I had no intention of including it. I would also use it to hold up a mirror to my own work.

One such observation was one of Jayson's Life Clubs. It was for low-level TB's, and the theme was 'utopia'. At the start he had the word on the big screen, and asked them if they knew what it meant. He tried to elicit ideas, but the kids had no clue, and when he tried to explain, he used language too far above their level. Then he showed them a film, *Lord of the Flies*, the classic adaptation of William Golding's awesome novel. He didn't show all of it (it was only a one hour session), but he didn't show a small portion either. He scrolled through the film for half an hour, before getting back to the kids to talk about the subject and eliciting their ideas about a 'perfect society'.

I think I was the most critical about this one than any other observation I did, but it served to remind me of some of my own mistakes. Life Clubs were often an afterthought for us because they weren't part of the standard curriculum, and they were much more informal than a proper lesson. However, they were still necessary for students, and they were part of the packages we sold, so students were entitled to a properly planned session.

There had been many times where I had planned a Club in a couple of minutes, throwing in some task that would easily fill twenty minutes of the session without much thought. I had been especially bad like that with the HF clubs, often reverting to colouring tasks or dragging out some game on PowerPoint, or even relying on the IWB games and the foot pads on the stage. They were often fun, but I wondered how useful they were. I was honest with Jayson when I gave him feedback, but I tried not to be brutal about it. The way he had shown the film was pretty bad and it didn't really convey the subject matter. He took it diplomatically; I just hoped he didn't take any offence.

Our weekly teacher meetings got back up to speed, and Rory and Julie kept pushing the teacher training. One Thursday they gave us some homework, which was to prepare a sample lesson based on what they had been demonstrating.

Let's just say this was not our finest moment. Only a couple of us actually got to present our plans because Julie put a stop to it pretty quickly with a combination of anger and exasperation. She had wanted proper demos, with everything planned out and prepared. Jayson and Maria had kicked things off, and it was clear they hadn't even come close.

It was clear that they had planned theirs at the last minute, as they were having to describe what would have happened had they sorted out a PowerPoint presentation, or had bespoke cue cards sorted. The rest of us were acting as students, but instead of doing tasks in the plan, we were being told what they would have been.

Julie was livid. She berated us for not doing something as simple as plan a 10-15 minute task that we could have easily sorted in our normal time. She took the training seriously, and was doing it for our benefits more than hers or Rory's, so us failing to pull our weight was a serious affront to her. She clearly felt personally offended by our lack of effort, and told us to get it done properly the next week, before she and Rory headed out for a long period of fresh air.

I say 'we' and 'our' because, even though only two of us had presented, we were all in the same boat. I had only finished my rough plan a few minutes before the lesson and didn't have the materials I would have needed. It was only by blind luck that it wasn't me who had been the one to upset Julie, so I'm not making any pretence of innocence.

The next week we were back, and we all got to present our examples. Every one of us was properly prepared this time, and Julie actually thanked us for it. It wasn't fear of a dressing down that pushed us though, it was genuine guilt.

There were more lessons and Life Clubs, and I was feeling infinitely more confident than at the start of my time. I was especially getting comfortable with the *Marco Polo* videos, and they were turning into an especially good tool to use in HF clubs. Whatever video I chose, I wouldn't just play it through and hope they understood. I'd pause it at key moments and ask questions e.g. "What animal is this?", "What is he eating?", "What colour is that?". Then, when the introductory part finished, I would often ignore the relevant-level middle portion in favour of an activity, and then finish up with the final part. It was a really excellent resource, but I had one big problem with it; Coco.

As I've said before, the videos were presented by two EF teachers – Cristina, a Chinese-American, and Coco, a Frenchman. I'm not being Francophobic; there is nothing essentially wrong with having a Frenchman teaching English. The problem was his accent. It was a thick, nasally French, the kind that English people perform when they want to do a caricature of our Gallic cousins. It's a difficult accent at the best of times, but it seemed a very, very bad choice when making videos to help teach English. Even I as a native speaker had trouble understanding what he was saying at times.

Also, I was really jealous of them. These two had been selected from hundreds of EF teachers and were given the cushy job of travelling around the world to some of the most exciting cities to make simple videos about subjects such as animals and eating. I'm not saying they had it easy, but they must have thought they'd hit the jackpot when their names were called out. If only I'd gone into teaching earlier; it could have been me!

Not all Life Clubs were a great success, but that was often because of poor attendance. I had a TB club about pirates with only one student, and so had to think fast to make it worthwhile. At least I was mentally able to do that. There was also an adult Club that required quick thinking to deal with just one student and, to cheer myself up, I decided to play on another characteristic of the Chinese; always saving face.

The theme was arguing, and for this I chose the awesome *Argument Sketch* my Monty Python, where Michael Palin goes to an office to pay to have an argument. Dana, Chongqing's chief prosecutor, turned up, and this was lucky, because if anyone could talk about this subject it was her. I decided to see what I could get away with. The sketch is set in an "argument clinic", something that doesn't exist anywhere in the world, so I asked her if they were in China. She said no, so I told her about the clinic in Havant (do you get the pun?), a town next to Portsmouth, and about some of the times I had paid for the service.

She looked blankly at me, like I was some kind of freakish moron who was talking total gibberish. I'm sure she was thinking "This guy is talking shit", but she didn't let on. I kept a straight face and a matter-of-fact tone, and eventually I asked "Have you never heard of these?". As I had predicted, she couldn't lose face, and just nodded saying "Yes, I have read about these places before. They are very interesting.". I'm sure she didn't actually believe they existed, but rather than call me out on my bullshit she just played along, not wanting to even risk looking ignorant.

There were other Life Clubs that were a mixture of success, failure, great planning and unintended awkwardness. Another adult Club was about current affairs, and all I did for this was write some statements about society, economics, sport, science etc. and got the students talking. I can't remember what statement kicked it off but Hank, one of the better students, suddenly brought up the biggest no-no topic in China; Tiananmen Square.

The 1989 violent suppression of pro-democracy protests is the hottest potato in the country. Discussion of it is officially banned, to the point of legal action. When Hank started talking I actual felt a shiver run through me, especially when he described the event as "terrible" and "such a missed opportunity". The others, who included Dana, a high ranking public official, didn't react. Thankfully, Comrade Rose wasn't there, and even more thankfully, it wasn't the last we saw of Hank.

And then there was another of what I would call my big successes. The title was very prescriptive, *Project Catwalk*. This is an American TV show, in the vein of *The Apprentice*, which had cropped up in conversation a few times, mainly because of the uber-camp presenter. I'd watched a couple of episodes and, despite it being a contrived reality show about a subject I had no interest in, I liked it. Unlike the others if its ilk it actually involved people doing something useful and creative, using their skills, imagination and talent.

The language I focussed on was clothing, and it was for mid-level RE's. I picked an episode at random, thoughtfully shown on Tudou, and showed portions of it, cutting out all the guff these shows are loaded with. Then I gave each student a croquis – featureless picture of a human figure used by designers to show their ideas. Everyone did a design of their own, and then we discussed a few of them, before watching the rest of the show and discussing the winning design there.

Once again, the students were really engaged, and a few of them tried to lighten the mood by coming up with outfits that were completely mental. Most of them drew relatively conservative designs, and when we talked about the dresses on the show they all chose the same one to win, which turned out to be the winner that episode. For me, the best thing about it was that, despite a few jokes, none of them suggested their tastes were anything like the gaudy and hideous wedding dresses on sale at New York New York.

We had another job to do. On a Thursday morning in our teacher's meeting, Julie told us about the upcoming Christmas party that would be held at the Marriot Hotel. We had two tasks. One was to figure out a performance that we would give to the parents and students. The other was to pick one of our classes and organize a performance they would give. Here was the problem; I don't do performance. I could do KTV because I was only doing it with my friends, but this would be in front of hundreds of people I didn't know, and I would be stone cold sober. On the other hand, I was living in a heavily polluted city of thirty million people doing a job I had always thought ill-equipped for, so in for a penny....

Not many ideas were put forward for our turn on stage so, when Jamie made her suggestion, we were up for it straight away. Chinese kids are, in many ways, no different to Western kids, especially when it comes to pop culture. Justin Bieber, that rancid little Canadian sod-face, was pretty popular there, so Jamie suggested a song and dance routine about learning English at EF, using the music to his monstrous attack on the soul of human culture, *Baby Baby*. Jamie would work out the lyrics and together we would figure out the routine.

Then there was the class performance. For me it was simple; TB3B. My only problem was what to do. I knew that to ensure it got done I would have to be the creative one and they would have to perform, so that limited us to a play, as singing and dancing are just not my thing. I told them the good news in our next lesson and they seemed pretty cool about it, but I needed to get some inspiration soon. There was only a few weeks to get it sorted.

The week ended with me slightly ahead of Rory in the donation race. Rory, being fair-haired, should have been at a disadvantage as his beard was barely visible at first, whereas my thick, dark hairs were standing proud the moment they poked through my skin.

Jamie had written some lyrics for our performance and that weekend, I spent a couple of hours listening to Justin fucking Bieber while trying to sing along with it. I felt dirty, and I don't mean the good kind of dirty you feel after having unconventional sex that was surprisingly fun, I mean the bad kind of dirty after a drunken quickie in a piss-soaked back alley that leaves you with the poisonous after taste of shame and self-loathing.

Talking of drunkenness, I found myself engaged in a new routine. With my stool well and truly chosen at Harp, I'd head there most weekends and often Rory, Julie and Jamie would show up where, once again, their wallets would open up and I would have to insist to get a round in at some point. Their drink of choice was Jameson's whiskey and so, on many Sundays, I would consume 5 or 6 of the bad boys. Monday mornings were often a nightmare, but at least I wasn't puking on JD.

On the Wednesday I was on a mission. I had planned ahead a bit, doing some lessons on Monday and Tuesday, just in case my creative juices took time to drip out. I arrived at the usual time, did some planning in the morning, got my usual spicy egg-fried rice from the supermarket and, feeling refreshed and right-headed, I sat down at my desk, in front of my laptop, and began.

I had already decided on the theme; a news report about the menace of Santa coming to China. I had a fixed number of players, of varying abilities and confidence, so I had to make sure I got the balance perfect and the language wasn't too much for them to learn. It was a tricky one, but I felt we had enough time to iron out any problems.

With the basic plot in my head, I began. My MP3 player was plugged into my ears and Jean Michel-Jarre was buzzing away. My fingers began to dance across the keyboard as the words began to spew out of my head and onto the screen. In my head, I pictured the attractive and smart readers on CQTV, sat at their desk, reading the latest headlines about the menace that was heading towards their beloved city. I imagined the concern in their well-manicured faces as they relayed to the populous the dangers of the impending visit by the big, fat white man with his daemonic flying animals, breaking into people's homes and filling them up with stuff nobody needed, before stealing food and booze and then moving on to his next victims. It was dark, but humorous too, and after an hour I had the first draft of a five minute script.

On the Saturday I gave the kids the script and they all seemed pretty content with my choices for the parts. Henry and Jo were to be the anchors as they clearly had the best English, but all the others had a good few lines to speak too. We ran through it a couple of times, they asked for some changes and we finished, feeling confident we could pull it off. We repeated the next day and I ended the week smiling, confident they would nail it.

Then I received a slap in the face from the other teachers. Most of us headed to Harp for our usual Sunday night/pre-weekend drinks and, chatting to the others, I soon realized one thing; I was a freak. Every one of them, to the person, was working out a cute little song and dance number. Even Phil, who was the only other teacher to pick a TB class, was going to get them on stage with microphones and some Christmassy pop song. My performance would be devoid of any soundtrack, any active motion by the students and, most tellingly, any joy. Suddenly, I didn't feel so confident.

1-6. The progression of the Movember moustache. The full SAS, or the gay biker, depending on one's preferences. 7. Dancing fountain in JiangBei.

25 第二十五章

For a few months I had been missing something that I had quickly taken to from the first time I had seen it. The view from Starbucks in Monument Square was one of the best I had ever experienced, with its long window looking down from the first floor onto the life below. I had hoped they would build a platform to raise the comfy chairs to give a better view, but other renovation work had taken place.

For months, the whole building had been covered in an ordered mesh of scaffolding as the exterior was being remodelled all over. Late on in the work, panels had been fitted over the windows, which I had assumed to be a temporary set up for protection or to change the panes or something. Inside, it was so devoid of natural light that it was often confusing to leave and be faced with a bright sun.

The scaffolding eventually came down and the new, smooth, sleek, colourful and modern exterior was revealed. It was looking great as the strong metal staffs disappeared, but when it got to the first floor, something seemed to have gone badly wrong. There were no windows, just a big, long, gaudy panel, made up of sections about the same size as the ones that could be seen through the windows of Starbucks. It looked like they were in the same spot, but that was ridiculous. Surely they couldn't have covered over the big window, the best asset the branch had?

Inside, it was revealed to be exactly the case. The owners of the building had decided that signage was more important than quality of experience for the customer. I was amazed because Starbucks is a huge corporation, and I'm sure other property owners would have got on their knees and begged for the big chain to move to their premises. But no, apparently this building owner was confident enough to destroy the biggest past time people enjoy in coffee shops (other than writing books) – people watching. Oh, and the signage that had destroyed one of the best Starbucks views in the world? It read 'Starbucks'.

The month ticked over and our beards got thicker. I had grown a fine face of black bushiness, speckled with a strong splodge of white on either side of my chin and sculpted to utter perfection. Rory had gone for a more retro look; something that would be perfectly familiar to any nineteenth-century Hussar. The pots filled up each day and we eagerly checked our totals on a regular basis, frantically looking for the higher denominations of notes. It was clear that it was a two-horse race between Rory and I. Greg and Jayson just weren't producing the goods.

It should be pointed out though, that Rory used slightly duplicitous means to inflate his donation total. One of my Small Stars, McQueen, persuaded his mum to put some money into my pot. Good lad. However, Rory saw this and reminded the cute little fella that auditions for the new EF Angels choir had only just taken place, and they hadn't decided who would be in it. McQueen had tried out and, keen to make a good impression, asked his mum to put more money in Rory's pot, just in case. I suppose it was payback for slapping Rory at KTV.

Remember I mentioned how the Chinese seem to have a penchant for impulse-buying pets? Well, one day I came into the teacher's room to find Jamie sat at her desk, with a small puppy on her lap. When I say "small" and "puppy", I mean really, really new born. Its eyes were barely open and its fur was so thin that it looked more like rough skin. A student had just bought it before class and had assumed she could take it in with her. Thankfully, the PA said no, and Jamie was left holding the puppy.

We also kept up with our dance practice. Every Thursday morning, after the weekly meeting, Rory and Julie would leave us in the Life Club Zone and we'd get our dancing shoes on. Not everyone was particularly happy about being compelled to do it, but this wasn't like working for any other kind of corporation.

If it had been Ford I'd have told my manager where to stick it, but at EF us teachers were a lot more important than the average IT or HR professional. There was only a few of us, and the success of the schools primarily depended on what we did. Our photos were proudly displayed on the wall in reception, so we were genuinely important to the business, and businesses need customers. Not just new ones either, but the ones we already had.

So we worked on the dance routine every week, trying to get something that looked like we had made a real effort but didn't make us look too foolish. I think most of us were somewhat less than thrilled about getting up on stage, but most of us were keen to please too, even when we found out we would be doing it twice, the second time on the ground floor of the mall on Christmas Eve.

Working on the play brought me a great deal of pleasure tinged with a hint of apprehension. As we spent time at the end of each lesson I was so impressed with the way these kids had taken it so seriously. They really wanted to do well, so much so that they were making a genuine effort to learn their lines off by heart.

Learning lines to a play is hard enough in your own language, but these guys were doing it not just in a foreign language, but in one that is so disconnected from their own that it might as well have been made up, like Klingon or Welsh. It still worried me that we were the only ones doing a play, but that's what we were doing and that was that. There was no going back.

I needed a break, so on a Monday, late in the month, I joined a few of the others for a bit of hotpot, but with a difference. I met Phil, Danni and her friend Sarah (on a visit from the old country) in our apartment's courtyard, and we headed to Hongyadong to meet Jayson and Greg. We met up with a few of the RE students at a hotpot place nearby, but it was for something rather different. We had the usual collection of sliced meats and vegetables, but then Danni suggested we try a few "alternatives". Hannibal, one of the better students, got the message, and placed a special order with the waitress.

A few minutes later, three dishes were brought out. One was full of what looked like pink tagliatelle, but was on a dish shaped like a duck. This was duck's intestines, and it was ok, if a little tough and plastic. The next dish had what looked like dark grey flannels, rolled up tightly. These were cow's stomachs, and looked the way they did due to the hedgehog-like spines. I was told one can feel the chunks sliding down one's throat, so I gave it a miss. The third dish had a brain – a whole brain, all pink and juicy and jelly-like. The brain was not to be passed on, and to be honest it tasted ok, with a porridge-like consistency. It was a weak taste, and the sensation didn't make me feel sick, but I wouldn't rush to eat it again.

As November drew to a close there was a special celebration that, while completely unique to just two of the many expat groups, actually served to bring us all together: Thanksgiving. I should take this opportunity to point out to any Americans (Canadians tend to already know this) that no-one in Europe celebrates this holiday. It's only celebrated in the USA, Canada, Liberia, Grenada, Puerto Rico and Norfolk Island (open an atlas), and on different dates. It is completely irrelevant everywhere else.

In the morning, Julie and Rory called us in to the big classroom in the middle of the school. For Thanksgiving, and for all our hard work, they had splashed out (with their own money as always) on a shed load of Subway sandwiches and a showing of *The Other Guys*. As bosses, they could be very strict, and hard at times, but they were serious about their jobs, and they were the most generous people I had ever worked with. It was a lovely treat, and the film was hilarious.

However, there were a lot of Americans and Canadians in the city (but, to my knowledge, no Liberians, Puerto Ricans, Grenadians or Norfolk Islanders), and I worked with a few of them, so it seemed only right to join them, especially as it required the consumption of copious amounts of food reminiscent of Christmas dinner. Harp was crowded to over-spilling, but myself and Tanja managed to find some space with some of the guys from the British consulate, and we feasted. Apart from eating, it seemed to be just about being with friends and family, and really, is there any better reason for a celebration?

It was also in November that Rory and Julie made an announcement that could have changed my whole life in the country. In our weekly meeting they announced that they were creating a brand new role; Life Club Coordinator. Basically, this person would be responsible for setting all the themes and promoting the sessions, as well as being the first point of call for any help teachers needed. It sounded interesting as it would be more money, but it would also mean a new contract, so whoever took it would be committing to the school for at least another year. I had been thinking about my future, but it was pretty much decided from my early weeks, solidified by my holiday with Miisa.

Lessons continued unabated though. Our teaching ranks had increased further, with the addition of Vivian in New York New York and Ruby and Joy in Paradise Walk, all of them Chinese. I also had a new RE00 class for a few weeks, kicking it off for Joy to take over. Sherry was one of the students, and she seemed pretty happy.

I had started taking on something completely different – SS Green and Blue Life Clubs. This was daunting. There seemed to be more than a cognitive difference between Blue/Greens and Orange/Reds; there was also a physical difference.

I finally got to use the Small Stars rooms, and everything about them was smaller, including the height of the whiteboard. For the most part, they were remarkably easy to deal with. They were shy, and a new face seemed to intimidate them a little. There was the occasional crier and one boy, Alex, even pulled his shorts down to take a piss against the wall. Thankfully I managed to grab a passing PA to take him to the toilet.

It was in one of these classes that I learnt something about language, something that made me feel like I'd been a bit of a bigot during my time there. I started a Blue/Green Life Club as normal – asking the kids their names and writing them on the board. There was Alex, Cassie, Jenny, Tim and a boy whose name I didn't understand. I asked again and it made no sense. It sounded like "table", but that was ridiculous. However, the other kids pointed at the small plastic tables behind and laughed. I tentatively wrote it on the board and carried on.

At the end of the club, I borrowed Vannie, one of the PA's, to translate to the boy's dad. Yes, he had chosen Table as his son's English name. From his laugh I guessed he thought it was cute. I didn't. The other kids in the class knew what it meant and I was worried it would lead to bullying, so I strongly suggested he change it. It got me thinking about names, and how ours are perceived in China.

Western names tend to be derivatives of words from other languages or older traditions. My name comes from the Greek *andros*, meaning *man*, but it has changed over the years to become Andrew. Chinese has not developed in the same way, so the meaning of a name can be quite direct (though still open to some interpretation). For example, the name of actress Zhang ZiYi can be translated as *Gentlewoman should soothe her spirits and be happy and pleased*. Maybe there is a common Chinese name that means "table".

It also got me thinking about the twins in my first HF class, Annie and Anna. I had been baffled by the name choices, and had talked about it to the other teachers in disparaging terms. Julie had even suggested I get their parents to change it, but I wasn't confident enough at the time. Now, it made more sense.

For example, Annie and Anna may be diminutives of the same name, but they differ by a single phoneme. Two names that also differ by one phoneme are Tim and Tom, both diminutives but from different sources. All four examples are often used as proper names, as opposed to their augmentatives (Annette, Timothy, Thomas). Even my RE's struggled. For a while they had thought I had the same name as Student Audrey, until I wrote our names in phonetics.

The question is, why would I have expected Chinese people to recognise Annie and Anna were the same name? Why should they? The names are similar but are not exactly the same, and many words that sound similar have no semantic relationships.

I genuinely felt like a bit of a dick for slagging off their parents for the name choices. In fact, I had put it on my mental list of things that annoy me about China, along with being followed by shop assistants, lack of queuing, gobbing puddles of mucous, jet-washing the streets while some places are in drought, walking while repeatedly clapping, chomping and slurping food, shouting to talk to people less than one foot away and staring at foreigners. Really, it didn't deserve to be there. The choice of names was perfectly logical and reasonable from their perspective and understanding.

It soon became clear the Small Stars Clubs were either/or affairs. They were either great or a nightmare. One club I gave was about Christmas trees, where I tried to get them to make their own with paper, scissors, glue, sprinkled glitter etc. It became an almighty mess. Another involved getting them to make hats out of the same ingredients, with the same results. Thank God I had only started doing them late in the year.

My TB's were still awesome. They continued to be intelligent, hard-working, thoughtful, enthusiastic, reliable and funny. I always looked forward to their classes, especially so I could try out new ideas I'd discovered. One task was a way to help students focus on their listening skills.

It was a simple description task, where each student had an item on a card to describe and key words they couldn't use. The trick was to only allow one student to answer, and they had to sit at the front of the class, with their backs to the rest. It meant that the student could only rely on their listening. There was no reading of gestures, or lips, or any non-verbal cues that could ordinarily help them. It was purely about what came in through their ears and got processed in their immense brains. Thankfully, they struggled a little with such an alien task, but they still succeeded too, as always.

However, they were somewhat overshadowed by Petal, my one to one TB who was the highest rated student in the school. I will state, without any shadow of a doubt, that she is one of the most intelligent people I have ever met in my entire life. Every time I finished her lesson I would go back into the teacher's room to tell everyone something awesome she had said, usually some intellectual insight or philosophical reasoning that she had plucked out of thin air.

In one class, I showed her an episode of one of my favourite sitcoms, *Coupling* (the UK original that was actually good). Part of it was to make it a more light-hearted session, but I also wanted to talk about syntactical structures. As I had predicted, she knew it all, and I'll admit that I was a bit lost at times. This was the only time I ever tried to review the subject of phrases and clauses, because I've always struggled with which is which. I had to bluff my way through it – now I was the one saving face.

In another lesson she had asked for help with an essay she was writing for a competition, which she would have to do a presentation about. When I read it, my eyes nearly fell out. The subject was about freedom of speech and freedom of information. WOW! This seventeen year old girl was nonchalantly going to submit an essay about two subjects the government is not known to have many sympathies with. I was a little gobsmacked and had to think hard before responding. Needless to say, I was full of praise for her well-written and well-reasoned arguments, and I just kept my mouth shut about the rest. If there were any risks to her ambitions from the essay, then she knew them better than I did, and I wasn't going to discourage her.

I talked to her about public speaking (not something I've done much of), and I made some suggestions about do's and don'ts, talking about posture and presentation, giving tips on what to focus on when rehearsing. After the lesson, I once again regaled the others about her talent, and made a prediction.

"That girl is so freaking intelligent, and so lovely. I swear to God though, that if things go wrong, she will end up ruling the world and enslaving all of humanity while sitting on a throne of skulls."

I stand by it.

Business was booming at the school. When I had started, the school had felt quite quiet at the weekends, but now it was rammed with students. All of us teachers had a full set of classes and new students were coming in thick and fast for OPTs. A day didn't go by when a PA didn't come into the teachers' room, with an OPT form, looking for whomever was on duty at the time.

They were usually pretty straightforward. It was just a case of reading the sample questions on the sheet, finding the ones they couldn't deal with and settling on the lowest of those levels. Sometimes the students wouldn't say anything, either because they had no English or because they were nervous and had a brain freeze. In those cases there was no option other than to put them in the lowest class. Sometimes they got weird, and for some reason it was always when Rory was doing the interview. One day he came back into the teachers' room, a little confused.

"I just had to put a girl in TB1A, even though Scarlet thought she was a 2B." He said.

"Why the big difference?" Julie asked, probably thinking it was the fault of the PA for being too generous in her assessment of the student.

"The girl barked like a little dog through the whole thing?"

I'd heard the words but couldn't quite grasp what he meant. I butted in, intrigued, asking him what he meant.

"She actually barked like a little Chihuahua. I shit you not."

He proceeded to re-enact the whole episode, repeating each question and responding to himself with the hideous, squeaky yapping of one of those stupid little bastard mutts that annoyingly trendy women like to carry around in their handbags. Amazingly, that wasn't even the weirdest.

One day I walked past the little room where the OPTs happened and Rory was sat there, with a teenager who was wiping tears from her eyes. I assumed that he'd put her in a level that was way below what she thought she was and she was a bit over sensitive. When Rory came back into the teachers' room, he had one hell of a story to tell.

"I was asking her the usual questions on the list, and I asked her what she thought about the environment. She told me that she was worried that it was going badly, and that she tried to get her friends to recycle and be careful what they do, and then, as she started talking about how the planet was dying, she burst into tears. I didn't know what the hell to do. I just asked if she wanted to take a break but she said she was okay, she just loved Earth so much that it upset her what people are doing to it."

Well, at least we knew there was one person in China who cared about the environment, but if she was that emotional about it, I wondered how she could possibly survive in a city so heavily shrouded in a thick, poisonous smog.

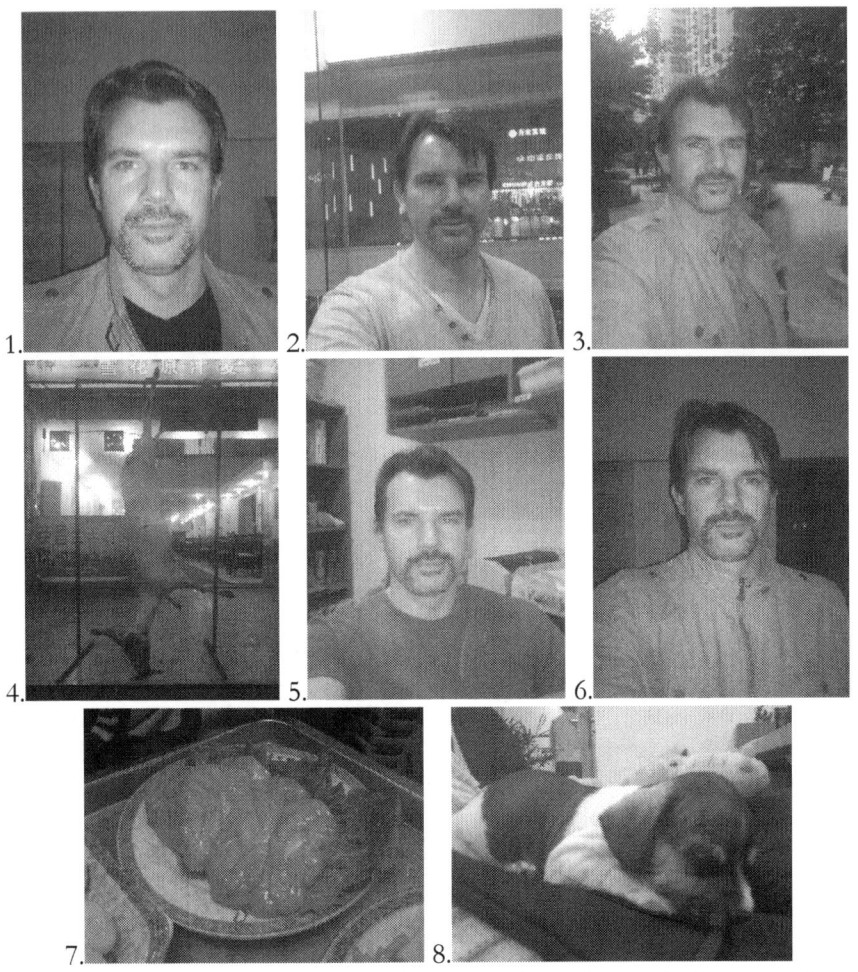

1-3. The facial hair continues its glorious growth. 4. A freshly slaughtered goat (or something) left to bleed-out on the street. 5-6. More moustache heaven. 7. The pig's brain. 8. The impulse-bought puppy.

26 第二十六章

November ended, and something important needed to be declared. We'd been growing our facial hair diligently all month, but now it was over, and it was time to find out who had won. Julie had been keeping a running total, so the final pots would decide it. Greg and Jayson were out, their beards deemed inadequate for the local population's tastes. We waited for the totals and, after a few minutes counting, Julie made the announcement. Rory had won by a hair's breadth. Clearly, his leverage over McQueen had been strong.

That wasn't the end of it though. In the first week of December the expats got together to celebrate the month and handover the big fat cheque to the charity. We were entertained by some of the residents of the care home with singing and dancing, and it was great to see how they had been able to thrive in a country not known for giving much help to the disabled. I gave a presentation about our competition and we were genuinely proud of the couple of thousand Yuan we had raised, despite other groups raising two or three times that. At the end of the night, we had all raised over forty thousand Yuan, and I came second in the "Manliest Moustache" contest.

Weirdly, I had grown accustomed to my facial hair. Instead of taking a razor to it the very next morning I decided to leave it on, with the intention of trimming it off on a gradual basis. I was actually quite chuffed with the way it had turned out. It was bushy, well-maintained and had quite a distinguished contrast between the black fibres on the lip and the grey on the chin. I was reluctant to let it go, but I knew I would have to say goodbye one day.

The evening of the Christmas party quickly approached. The kids were learning their lines excellently and Linda provided me with a full translation of the script, so that I could put it into PowerPoint to give the parents subtitles on the big screens in the Marriot's ballroom. Everyone was working hard and stressing out with the added pressure on top of our lessons.

We got our dance routine sorted too. It was nothing complicated, or too energetic, and it was my genius idea to include something called "double dream hands". Look it up on YouTube. It's a video by an American life coach/motivational speaker/overly enthusiastic instructor showing some dance routine instruction. He's bleach blonde, fake tanned, has the whitest teeth in the known universe and an effervescence that's akin to someone on crack. In short, he's a stereotypical American.

My moustache was looking great, but gradually became shorter as I shaved little bits of it over the days. The handle bar shrunk, rising to the top lip so that, for a few days, with the tuft under the bottom lip, I looked like a dashing cavalier. Eventually the tuft went and I had the full Tom Selleck. I think you can probably guess where this is all leading to.

One morning I decided that it would go for good, but I had one last task. I showered, combed my hair in the right way and shaved off the two ends of my whiskers to form the toothbrush moustache, more commonly known as the Hitler. I took a photo for posterity and then shaved it completely. I regret not going out for the day with it. I could have gone out and not been bothered or attacked, and I'm sure the expats would have had a good laugh about it. After all, it's just facial hair, and Hitler wasn't the first (Charlie Chaplin, Oscar Deutsch – founder of Odeon cinemas and Jewish, the bloke from Sparks).

We also had one other job to do. Audrey had been so impressed with the Movember activities that she decided we should raise money for the same good cause. The plan was that each teacher would donate something to be auctioned at the Christmas party. A lot of the others offered time; Jayson would spend a few hours with a kid in the adventure play pen in the mall, Dulce would give a kid dance lessons and Tanja would give an art class. Nothing spectacular, just something fun. Despite being a teacher, nothing like that appealed to me, so Rory suggested something simple; I should print five really good photos of places I've travelled to and put them in frames. Job done. It cost me 100 Yuan - £10 – and just a few minutes of my time.

The expats were a pretty good crowd to hang around with, especially the Brits. Geordie Rory had been on a six-month contract, and it was coming to an end in time for Christmas. There was a get together at Harp to send him off, and a good crowd went along. Among them was a middle aged Maccam (from Sunderland) known as Bacca. He'd been making regular visits to the city on business and was one of the biggest partiers, entertaining us with his improvised *Bacca Rap*. John, Rory's cousin, was there too, as was Steve and an American astronomer/cosmologist he'd gotten to know. Ryan, as always, was in the mix, and both Amy's (Neighbour and Crazy) showed up for a few jars to say goodbye to the ever popular Geordie Rory.

There was another woman there whom I'd never seen around, and for very good reason. She lived in Shanghai and was just visiting the city. I don't know if she already knew anyone there, or if she'd just met people and tagged along, but I was more interested in why she was in the city. She was also an English teacher, but she worked for a certain school called Disney English.

That "Disney" in the name is not Chinese plagiarism – it's the actual Disney of Mickey Mouse and Simba. EF had created some very cute cartoon characters for the kids' courses, and they were very popular, but there was no way they could compete with Donald and Goofy. EF had announced a plan to open a thousand new schools over the following 10 years, and one of the reasons seemed to be staring me in the face.

Disney popped up on the radar at school: the Disney English cartoons. I had used them a couple of times in HF Life Clubs as an easy option to ask questions and elicit answers. It was a good tool, but it was Disney, and Julie put her foot down and banned it, and any other Disney material, from all lessons. I forgot that rule once though, but it was fair enough, if only for the issues of copyright infringement. It was giving a competitor just a little bit too much free advertising.

Then it was time for the big night. The ballroom was huge and crowded with tables, and the stage was pretty big. It seemed that no expense had been spared. The hallway outside was where the buffet would be, and we were all intrigued by the delights that would be on offer. We were going to have Christmas dinner there, so we considered it a trial run.

In typical Chinese fashion, getting the party started wasn't going to be straight forward. A "red carpet" had been laid out, and the parents and kids got to walk down it, while a photographer took pics of them like they were Andy Lau or Michelle Yeoh heading to a premier. It took ages to get everyone seated and we were behind schedule from the off.

The evening kicked off with some introductions and announcements, a performance by the EF Angels choir (all the hassle for Rory and Julie actually paid off) and then a few of the class performances. As I had feared, each one was upbeat, cheery and full of smiles, and the audience applauded loudly. My heart was sinking by the minute. I just hoped the kids had thick skins.

Dinner came eventually, and we all tucked in. It was a pretty lavish buffet layout, and the hotel had done a great job of providing a mix of local delicacies and Western tastes. The vegetables tasted superb, and there was plenty of meat that hadn't been cooked in a freaky sauce. There was even lung, but I never found out from which animal. At least I now know that I don't like lung.

My kids were at their table, but Andy and Jennifer were missing. I got Linda to call them and that's when my stress boiled up. Jennifer was sick (her parents didn't think to call) and Andy had panicked and decided to pull out. I had thought he might; despite being very good at English and being able to produce some of the funniest moments in class, he was always the least confident. I had to think fast. Salvation came in the form of Chris, a TB5A on their table. I roped him in to taking Andy's place and, with a bit or rejigging, I was able to deal with Jennifer's absence. We had a couple of extra rehearsals in the corridor and that was it. We were as ready as we would ever be.

During the performance before our turn I got them to the side of the stage, commandeered some furniture, and the moment the stage was free we set it up and I got on the other side, ready to operate the all-important subtitles projected on the screens either side of the stage. The kids were utterly and indisputably amazing. They didn't just say their lines; they delivered them, in character.

Henry and Jo played the newscasters perfectly and the others, playing reporters and analysts, acted brilliantly and were word perfect. Bella, who was a location reporter, even had a prop microphone and stuck her finger in her ear to simulate an ear piece. I just wish the parents had been a bit more responsive. Maybe they didn't understand the whole Santa Claus thing, and annoyingly none of the kid's parent's had come along. If they'd been happy with my teaching before, they would have been ecstatic with me after.

At the end of the performance, the kids took a bow in unison and the audience clapped, sadly not as loudly as with the other groups. I walked away from the stage, delighted and relieved it was over and so impressed with the guys. Back at the tables Rory was waiting with a beaming smile.

"What the fuck Andy". He said, his eyes lighting up. "That was awesome, freaking awesome."

"That was amazing." Phil joined in. "Did you write that?"

"Yeah." I said, a little perplexed. I had expected some disappointment, seeing as the audience wasn't exactly overwhelmed with joy.

In fact, the overwhelming response from the other teachers was the same; they all thought it had been a fantastic performance by the kids and that the play had been great. I was now on a high, the best kind of upper that money can't buy. I went to their table and thanked every one of the kids personally. I was beaming, but they seemed quite relaxed about it all. *Yeah, we spoke English, big whoop, that's what we do.* It was Julie who put it in perspective for me.

"You showed the parents exactly what their kids can get out of this school. Thank you."

When I thought about it, I realized that I had gotten it the most right. Don't get me wrong, the other teachers had done a great job and put in a lot of work getting their kids to learn a dance routine, and they had been very entertaining. I, however, was the only one who got the kids to show exactly what they had learned at the school. My class had been the only one to put into practice what those parents in the crowd had paid so much money for. It was just such a shame that their own parents hadn't been there to see it.

Then came the auctions and, for a short time, my stress returned. The initial offerings went for a thousand or so Yuan, and all I could think about were my five basic prints in cheap frames. There was still time for me to look like a chump. Jayson's play time when for 1200 and then Rory, the auctioneer, with Audrey translating, held up my framed photos, described them and set off the bidding at 350 Yuan, as suggested by the local staff. £35 minimum, for £10 worth of photos and frames. Immediately the hands went up and so did the price. 400, 450, 500, 550. 600, 650. Up and up it went until it hit that magical 1000 Yuan, then it went higher and higher. It quickly passed Jayson's lead and went beyond, eventually stopping at an insane 1700 Yuan - £170, for five basic prints in five cheap frames. It was turning into a great night for me.

My lead didn't last long, but the insanity continued. The next went for 2000 and, at the end, Julie and Rory sold a CD of music by the band they had been in back in Missouri for 5000 Yuan - £500, $750, for what was essentially a demo. I think this madness speaks to the idea that the Chinese don't like to lose face and so none of the bidding parties could really back down. We didn't care though; that was a ton of money for the charity.

Boss Audrey had made one mistake on the timetable; she hadn't allowed for prep time between performances, so by the time we did our Justin Bieber inspired dance routine the hall was half empty. We gave it our all though. We had been working on it for weeks and some of us were really fighting through aversions to public performance to be on stage. Like most such things it was a case of throwing one's self into it from the first second and, like most such things, it wasn't so bad either, confirmed by the round of applause from the few people who remained.

The night finished with Aurora singing a tune in her excellent English, and then Julie singing a Christmas song with Rory on guitar but, sadly, most of the audience was gone by then. It had been a long and trying few weeks, but it had all paid off that night.

A little over a week later it was Christmas Eve. On the ground floor of Paradise Walk a small stage had been set up with a few tables around it for some kid's activities. In the school we were in a festive mood. Lessons had been cancelled but we still had some stuff to do; Christmas Day was our only day off, but lessons needed planning and we still had to get involved in the promotional stuff. I however, was looking forward to Bangkok and spending New Year with Miisa.

Generally I'm not that interested in Christmas, apart from the food, but this time it felt a little different, almost fun. For the preceding weeks I had noticed a lot of decorations going up around the city, with some of the bigger malls and department stores really going to town with the flashing lights and images of Santa. I was somewhat confused, as I had assumed that Christmas was a nothing time of the year for the Chinese, which had been confirmed by my TB3Bs, who told me it was always just a normal day for them. We teachers planned to make a big deal of it though.

The day moved along, and every now and then we would pop down to show our faces in the school's promo area to encourage passing families to pop in and have a go at some of the activities, and for the local staff to talk to the parents and drum up some business. It always amazed me how confused China's perception is of the West. On the one hand they are economically powerful and superior and often sneer at our cultural norms, but on the other there can be a lot of kudos with being associated with a "laowai".

Eventually, the festivities began. With crowds gathered around the stage and on the balconies overlooking us from three, four, even five floors up, Julie and Audrey took to the stage to give their spiel about how great EF was and what it could do for their kids. The EF Angels did their singing and Aurora, the star pupil, sang a solo in English. Students from New York New York also did a performance, and after a few more ditties it was our turn. Once again we got on stage, took deep breaths and let the magic happen as we danced our way around the stage to the tune of that awful Justin Bieber song, beautifully bastardized into something meaningful and with actual soul by Jamie. Our audience looked a lot more bemused than at the party, but it was enough that we looked like we were genuinely enjoying ourselves.

After packing up our stuff, most of us headed straight to Harp. By the time we got there it was packed out, but we managed to bag a table in a corner. It was gone 10pm, but the kitchen was open and, seeing as it was nearly Christmas Day, we ordered Christmas dinners. Chris and Shang had done a great job of teaching their locally born and bred kitchen staff how to make good American and Mexican food, but they really outdid themselves with this meal. While it was nothing like my mother's cooking, it was still just what I would have expected from a pub. The turkey, roast potatoes, stuffing, carrots, peas, pigs in blankets and gravy were fantastic. It was a great Christmas meal.

By the time we decided to leave, Dulce was quite drunk, so I walked her back to our building, fully intending to hit the sack too. Instead, feeling wide awake and stuffed, I dumped my bag in the flat and headed out to the Cotton Club, where I partied hard with the other expats in what must have been the club's busiest night of the year so far. I got home at about 5am for a sleep that was almost worthless.

There was something I missed though. In the days leading up to the 25th I had noticed a lot of street hawkers selling inflatable items such as bananas and hammers. It was weird, but I learnt the reason was actually pretty cool. Despite Christmas Day not being a big thing in China, the people of Chongqing (and maybe other cities) had come up with their own way of joining in. On Christmas Eve, thousands would gather in Monument Square, and at the stroke of midnight they would engage in a mass inflatable fight, whacking each other at random with their harmless, air-filled toys. It seemed utterly crazy, and worth a look, but at the stroke of midnight I was in Harp, eating a hearty Christmas dinner and drinking with my friends, so I didn't miss out on anything.

In the morning it was Christmas Day. I woke up from what was essentially a long nap, had a light breakfast and headed down and out. Phil was already outside so we headed to JieFangBei together, climbing the steep steps and walking through the staggered housing estate that led to the grubby old street that took us to the Marriot. When we got there we realized we were supposed to meet everyone at New York New York so, after calling Julie to let her know our error, we headed round the corner to another one of the city's brand new shopping malls where, in the square outside, there was a plush-looking coffee shop. It was expensive but good, and my favourite thing about it was sitting by the window with a view of the huge Bulgari advert featuring the ever beautiful

Julianne Moore, one of my favourites. In China, her pale skin and striking red hair made her incredibly exotic.

Eventually, we headed back and met up with the others. Inside, the restaurant wasn't exactly busy, no doubt because international travellers had studiously avoided that date. The dinner itself was "interesting" to say the least. All the normal vegetables were on offer, but on tasting them we found they had been cooked in whatever local sauce it was that local taste buds were so attuned to. There was freshly carved turkey though, that was the main thing, but I also took the opportunity to try crab for the first time in my life.

It was a fantastic lunch, where we were all gathered as our own little family for that day. There was no secret Santa though, which would have been a nice little touch. Somehow I managed another whole meal after the night before, and I was grateful I had taken that opportunity, or I would have missed out on a real Christmas dinner for the first time in my life.

After lunch we went our separate ways. Phil, Dulce and I took a walk through Monument Square to one of the many small vendors selling pirated DVDs. It felt so odd walking through the streets on Christmas Day and everything being business as usual. It was a Saturday and, just like back home, it was the busiest shopping day of the week. People were out and about walking from mall to mall, restaurant to coffee shop and even to their offices, just like they would on any other day of the year. I had known it would be like that, but I was brought up in a world where pretty much everything shuts down on 25th December and hardly anyone goes out, so it still felt odd.

I then headed to Harp to see if any expats were around, but I found myself all alone, drinking homemade mulled wine and watching football highlights on the big screen. Then it was back home to chill out and pack. It was cold and quiet in the flat, and I was flagging after the previous night's party exertions. In the evening I called home on Skype to wish my mum, sister and aunt a Merry Christmas. Sadly, the quality of the line from Skype to mum's landline was pretty poor. It was crackly and broken, and eventually cut out of its own accord. I managed to get the message across though. No doubt they were preparing for mum's annual, epic feast. Thankfully, because of Harp, I didn't feel like I had missed out, though mum's cooking was still the best. After watching a film on one of China's video web sites, I dragged myself off the sofa to pack, ready for the big trip the very next day, for my real Christmas present.

1. The final version of the full SAS/gay biker. 2. The trimming begins. 3. The cavalier look. 4. The Tom Selleck. 5. The Adolf Hitler. 6. The crowd of locals waiting for our amazing performance. 7-8. Christmas decorations. 9. My Christmas lunch crab.

27 第二十七章

I don't particularly like Chongqing International Airport. Don't get me wrong, it's plush, clean and fairly new, but it's still set up for locals, so apart from a coffee I was going be stuffed for refreshments. My opinion wasn't helped when I saw a mum help her toddler daughter take a piss on the floor inside the terminal. Ok, it was against the wall of an internal office unit, but she still could have taken the little brat to the proper place.

  I got there in plenty of time, got to my check-in desk, handed over my passport and was promptly told that my flight had been cancelled due to mechanical problems. Oh good God I was pissed off, really bloody pissed off. Annoyingly, the check-in attendant didn't continue, as if that was it, end of story. I had paid for the flight but that was just tough. I wasn't going anywhere. I had put up with so much of the poor customer service in China relatively stoically for the year, but now I was impatient, especially when she said there were no alternatives and I wouldn't be flying that day.

  'Bullshit' is what I thought and I began arguing with her as politely as I could, telling her there had to be an alternative, but she insisted that there wasn't because I had paid for that flight and it wasn't flying. Apparently, looking to get me onto an alternative flight hadn't occurred to her, but her supervisor stepped in, taking me to another desk where I was given a new ticket. Instead of connecting at Kunming, I would be flying across the country in the wrong direction to Beijing, before heading south. I would be a few hours later than planned, but that was a small price to pay.

  In a few hours I was back in Beijing Airport, coming out into the brand spanking new Terminal 3 to transfer to the crappy, old Terminal 1. I had a good few hours to spare, so I decided not to rush to the older building. I had a hunger to sate. I was sick of Starbucks, MacDonald's and Subway and I needed something different. Up the stairs, above the shops, in the food court, I queued up at Burger King, ordered the largest bacon double cheeseburger and fries I could, and devoured them with a ravenous hunger. I had been craving it, which is really weird and incredibly sad, but I was happy that I finally had it.

  I headed out front, full of highly processed meat and something that claimed to be fried potato strips. I caught the bus and headed to Terminal 1, where I spent a couple of hours drinking coffee and talking to a couple who worked for Angolan Airlines. It was interesting to hear about the place; how it was an insane mix of wealth and poverty, how its capital, Luanda, was the most expensive city in the world for expats, and how the influx of Chinese money had plenty of negatives as well as positives. It perked my interest in the country, but I still don't see myself visiting for a long time.

  I was glad I had eaten in Terminal 3. The only other time I'd been in Terminal was when heading home from my 2007 trip. In Hong Kong I'd told my friend about the glory of the full English breakfast, and how it was so simple it was impossible to fuck up. She'd been sceptical, and in Beijing T1 she had been proved right.

Eventually, I boarded my plane and a few hours later, on a balmy, tropical evening, I passed through customs and entered arrivals, where Miisa was waiting for me.

Miisa was staying in a small, one-roomed apartment just off Silom Soi, near the notorious Patpong district. Personally I could have lived in the place. It had a good sized bed with a TV and DVD player opposite, a wardrobe, a WC with a shower, a kitchen area and a dining table, all in an area the size of a comfortable living room (by UK standards). The best bit of the apartment complex was the outdoor pool on the roof, which was also home to the laundry room and gym. The first morning was hot and sunny (I remembered my shorts this time) and the pool was looking tempting, but there was plenty of time for that.

On our previous visit we had spent most of our time around the historic district of Thonburi, but now we were all about the modern. We took a walk through Lumphini Park, where I was excited to see a large lizard in the wild for the first time in my life. We followed the line of the Sky Train past the Royal Bangkok Sports Club and onto Rama I Avenue, where we took another browse through the mighty Siam Paragon, especially in the bookshops, which had ensured they were fully stocked with books about Justin Bieber. I swear to God that little shit was trying to haunt me.

During my stay we got to see all the places we'd missed in our last visit (which Miisa had been to since). There were the usual temples all over, and the streets were a crazy conglomeration of people, overhead cabling, spicy smells, traffic and smog. We negotiated the back streets of a cramped, narrow canal district ("canal" being generous, considering the channels' widths) and had a look at the Royal Barge Museum. We could only assume that it was meant to be approached by boat, but the exhibits were impressive.

When we weren't wandering from golden-domed place of worship to cheap restaurant to market to mall, we spent a few hours by the pool, me swimming and Miisa soaking up the sun (when she wasn't losing her mind at the site of the tiniest spider in the world). In the evenings we headed out for dinner in Patpong, with our favourite place being Le Bouchon, the French restaurant in the middle of the sex and party district that served some of the best chicken I've had anywhere in Asia.

We quickly got used to the hazards of walking through these streets – guys holding menus trying to get people to see the "ping pong" shows and other assorted delights. I'm no prude, and I've had my fair share of fun in strip bars, but I have absolutely no interest whatsoever in a ping pong show. I cannot think of anything more stupid or less erotic. We also took in a spot of Muay Thai boxing, that other vice that draws so many people to this great metropolis.

The next day we continued our exploration. Wat Benchamabophit Dusitvanaram, also known as the Marble Temple, is a relatively new complex, completed in the early years of the 20th century, but still as ornate and gilded as every other in the city and blessed with a little canal. Not far from that is the Ananta Samakom Throne Hall, an incongruous Neo-Classical palace that would sit better in a US state capital.

New Year's Eve was the other reason for being there and, after another day of touring, we headed out to the city's other party district, Kao San Road. Every bar we went to was either packed out or dead, and we didn't want to party anywhere without a good atmosphere. Somehow, we eventually found a table in a bar and the atmosphere was electric. As the minutes passed, the street became more and more crowded, with walking being a chore all of its own.

When midnight struck, the party really kicked off, but the atmosphere was joyous and friendly, and there was no hint of trouble. Everyone was good natured, with one group of English guys going from table to table sharing their bottles of Jack Daniels and Smirnoff. Like everywhere else in the world, the party lasted well into the early hours, gallons of booze was consumed, and we headed back to the apartment, drunk and exhausted.

We woke up pretty late the next morning and did our very best to do as little as possible. We had a late breakfast in an Irish pub on Silom Soi, and were amazed at how dead and quiet the area was, even by New Year's Day standards. We hopped on the SkyTrain and headed out to Chatuchak Market, a utopia for the budget consumer. The large and messy book and magazine stall was fun to browse through, but the highlight for me had to be the stall that sold t-shirts, sow-on badges and flags, including three different types of Nazi banner (standard, Eagle-crested and Nordic Cross). It made me wonder if there were any images commonly on offer back home that really pissed-off Asians. I suppose the Japanese flag would annoy quite a few people in China.

My biggest adventure happened when I headed home. We got to the plush and magnificent airport in plenty of time and, after an emotional goodbye, I headed through security and was air side. After a much needed Burger King, I browsed a few of the shops and then, with time ticking along, headed to my gate. That's when the fun began.

As the time approached I realized that there was no plane in position. Usually they are parked well in advance to be cleaned and prepared, but there was nothing. As departure time got closer it was clear that something was wrong, and then the announcement was made by a woman with a very thick local accent. I got enough of it though – delayed for two hours. It turned out the plane was still in Kunming due to mechanical issues but it wouldn't be too long, though I had the option of transferring to a flight the next day. She was sure it wouldn't be much longer, so I chose to wait.

I called Miisa and she suggested I transfer, but I'm not the best of travellers and I usually need a day or two after long flights to get back to a clear head, even without jet lag. I had another slow round of browsing, sat in a coffee shop and read, got online for a while and when the new boarding time approached, I headed to the gate, only to find it empty. No plane, no staff. Eventually, the time on the boards disappeared, and I began to fear the worst.

The following minutes became hours and there was only so much browsing I could do without feeling like I would go completely mental. The time dragged on and on and on, and it became clear that the assurances we had been given were complete and utter bullshit. I returned to the gate a few more times and there was staff there, who kept informing us that they expected the plane in an hour or so, but even they eventually gave up on this. One of the first-class lounges was opened and we were given free access to the tea, coffee, soft drinks and beers. It was clear that we were going to be there for a long, long time.

Thirteen hours. That was how long we were delayed. It was gone midnight by the time we boarded and I was tired and drained. I just wanted to go home. Most of us grabbed our seats, but some of the Chinese passengers stayed at the gate, remonstrating loudly with the airline staff and holding up our departure for at least another half hour. A few of us had decided, out of our own protest, to bag business class seats and to hell with anyone else. Eventually we took off, tired and hacked off with the people who had held us up for just that little bit longer.

As it turned out, we should have been kissing their feet. Their annoying intransigence and aggression had ensured that every passenger received a full refund for that trip – 700 Yuan. As much as I had been furious with those people, I was now utterly grateful. Money talks, but when it's the Chinese, they shout the loudest.

We touched down at an ungodly hour and, after receiving our cash, I headed into the departures lounge. It was the very earliest of hours and I had a few more to kill in Kunming Airport, another Chinese hub more geared towards local tastes. Also, it was small, so by the time I hopped on the bus for the plane I was going mentally nuts. In no time at all, however, I was back in cold, smoggy Chongqing, ready for the final leg of my life in China.

I only had a few weeks left. Winter was in full swing, and unlike Bangkok it was cold and miserable for most of the time. The sun was firmly hidden behind the winter smog that had greeted me on my arrival, and it wouldn't be out for a while.

It was cold, but no-one seemed to have told the restaurants. They seemed very reluctant to switch the heating on, despite the temperature being about 5 Celsius. It was a little unpleasant and odd to have to sit at a table, waiting and then eating, with my warm winter jacket on and buttoned up, and my scarf wrapped around my neck. I guess the one benefit was that it saved a bit of electricity, and bearing in mind the smog in the city, that wasn't such a bad idea.

Sitting in one restaurant, chatting with a few locals who wanted to practice their English, I learnt something shocking. I was in a restaurant on my street, Huayi Lu, wrapped up and shivering. They came and said hi, the usual stuff, but this time I was more amenable to them bothering me, so I took up their invite and joined them.

The usual get to know you questions were exchanged, and when I revealed I lived a few doors away, one of them told me about her childhood. She was about my age, and she had grown up on that street. In her younger days in the early 80's, the street was all houses, all the way up. I knew that the skyscrapers were very recent, but I had assumed the old, grubby, crumbling mid-rises had a few years on them. It turned out that they barely dated from the mid 80's, but extreme neglect had seen them age worse than a heavy smoker, and be targeted by the property developers and their friends in demolition.

That wasn't even the most incredible story. According to her, back in those days there was only one toilet for the entire street. Whenever anyone on the street wanted a piss or a shit, they'd had to go to the same, shared facility. It was enough to put me off my food. I'd used the public toilet on the street once and it was beyond revolting, but that was mainly for customers of the barbeque restaurant. The Chinese must have been an incredibly hardy sort back in those oh so recent days.

My not being able to get the air-con in my bedroom working meant that I also had no heat there. I'd been going to bed wearing my full tracksuit, but eventually even that didn't keep me from shivering, so the school bought me a heater. It was a great little standing three bar piece of kit and kept me toasty warm, so long as I was right in front of it and up close. The heat seemed to vanish if I stood to the side and the turning action didn't seem to spread the warmth. As the winter progressed I needed to wear my warm winter coat to bed too.

I had made a final decision that I would not be renewing my contract and I would be leaving in February. The Life Club Coordinator role had been very tempting, and I really liked being there and working with everyone, but I had never intended to stay longer, and Miisa and I had plans. It was sad because things had really settled down at school. It had been a few months since anything major had happened in my classes and I had really gotten the hang of some of the trickiest students.

Jake, from my second HF1A class had been such a horrid little pain in the arse at first, but now I found him one of the most delightful kids I was teaching. Hero, in my second SS Red group, was another horrid little sod in the beginning who I was now very fond of. In fact, all of the young kids had surprised me a lot. They were clearly learning, and they seemed to be happy to be my guinea pigs for my ideas.

One task I tried in my original HF1A group was for teaching prepositions of location. The usual fifteen kids was reduced to seven one evening, so I had to rethink my lesson fast. I had a few cue cards but, annoyingly, I needed a full class, so I had to come up with a new exercise on the fly. I went through the plan as intended until the break and then, after letting the kids out, I grabbed a load more cards of various nouns that they knew (and one or two they didn't) and then gathered the kids up for the next half.

First of all there was a review, holding up each card and asking "What's this?", to which they replied "It's a ......". I then placed a few randomly selected cards on the floor, neatly arranged in a grid, and stood on the middle one (an apple), asking "Where's the apple?" Thankfully I wasn't faced with blank looks, but the kids were having to think hard. I then pointed at the card in front of my feet, a pencil and said "It's behind the pencil." The lights were on, and I pointed to the card at my heel. I asked "Where's the cat?" Lucy answered "It's behind the apple." I asked "Where's the apple?" and pointed to the cat. After a short pause Jennifer answered "It's in front of the cat." Wallop! Job done, but I had a twist.

I got Sky to stand on the apple and I sat in his seat, then I raised my hand enthusiastically. He was clued up. He pointed at me and I asked "Where's the shirt?" He looked to his left, saw the card and said "It's next to the apple." Sorted! I then let the kids take over. They raised their hands enthusiastically, and Sky took a few identical questions, answering each one as best as he could. A couple of times he was wrong and I asked "Is it?" or "Is the apple behind the car?" Either Sky corrected himself or one of the others volunteered the answer. Then it was just a case of giving them all a chance and changing the cards to keep them on their toes.

It reminded me of how far I had come in less than a year. When I first started I was well up on the theory and the process of planning, but I was a naïve novice who was balancing on a tightrope between success and failure. Back then, when things had gone wrong, I was in danger of panicking and had to take deep breaths to calm down and think. My plan was sacrosanct, and anything that forced a deviation was my idea of hell.

Now I could just deal with it. Not enough students, students looking bored, students failing to grasp the concept, students playing up, none of them worried me too much anymore. I had alternatives dancing around in my head and when they were needed, I could usually just grab them and throw them out in the class whenever I was in trouble.

I also saw some big progress with my SS Reds. They were learning well, remembering all the nouns and basic verbs and, with less and less help, the formulaic expressions. I was able to change up the classes a lot more e.g. when doing the team races, I would often get a student to stand at the front, calling out the items, or asking "Give me a....." or "I want a......". The best show of progress came from Angel, one of the naughtier kids in class.

I gave them a simple, fun colouring task. I know I've mentioned this as cheating, but that was mainly in Life Clubs. The SS course books actually had colouring tasks, so the experts thought it was okay for some occasions. As always, I kept hold of the pencils, and the kids had to come to me. By this time I wouldn't accept them asking for "red" or "green". They had to ask "Can I have a red pencil?". It needed a bit of a push at times, but they got it.

In one lesson, Angel came to me and asked "Do you have a red pencil?". That was a shock. It's a structure that's very difficult to translate ('do' doesn't exist in many languages), but she confidently used it, without any prodding, like it was the most natural thing to do. That was a moment that showed me what a great decision it had been to teach.

1. The pool in Miisa's apartment block. 2. A view from Lumphini Park. 3. The lizard in Lumphini Park. 4. Me pretending to be a Belieber. 5. Muay Thai at Lumphini Stadium. 6. The Marble Temple. 7. The Ananta Samakom Throne Hall. 8. New Year on Kao San Road. 9. Patpong. 10. Flags on sale at Chatuchak Market.

28 第二十八章

There was another addition to life in the big smog. After months of waiting and hoping with bated breath, Cactus finally opened. It had been months since the Belgian restaurant had shut, and we expats were eagerly anticipating the expansion of Chris and Shang's empire. Harp was the place to go for us when we were homesick or too lazy to make an effort to get local food. Now we had another little treat. It was gorgeous inside, with a roaring fireplace, big leather sofas, a pool table, a long bar and big TVs mounted on the walls. It was billed as a Mexican restaurant but, like Harp, its décor didn't quite match its ethnic association. It didn't matter though: it was Harp on a grander scale.

They'd almost had a bit of an inauspicious start where they'd had to bar two people from the offset. One was the infamous Graham, the drunk ex-Rover engineer or whatever. He'd apparently gotten pissed and then started being an arsehole to Chris. Chris was an architect by trade, but Graham was going on and on about how he was much better because he'd spent so many years as a civil engineer working on big projects.

So, he'd been a prick to me because he'd spent so many years at Rover, and then he'd been a prick to Chris because he'd spent so many years in big engineering. Even if he was a genuine engineer, those are two completely different types of engineering and are not interchangeable. In other words, Graham was completely full of shit.

The other was Crazy Amy. I don't know exactly why she was known as "Crazy", but I knew she had a certain "reputation". It didn't bother me. I'm no-one to talk, and whenever I'd seen her she'd been perfectly nice and friendly. Apparently she'd spent a whole night in Cactus, drinking a lot of expensive spirits and wines, but when her bar bill came, she'd refused to pay it. I really don't understand what her thinking was. It wasn't like she was the daughter of a gangster or was well-connected to rich expats. She was a very attractive, vivacious, well-educated young woman, who was probably a bit up herself somewhat, but no worse than many other women in her situation anywhere else in the world. Worst of all, it wasn't even Chris she was dealing with, so I'm not sure how she thought Shang could have been persuaded.

January was also a month of arrivals and departures. I'd had it pretty easy for most of the year. After David had moved out to live with Maria I'd had the run of the flat on my own and it had been fantastic. During the summer I had spent most nights sleeping on the sofa, where I could be comfortable under the working air con and I could be as messy or as tidy as I wanted to be. Now, I was to get some company.

It was my turn to be the welcoming committee, as Rory and Julie headed out to the airport once again. I bought a few introductory supplies and on the Monday afternoon, after another busy week, I stayed in the flat instead of heading to Harp. Eventually they arrived with our new teacher, Stephen. He was Chinese, but nothing like the locals. He was from San Francisco and very much fell into the hippy side of the City of Love. He had long dreadlocks, baggy and scruffy clothes and wore one of those woolly Rasta hats. I don't think he could have been more Bohemian if he had come from Prague.

We also had ourselves a third Filipino teacher. Her name was Nochelle, and she had moved to Chongqing with her American husband. They knew EF well already. Hubby had been a teacher with EF for years, and he had even been the one to make a video of a demo lesson for the *Marco Polo Project*. Nochelle had the pleasure of working in New York New York.

Stephen's first week was pretty standard. Like everyone else he had a super easy week of observing lessons without having to worry about planning and teaching, while the rest of us were rushed off our feet with our normal tasks. In his second week he was given a baptism of fire, with his first class being a Small Stars Green.

Another arrival was of a non-human kind. During my short time in charge I had taken part in an online meeting about the new RE course. Now it had arrived, and we were given a preview of the new whizziness. It was a video, done as a montage about a world famous superstar, with shots of screaming fans, red carpets and a talk show host holding up a photo of the legend. We were shocked to see a photo of Greg, and to see his name on the placards held up by screaming fans all desperate to see their hero.

It wasn't really about Greg; it was an online tool EF were using. The video had a lot of green screen, and one could upload photos and personal details, which would be automatically added to the film. I don't know if it was a gimmick or actually used as part of the course material, but it looked like a pretty good selling point. EF is the largest company of its kind, so it seemed odd that the best they had managed until then were a series of low-budget short films that any student could have put together. The new courses looked great too, as they had been properly aligned with the Common European Framework for linguistic assessment. Sadly, I wouldn't get the chance to use them.

One departure in January was Tanja. Her contract had run out and, late the previous year, Julie had decided not to offer a new one. I don't know the circumstances behind it, but it was sad for me to see her go. I'd hung out with her more than anyone and she'd been one hell of a good resource for ideas, especially with the Small Stars. Luckily for her she quickly found a new job at a nursery in a new district on the outskirts, so we could still hook up.

Another departure that month was Theo's. He'd been there a few years, but late the previous year he'd decided to move on, taking on a job at a school in Beijing. He'd announced it before Christmas, and at the party it had been a bit emotional for a few when a video montage tribute had been played for him. We had a party in Dani and Phil's flat, where Stephen shared around some hash cookies he had somehow smuggled into the country. Greg actually managed to get high.

There was another party to get through. To celebrate another successful year of the school, John treated us all to a big night out in his usual, generous vein. Everyone – teachers, PA's, admin staff and administrators – gathered at one of the bigger, and more exclusive, hotpot restaurants, hidden away off one of the main streets in JieFangBei. Everyone gorged themselves on the meats and vegetables, and we all downed a few local beers and more than a shot or two of jinjiu. Afterwards, we all headed to KTV.

The room wasn't the biggest, and it was quite crowded, but it worked well, feeling a lot more intimate than the mega room he'd hired for after the competition in the summer. Prizes were given out for various aspects of our jobs, and I was lucky enough to have been chosen as the "Most Improved Teacher over the Year". Julie said some lovely and warm words about me, saying how, after a few early mishaps, I had quickly gotten to a point where she didn't feel she needed to worry about my work. John gave me a certificate and nice little envelope with 500 Yuan, about £50. It was tinged with a certain amount of sadness, as I knew that my time was running out there, and I was already feeling like I missed the place.

Chris and Shang were pretty much sealing up the expat dollar in the city, and at the beginning of February, they pulled in a few more, with a little help from loose Chinese licensing laws. Cactus was open on Sunday, February 6th as normal, but this time they didn't close for the night. It stayed open, despite going into Monday, in anticipation of the crowd of expats who would drag themselves out of bed and force themselves through the ice-cold air and nasty pollutants for the big one, the Super Bowl.

I'm a huge American Football fan – Washington Redskins through and through – so it was a no brainer for me. Traditionally, my first day off of the year was always the Monday after the Super Bowl, but this time it was my weekend anyway. When I arrived at Hongyadong it was still dark, but even then I could tell the smog was particularly thick – the lights across the river were completely invisible. Alcohol was being served, but I wisely stuck to coffee for the whole game. Dani and Greg came along too, but the rest of the teachers chose to screw the game and stay in their warm, comfy beds.

I really can't remember anything about the game itself. I was the Pittsburgh Steelers vs the Green Bay Packers, two of the grand old teams with a lot of championships under their belts. I found myself siding with the Pack, mainly because I wanted their quarterback, Aaron Rodgers, to get that title so that he could shove a big part of that "not as good as Brett Favre" monkey off his back, but also because I thought the Steelers QB, Ben Roethlisberger, was a bit of a dick.

It was a fun morning, despite the ungodly hour we had all decided to get up at. Cactus was packed out but only a small handful were obsessed with the game. Even I wasn't my usual transfixed self; it was as nice to hang out with Dani and Greg as it was to watch the match. When the sun came out (as much as it could with all the pollution) the scene outside was easily the worst it had ever been.

Even on a bad day, it had been possible to look across the river and see the outline of the museum, or look west along the Jialing and see the bridge. This time, it was all obscured, completely blanketed by a thick layer of God only knew what gases that were in the atmosphere. In my time there, I hadn't felt bad; there had been no respiratory issues to speak off and I'd only felt the need for a mask when I went out running. Now, looking at the ghastly scene in front of me, I wondered if I'd been damaged in anyway.

It seemed so inhuman, so unbearable, so terrifying that there were places with air quality like that. I understood why it existed – rapid and poorly controlled industrial expansion coupled with mass construction projects – and that it was just the growing pains of an industrializing nation. The West experienced the same thing right up to the middle of the twentieth century (e.g. the great smog of London in 1952), but in my closeted upbringing I had thought those days were a thing of the past. If it was happening to China then it would happen to India, and God help the environment then.

Oh, and the Packers won.

Later, I needed to sort out my departure. Student Audrey had offered to help me get through the minefield of buying a train ticket, so we met up in JiangBei, where she took me to one of the kiosks that were dotted around the city. Outrageously, I wasn't allowed to buy a ticket. I had heard some bullshit excuses for bad service, but the one the attendant gave Audrey took the piss. Because it was close to the public holiday, it seemed that foreigners were not allowed to buy tickets from the kiosks – we had to buy them from the train station. It sounded like horseshit to me, but Audrey didn't seem too surprised.

I knew I would be getting my train from the ultra-modern north station, but the main ticket office was in the main city centre terminal. The plaza outside looked like chaos, full of cars, buses and people with piles of baggage to take with them on their long journeys across the country. Above was a network of highways, stilted higher than a decent-sized office block, snaking above everyone's heads like a modern Sword of Damocles. Audrey got me the correct ticket, and as we left the melee, it felt even more real that I was actually leaving China in just a few weeks.

Back in my apartment building I shared the lift with an old man and what I assumed was his grandson. I was wearing a t-shirt Miisa had given me, specially made with the Finnish flag sewn on. He asked if I was from Finland, then where I was actually from, what I was doing in China, did I like etc. I responded each time, and when I got out on my floor I realized something: I'd just had a full conversation in Chinese, without thinking or referring to a dictionary. I'd been pretty lax with my self-education but, almost at the end of my stay, I'd finally done it. A small victory maybe, but still a victory.

Chinese New Year is the biggest event on the Chinese social and cultural calendar. This is the time when people travel round the country the most, mainly to see their families in other cities or the countryside. It's such a big deal that Boss Audrey and Julie decided to close the school for a week, as there would be so few students coming in. So, we all had an extra week of holiday available. Before the school closed though, Jackson, one of my second HF1A's, gave me a toy cuddly rabbit as a New Year present (it was the Year of the Rabbit). It was a sweet thing to do, and he was one of the chubbiest, cutest kids in my classes (as well as a bit of a bugger at times).

This was a golden opportunity to see more of the country, and so I decided to hop on a plane and get touring. My first stop was Kunming, capital of Yunnan province, a mere 380 miles southwest of Chongqing and the place where I had been so bored waiting for a connecting flight just over a month before.

When I arrived I was amazed to find it a sunny day. It was mild too, but not shorts weather. The taxi was quick and cheap and I was soon in the city centre and checked in to the Hump Hostel, a very typical backpacker style establishment in the heart of the city. It was moderately built up by Chinese standards, and the high rises didn't go that high either. The central business district was mostly pedestrianized and, wonderfully, the sky was a bright, rich blue.

One of the highlights should have been Yuantong Si, a Buddhist temple complex that was popular as a pilgrimage destination. Sat at the foot of Yuantong Hill, it would have been one of the most picturesque and tranquil spots in city, had it not been for the scaffolding for the mass renovation work. The large artificial lake had been drained so that all one could see was the stone bed passing underneath the arches and around the steps of the pavilion.

Another highlight was Green Lake Park, an attractive public park full of lakes and pavilions that is more popular with seagulls than people. Unlike a lot of cities in China, Kunming still had an "old town" area in existence. Sadly, it had become somewhat run down, but it seemed like there was a desire to keep it going. So much had been lost in the country through the years of ultra-fast development, but there were signs they were getting attracted to the idea of preserving some elements of the past.

I also saw one practice taken to a new extreme. Just like in Chongqing, walking past some of the restaurants in the morning I saw the staff lined up in three rows, military style. There were the usual pep talks, chanting and finger pointing, and it all seemed a bit over the top and needless. One went a step further. With the staff lined up, one of them stood in front, waving a conductor's baton, while the others sang. I swear to God, the restaurant had its own anthem. She wasn't exactly conducting – more like waving the baton around in a vaguely rhythmical manner like one does when they want to pretend to be a conductor. Somehow, I just don't see it catching on at Ken's Kebabs in Portsmouth.

I visited one late bar while I was there, but I didn't exactly party the night away. On my second night I headed back to Green Lake Park, hoping to see a massive fireworks display, but when I arrived there was no sign of life at all, so I spent the evening in the hostel bar, sitting out on its large veranda in the clear night sky. That was when it all kicked off as, from all sides of the city, explosions popped up every few seconds, lighting up the sky with a myriad of dancing colours.

It was spectacular and shocking too. There seemed to be no regulation whatsoever (not a big surprise) and some of the fireworks exploded just a few metres from the balconies of people's homes. If anyone was sat out watching the displays, they were in for a dangerous shock, though I'm sure many would have expected it and stayed away.

From there, it was on to Beijing. I had thought about going to Suzhou and Hangzhou, but in the end I decided to get to a few places in the capital I'd missed out on in my last visit. When I arrived it was freezing, but bright and sunny, and the train into the city was delightfully modern and efficient. My hostel was in the Qianmen district, a restored old part of the city adjacent to Tiananmen Square. It was a delightful, traditional looking paved thoroughfare, with a mixture of traditional craft shops, local restaurants and international brand outlets.

It was on this visit that I had a very rare disaster. I should have seen it coming. When I was wandering Kunming an old man had approached me, pointing at the satchel I had slung by my side. Shock horror, it was wide open, but nothing was missing.

So, in Beijing I hopped on the metro and headed out to the Summer Palace, home of successive imperial families over its most glorious centuries. It was an amazing place. Rather than one palace, it was a complex of grand buildings, gardens and pavilions sprawled over a vast estate.

All the lakes had frozen over, and people had hired out little sleds to enjoy scooting along on the thick slabs of ice. It's not something I've ever done before because it's never happened to Canoe Lake in Portsmouth, but I was determined to give it a go. After visiting a number of small museums dedicated to the treasures of the former imperial court, I found myself at the palace lake, a vast natural pool that had turned to thick ice. After some tentative steps I was walking across it, but it was still tough, so I decided to hire one of the sleds.

Reaching into my satchel I was greeted with my guide book, my documents wallet, but no normal wallet. I frantically searched, then hunted every pocket I had, but there was nothing. Then it hit me; I hadn't needed to unzip. I had no idea if I had been robbed or it had dropped out from picking out my guidebook, but it was gone, and along with it 1000 Yuan – £100 – in small notes and loose change. I had a panic, but to be honest I over reacted.

My panic was more out of shock and fear. First of all, I was sure I had left all my important cards in Chonqging, but I wasn't one hundred percent. Secondly, the document wallet contained ALL of my money in China, about 20,000 Yuan - £2,000. I had kept it because I thought it was safer than leaving it in my hostel, but now I realized just how close to disaster I had come.

It was the only negative of the trip. That night I headed into Bar Street, another zone primarily serving the entertainment needs of the Western expats. It was nice, but it lacked something. In Chongqing, if I was in Harp, Cactus or Starbucks and I saw another Westerner, I could happily say hello and they would be equally as friendly. It was a great atmosphere because there were so few of us and we were all in the same boat. That was one of the best things about being in Chongqing.

Beijing, however, is far more cosmopolitan, and with so many expats around, there just isn't the same incentive to get to know people. I struck up a conversation with a Canadian woman, but as soon as her friends turned up she switched to them and ignored me (she didn't even give me a Canadian "*sooooory*"). After a couple of hours and another bar, I walked on to The World of Suzie Wong, a bar situated in delightful isolation. It was a small venue that tried to capture the essence of China in the 1920's and 30's, and was the perfect place to down a few G & T's.

The next day I headed to the modern business district, primarily to see one building. The headquarters of Chinese Central Television (CCTV) is one of the craziest constructions ever. It's not the tallest in the world, but it looks like the most impossible to exist. Imagine two "Z", with the middle stem upright, joined at right angles at the top with two extra stems connecting at the base. It's a staggering piece of engineering that should remind everyone why China is taking over the world.

I thought about the disgusting and damaging out of town business parks that are digging up precious countryside all over the UK. That's bad enough, but the architecture is so boring; it's just flat-pack cut and paste drivel that somehow earns architects a tidy packet. I'm amazed at how these people can get away with designing the exact same buildings other people design everywhere else, and how the developers pay for it. I'm sure the designs come from just ten templates that architects spend six months tinkering with in between coffees and five hour lunches. No wonder Chinese cities are dynamic and flourishing while British cities are dying a slow death.

I then headed to Beijing's other pride and joy, the Olympic Park. It was 18 months before London was to host its own extravaganza and, ever since Beijing dazzled the world, there had been endless negativity about what Britain had to offer. I must admit, this park wasn't as impressive as I had imagined. The Bird's Nest Stadium is another stunning example of engineering, but it didn't look as big as I had thought, probably because much of the interior is below ground level. The Water Cube lives up to the hype though, with its plastic walls so thin the sun shone through two sides of a corner.

That evening I had a few drinks in the hostel bar and hung out with some English teachers from Shanghai. They worked for Disney English and the more we talked, the more I wondered how EF would deal with the threat of this big corporation trying to muscle in on the market. It was clear they paid a lot more to their staff, which could have been because of the local cost of living, but that would always be attractive to potential recruits, not to mention the characters they could use.

The following day was filled with more sightseeing, a wander round the main shopping street and more food and drink in Bar Street. I'd had another wonderful, exciting time, but I was on a downer too. I could see the end of my adventure in sight, and my head was full of memories that I would barely comprehend were real. I wasn't just going to miss Chongqing, I was going to miss China.

In the morning I caught a taxi to the airport and, as we headed along the highway, my fears for EF were brought into perspective. The cab drove past a Disney English school, emblazoned with the internationally iconic characters that made that studio a media monolith. No wonder EF had a plan to quadruple the number of schools in ten years. Mel, Vic, Kevin, Ben and Roddy just couldn't compete with Goofy, Pluto, Simba, Belle, Donald, Arial and Mickey.

1. Theo's party. 2. Downtown Kunming. 3. Yuantong Si. 4. Pagoda. 5. Old town Kunming. 6. Beijing Summer Palace. 7. CCTV HQ. 8. Poster for EF in Beijing. 9. Olympic Stadium. 10. Water Cube.

29 第二十九章

I didn't have long left. A whole year was almost over and my mind had firmly wandered to the few weeks Miisa and I would be travelling together before I headed home. There were so many places to see and it was difficult to choose, but we soon settled on a schedule. I would leave Chongqing for a few days in Guangzhou and from there head to Shenzhen. We would meet up in Hong Kong and then travel to Singapore, Ho Chi Minh City, Phnom Penh and Siem Reap and then finish in Bangkok, where I would head back to Blighty.

There was plenty to sort out at home too. I hadn't exactly been on shopping splurges, but I had accumulated enough new stuff to know that there was no way I was getting it back home in the baggage I had come with. I was going to have to spend some of that Yuan on postage. On my penultimate weekend I spent a day sorting stuff out, deciding what I could take with me and what I could do without. I didn't really fancy spending too much, but eventually I had a pile of books, CD's, and clothing items that seemed dispensable for a few weeks, as well as a pile of books and magazines I didn't need anymore.

On the Wednesday, with the help of Grace, I packed the items into a regulation box and filled out the forms in the post office. It was bureaucratic, as the staff had to see what was in it before I could seal it up. They wouldn't let me send any CD's or spare currency so, annoyingly, the box wasn't as full as it could have been. It took over half an hour to get one box in the post, and that didn't include the waiting time. The remaining books and magazines I gave to Echo at Coffee for Two.

I was somewhat apprehensive as the final week approached. I had no idea how sensitive the students were, or if they really liked me, but I had a feeling they did. I had assumed the students would be told in advance, so I didn't really think about it until the Sunday of my penultimate week, right at the end of my TB3B class. When I told them the following week was my last their reaction was genuinely heart-warming. They were shocked – gasping, open mouthed and looking at each other. They had no idea, and it was a big deal for them.

The following week was the final leg of my year-long adventure in the Middle Kingdom. On the Wednesday I had my second HF1A class as normal and Linda came in at the end to translate the news. They were, like my TBs, shocked. I was heartened by this; I'd struggled with this group for a while and it would have been easy for them to hate me. Clearly they liked me though, and I had grown to like them, from the hard workers to the lazy ones, the well-behaved to the little sods.

Thursday was my final RE01 session. I liked them as people for sure, but it had been a nightmare teaching them. SS Red was the first class I was worried about. They were very young, and I had no idea how they would take it. I just had to go for broke. Kathleen translated for me and their reaction was "interesting" to say the least. They didn't seem particularly bothered, but they gave me a wave on their way out. Angel cried, but that was only because I gave her a bad behaviour mark in her report book and she was worried her mum would slap her. I was generous and "corrected" myself.

My final, super busy Saturday had arrived. In the evening, Linda came into class to help me say goodbye to my first HF1A, the very first class I had taught. They had been a great introduction to teaching for me, both in terms of lesson planning and class management, and I was grateful to all of them, for all the good and bad things. I think teaching this level had been the most educational for me regarding the joys and perils of this job. They were all smiles as they left the room, with a few saying "Bye bye teacher" and a couple giving me a hug. It was nice to be appreciated.

Sunday was it, my last day in school. The adventure was soon to be over. In the morning I had my second SS Red class and, with the help of Kathleen, I got the kids sat in a circle, holding hands. I thought it was a nice touch, just in case they got upset but, just like the others, they took it all in their stride as if it was no big deal. I suppose I was asking too much, or thought too highly of myself, but at least they were nice to me when they left.

Saying goodbye to TB3B was the hardest for me. They were great kids, really great kids, and I was going to miss them so much. When the lesson finished I was genuinely choked up as I thanked them for being such great students and told them how much of a pleasure it had been teaching them. Every one of them took my email address as they left. Last of all was an RE Life Club and then, in the late afternoon, I was done. No more classes, no more teaching. It was over.

Despite my teaching being done I wasn't in any rush to leave. I hadn't really gotten to know the PA's well, but I was still going to miss them. Kathleen had given me a goodbye present earlier. Actually, it was for Miisa, which I thought was a lovely little touch on her part. Boss Audrey had also given me a gift; a nice, big wooden comb. I was grateful, but a little confused by the choice. It was clearly for a woman with long hair, not like mine (Miisa had very short hair). Joy gave me a bracelet, with beads that felt like golf balls.

I made the rounds, giving the PA's hugs and kisses on the cheeks and taking photos and then, after making sure my desk was completely empty, I headed out. Kathleen and Scarlet were in the reception and we chatted about how the year had gone so quickly. Scarlet said how sad it was to see me leave, and that's when Kathleen lost it.

She started speaking, and then her voice broke as she fought back tears. This was a new experience for me. I've had a few girlfriends, and a couple of them have actually shed tears when we broke up (cross my heart), but it's still rare for me to generate such emotions from anyone. My last sight of her was as she walked around a corner to hide her tears.

And so it was time for the big goodbye, and there was only one way it could be done properly. I headed home and, after a luscious shower and a change I headed into JieFangBei, popping in to New York New York to say goodbye to anyone I knew there. Yogi was the only one. Destination for the evening was the best food in the world; shrimp pot. We teachers met up at a restaurant nearby and the beers started flowing. All we needed was that large metal bowl of vegetable broth, filled and piled high with shrimps cooked in numb and spicy chillis.

The first bowl was delivered, along with a bottle of jinjiu for each of us, and when the others showed up, another bowl was brought out with more beer and more jinjiu. This was the perfect way to end my time in Chongqing; amazing food, litres of booze and good friends. We were rowdy, but that was perfectly normal for those places. We had seen some very aggressive behaviour at times from the locals, but we were just partying the night away. At one point, I drunkenly demanded that Jayson give me his New York Yankees baseball cap, to which he duly obliged.

As the night ended there were some heartfelt – and even tearful – goodbyes. It would be the last time I saw Grace, Karen, Vivian, Joy, Ruby, Rory and Julie and I was incredibly sad to see this day. Dani, Jamie, Phil and I decided to head to Cactus for a few more beers, where I got to give Chris and Shang a hug and a kiss, after necking a few more drinks for the very last time in their wonderful place.

Eventually it was just Dani and I left, and in the early hours of Monday morning we headed home. There was a certain irony and justice that night. After all those nights out where Dani had been so hammered she couldn't avoid sitting in a puddle or know where she was, she finally took me home for once, knowing that I didn't have the faintest clue what was going on.

The following morning my brain felt like it was leaking razor blades. I had no memory of leaving Cactus, but it did make me smile thinking that Dani had finally taken her turn to get me home safely. I woke up late, really late, but thankfully I had absolutely no need to be anywhere until the evening. I headed out to JieFangBei for one last time, grabbing a coffee in Starbucks, having spicy beef in noodles in CSC, taking a walk through the malls and the warrens of streets, down to Chaotianmen and on a bus to JiangBei, where I took one last walk around the park and its underground shopping mall.

I was beginning to realize just how fond I was of the city and how much I was going to miss it. This had been my first extended period outside of the UK where I'd worked and had to survive. I had always imagined that my foreign working experience would be via the corporate environment, when daily commutes in a suit on a metro carrying a big fat latte were the fashionable norm. Instead it was done in jeans and t-shirts, on filthy buses eating cheap food. It didn't matter one way or the other though. I had done it.

I was going to miss the thick smog, the slippery streets when it rained, the incessant drizzle, the bang-bang men, the young women standing outside shops shouting the latest deals and clapping, the stinky dofu, the horrid traffic, the spicy smells from the restaurants, the stench of human faeces from the broken sewers, the litter, the spit and mucous on the streets, the car horns, the steep streets, the mass of people and so many other things that I know are in the deepest recesses of my memory but haven't quite come to the front.

That evening I had my last, arduous experience in the city when I headed out to see Tanja. I got the bus to JiangBei and then got on another to one of the newer districts where it seemed pretty clear that I was lost. The taxi ride from there was over half an hour, and then the driver still drove around and around the streets, looking for where I needed to be. Chongqing taxi drivers were miles better than in Shanghai and Beijing, but they were still far behind even the worst in the UK.

She was living in a plush looking complex and working in a kindergarten within. Everything she needed was on her doorstep, and the area seemed pretty clean and well looked after. It was too nice for my liking. There was no-one on the streets, no activity, no life to speak of. It was pleasant enough, but it wasn't my cup of tea.

We had dinner in the restaurant and talked about her new job and how well it had started. I was really happy for her, and she seemed to be enjoying her new life out in the metropolitan sticks and that was the main thing. We headed up to her flat for coffee and I got to say goodbye to cute little NanGua and then, with a big hug, I hopped in a taxi and headed back home, via JiangBei Cheng for some night time photos of the city. I was going to miss Tanja a lot; I felt that I had gotten closest to her than to anyone else.

I finished my packing at home, and was worried that I needed to sit on the suit case to get it shut. Clearly some drastic action was going to be needed, but my main concern was getting to the station in the morning. I took one last walk around the bars and clubs of the city centre, then headed home. It was time for my last night in my beloved Chongqing.

It was a dull and cold morning, almost exactly as it was when I had arrived a year before. After freshening up I was finally all packed and ready for the day ahead. I had lunch at a fancy restaurant under the Three Gorges Museum, and after coffee it was back to the flat, where a send-off committee was waiting. Stephen, Dulce, Maria, Jayson, Greg, Dani and Phil were all there, and they carried all my ridiculously heavy bags down in the lift and out to the street, hailed a taxi and packed it all in. With hugs all round I hopped in the cab and we drove away, looking back at the guys as I headed down the street, turned left and was gone.

The trip through the city was surreal. Each spin of the wheels and each turn of a corner took me further and further away from the city that had been my home, and the people who had been my family, for a year. Metre by metre, mile by mile, I left my amazing life behind me and made my way ever closer to being with Miisa, and then home.

I arrived at the main train station in plenty of time for me to buy some supplies and then join the massive queue of locals waiting to board. There was no real need for anyone to queue; we all had tickets and the train wouldn't rush off. I had a super-heavy suitcase, a well packed holdall and stuffed rucksack. I really wished I had put more stuff in the post.

My cabin was a shared four berth with a lockable door. I had been hoping to have it all to myself, but sadly there was another passenger. I've stayed in hostel dorms with Chinese people before and, every time, they have been the most violently loud snorers I have ever encountered. I had ear plugs though, and I just had to hope they worked. As the train pulled away, I texted my final goodbyes. In about an hour I would be outside the limits of Chongqing municipality for the very last time.

The journey was pretty comfortable. It wasn't a modern train, but it was clean enough, and the bed was comfortable. Most importantly, it was warm. I tucked into my food and drink supply, always keeping in mind that the train toilets would almost certainly be filthy squatters. I watched a couple of films on my laptop and read, and then settled down for the night. It was as comfortable as I had expected and, in no time at all, we arrived in the great, southern city of Guangzhou. My Asian adventure had begun.

I had made a really dumb mistake: I had forgotten to print a map to my hotel. I exited the station wondering if I could find an Internet café, but none was obviously close. What I did know was the name of the hotel and the street, so I was in for another stressful Chinese taxi ride. Actually it wasn't so bad. He didn't drive around too far, and he stopped at another hotel early on to ask the doorman, and eventually we made it. I didn't venture too far that night, but I did find a Starbucks a mile or so away, though just outside it seemed to be a popular haunt for the local prostitutes.

In the morning I was treated to the familiar sight of a thick cloud of smog in the air. I took a ride on the metro and was soon in the CBD (central business district), the sun wholly obscured by the city's own, legendary pollution. It was very quiet, almost as if there was no business going on that day. Despite the forest of high rise offices there was hardly any traffic about, a lot like Frankfurt in many ways. I had one place in my sights; the Canton Tower.

Built as the centrepiece of the city's modern developments in time for the 2010 Asian Games on the banks of the Pearl River, it stands at 488m to the roof, and 600m to the antenna, and was briefly the tallest freestanding structure in the world. For some reason I cannot fathom though, I chose to see it straight away. When I got to the viewing deck at 449m, I was faced with a scene of utter nothing. The smog was so thick that even the areas just across the river were partially obscured. By the time I was back on the ground the smog had burned off a lot, and the sky was blue. I would have had a great view and I should have known.

I took a long walk around the city centre and was amazed at how quiet and dead it seemed. This is a huge city with a mega-population and yet, none of the people seemed to be out and about that day. Midweek it may have been, and a lot less packed in than Chongqing too, but I expected some semblance of commotion. I stopped for lunch in a nice little café and then continued my wanderings, realizing that Guangzhou was not a city littered with staggering landmarks, but it was pretty clean and there seemed to be a good quality of life.

The next morning I found my way to Shamian Island, an idyllic oasis of colonial-era calm in an older, busier part of the city. It had been controlled by the French and British in the 19th century and had escaped the mass redevelopments elsewhere. It was the perfect place to kick back with a latte and a book, and it seemed the rest of the expat community agreed with me.

The thing I loved most about the city, and this area specifically, was the smell. I love Chinese food and, as I've said before, most Chinese food in the West is Cantonese, and the air of Guangzhou reeked of that wonderful smell, just like in Hong Kong or Chinatown in London. There was no partying for me either. I was saving myself up for Hong Kong.

After a couple of days I hopped on another train and headed to Guangzhou's equally vast neighbour, Shenzhen. In 1979, after taking over the government and purging his Maoist enemies, Deng Xiaoping started his policy of "Capitalism with Chinese Characteristics". He created five Special Economic Zones (SEZ) which would allow for limited experimentation with market capitalism, and Bao'an County was one, due to its close proximity to Hong Kong.

It has often been said that it was just a small fishing community at the time, but actually the county had a population of over 300,000, but it was sparsely populated and poor, and what happened next can best be described as a miracle of economics, engineering and town planning.

Money and people flooded in and work began almost immediately on turning this barely populated soil into what would become one of the biggest cities in the world. Between 1982 and 1985 the population rose by 150% and by 1987 it had reached 1 million. Between 1990 and 1995 the population grew by 270% and in 2000 it hit 7 million. Growth eventually slowed to a more sustainable rate, but in 2010 it topped 10 million, all in the space of thirty-one years. It wasn't haphazard either. Roads were well planned and neatly laid out, with wide freeways connecting neighbouring cities directly into the CBD and spreading out to the suburbs. Large parks were given as much importance as industrial zones and the eventual addition of a metro neatly cemented its ambition to be a truly global city.

By the time I got to my hostel I was tired and sweating like a pig. All this stuff I was carrying was too much; I had to get rid of it. Before taking any kind of shower I dashed to the nearest post office, bought a huge box and stuffed it full of as much of my crap as I could fit in: books, souvenirs, my thick winter coat, jumpers, smart shirts, anything I wouldn't need in the hot Asian climate that I could also survive without for a reasonable amount of time back home. Once done, I showered and headed into the CBD.

Shenzhen is arguably the epicentre of the world's electronics industries. There are so many factories in the region, and even more malls dedicated to their retail, that it's like the city was built just to service the likes of Hitachi and Apple. I decided I wanted a new phone, as the cracked screen on mine was pissing me off, but I didn't have a great deal of money to spend. As I've said before, it is a myth that good electronics gear is super cheap in these countries. They are cheaper, but don't expect mega-savings unless you are happy to use the knocked-off stuff. I thought about buying a cheaper Chinese brand though, but I couldn't communicate my main concern: would it work with a UK SIM card? A local woman who spoke a little English tried to help, but I eventually decided it wasn't worth the risk.

I headed along the main road and into Lizhi Park, a landscaped open space surrounded by the high rises that crammed the people in. As is the norm, the sound of traffic died down somewhat the further in I got, and the large boating lake, with its elegant bridges and statues, made Canoe Lake in Portsmouth seem like a mud-filled puddle after a rain storm. Dominating the surroundings was the partially finished Kingkey 100, which was already the city's tallest building, but would only be so for a few years when an even bigger one would be completed. That evening I didn't stay out late. There were a few bars near the hostel, so I stuck to a couple of pints before hitting the much-needed sack.

In the morning I made another, almighty cock up. I had a plan to see plenty of sights, and so hopped in a taxi and headed to my first. Lianhuashan Park is another of the city's open spaces and this one is a little special. After walking around the boating lake, through the wooded areas and up the hill I reached the peak, where I was greeted by two sights.

The view of the city was pretty stunning, and the pollution had lifted enough to open it up for all to see. It's not the most beautiful city in the world, but it's not ugly either, and what it represents is far more important. On the peak was a large, heroic looking statue of Deng Xiaoping. This wasn't so surprising, as it was he who had ordered the city's existence, but what did shock me was all the praying at its base. It seems that in this city he had been elevated to a God-like status, and in a way I don't blame them. I mean, why not? At least he actually did something for the people.

It was then that my mind wandered. I had remembered taking my camera's memory card out and saving the pics on my laptop, but it suddenly occurred to me that I couldn't remember putting it back in. I checked, and guess what; no card. I headed back down the hill, into a taxi, back to the hostel, inserted card into camera (and metaphorical fist into metaphorical face) and then headed back, for a second view of the park and Deng's devoted worshippers, only this time at speed.

The metro took me back into the CBD, which seemed a bit busier than Guangzhou's, but not by much. Despite Kingkey 100 already being the tallest building in the city, and the Pingan Centre soon to take its place, the city's architectural landmark is still Shun Hing Square. Like the Empire State Building in New York or the Sears Tower in Chicago, it had been a major leap on the city's skyline and would forever be its icon, even if it was towered over by rivals.

This twin-spired, green clad and narrow giant was the city's first major statement to the world, topping off at 384m and giving the city a face that could be recognized as Shenzhen, and only Shenzhen. I liked it. It was different, being covered in green glass, and it was delightful to enjoy a coffee across the road, underneath its vast shadow. I walked further down the road, finding a couple of branches of my beloved EF and checking out the view of the mountains on the edge of Hong Kong.

That evening I decided to party. I took a long taxi ride to Shekou, the former industrial zone that had been turned into a Westernized entertainment district. This area was full of bars, clubs and restaurants and I chose an Indian, with one of the spiciest curries my tongue has ever been subjected to.

Annoyingly, after walking around some more, I found a Hakka restaurant. The Hakka people are one of China's minorities and are heavily associated with the Guangdong/Hong Kong region. The boiled pork bellies in mustard with vegetables and rice was the greatest food I had ever eaten until I discovered shrimp pot. It was also Six Nations day, so some of the pubs were crammed full of expats watching the mighty England shame the French and the heroic Italians just fall short against the Welsh.

It was also interesting to see how many young Westerners there were. They were very young, and numerous, and it was clear they were university students. I had met a few from Belgium in Chongqing, but Shenzhen seemed to have a large community of them. I must admit to a huge amount of jealousy towards them. I never had that opportunity in my degree, but they'd been able to travel to the other side of the world to study, if only for one year. I just hoped they understood how lucky they were. It wasn't just a great city to live and study in; it was a pretty good party town too, but I was in no mood to go wild. I had an important rendezvous to keep and I wanted as clear a head as possible.

1. In my train to Guangzhou. 2. Canton Tower. 3-4. Shamian Island. 5. Downtown Guangzhou. 6. Skyline of Shenzhen. 7. Statue of Deng Xiaoping. 8. Shun Hing Square. 9. Kingkey 100. 10. EF school.

30 第三十章

I left mainland China on foot. I know this isn't the most uncommon thing in the world, and it's not so incredible when you actually consider the arbitrariness of borders, but it still felt weird. I left my hostel on another hot and sunny day and hopped on the delightful metro, passing through the city centre and straight to the customs control at the border.

It's at this point that I want to reiterate a few things. Yes, I know full well that Hong Kong is a part of China, but I also want to make it clear that that's like saying that the Channel Islands and the Isle of Man are part of the UK (or that Hong Kong used to be). Hong Kong is classed as a Special Administrative Region (as is Macau). It has its own laws, its own police, its own government and its own currency, just like it had when it was a British colony. In pretty much every way, Hong Kong's status has remained the same; it's just controlled by a different country. That is why I class it as a separate country. I would do the same for Guernsey, Jersey and the Isle of Man (if I could ever be bothered to visit them).

I queued up patiently but expectantly, knowing that this was a big moment for me. I handed over my passport, waited for the official to finish looking at my beloved visa, dragged my suitcase through the 'neutral zone', went through the same rigmarole with my passport once again, and I was there. China is the fourth largest country by landmass, considerably bigger than Europe (minus Russia) and I had just walked out of it.

I hopped straight on the MTR, realising that it was exactly the same as in Shenzhen. Hong Kong's metro system is so efficient and successful that the company has been given contracts to run parts of the metros in Shenzhen and Beijing, as well as the systems in Melbourne and Stockholm. It's amazing how such a small territory can do so many incredible things. The train was comfortable and efficient and it felt like it took no time at all to cross from the border into the centre of Kowloon, one of the most densely populated places on Earth. A few streets later and I was in the hotel, and the lift took me up ten floors where I joined Miisa.

Our room was ridiculously tiny, with barely any floor space for our suitcases. I've never really understood why this is the case. They aren't scared about knocking down old buildings and constructing new ones, nor are they afraid to build high. I don't understand why floor plans have to be so cramped; it just feels like an artificial problem that could easily be solved.

It was already afternoon, so we took a quick excursion to the harbour, where we got to enjoy one of my favourite sights; the view of the skyline of Central (formerly known as Victoria). We did it again in the evening, when the buildings were lit up like Oxford Street in the silly season. It always reminds me why I love skyscraper architecture so much.

The next day we headed out in the heat and sun. I soon realized that my love of Hong Kong was pretty idiosyncratic and nerdy. Miisa showed little interest in the tower architecture, despite my enthusiasm. We hopped on the metro and took a wander round the glass and steel blocks of Central, before heading to the Peak Tram. Sadly it was closed, so after a one hour bus ride we were at the top, gazing out across one of the most iconic and stunning urban views in the world.

It's an awesome sight, full of towering constructions, reclaimed land and a surprising amount of nature. Don't be put off by the smog and grime you see on TV; Hong Kong has more than its fair share of natural attractions. In fact, 75% of it is countryside, and 38% is under statutory protection. We took another wander through Central and headed back to Kowloon where, in the evening, we had dinner in a Spanish restaurant.

The next day I suggested we go to one of the outlying towns. On my first visit, I had enjoyed half a day in the resort of Stanley and, from the guide books, I suggested Aberdeen, noteworthy for the floating Jumbo King Restaurant. However, when we got to the city centre we realized the restaurant was somewhere else, and that the area wasn't particularly exciting, except for the nearby striking cemetery built on a hillside.

Back in Central we decided to look around some of the shops and markets stalls around Queen's Road, stopping at the Western Market, where Miisa was shocked at my construction of a chip butty (sandwich). To all non-British women out there, if you put a plate or bowl of chips, some bread and some butter in front of a British guy, you should consider him weird if he DOESN'T make a chip butty.

I love Hong Kong, and I loved being back, but I could tell Miisa wasn't particularly impressed.

Our next destination was Singapore, another fashionable former outpost of the British Empire that had thrived thanks to years of cheap industrial labour and converting to high finance.

Our hotel was a few miles outside the centre, in an area relatively untouched by modern high rises. After a brief wander around St Andrew's Cathedral and the Raffles Hotel, we ducked into the Raffles City mall to escape a thunderous and explosive deluge of rain. It passed over quickly and we were soon back out in the open, browsing the streets of Chinatown and finding a shop devoted to all things Tin Tin. I hadn't even seen that in Brussels.

The metro took us into the city centre business district, another world famous high rise skyline that had put this country on the map. Across the bay was the newest edition; the Marina Bay Sands. To my eyes, this is one of the most revolting buildings in the world. Three towers stand at about 200m, connected at the top by a surfboard-shaped sky deck. This is where guests and tourists get to enjoy swimming pools, restaurants and bars, and the best thing about them is that patrons can enjoy the view without the Marina Bay Sands in the way. After a drink under the Andersen Bridge, we took a walk along Bridge Quay, returning that evening for a stunning curry and a few drinks in the warm, sticky evening.

The next day we were back on the quay for breakfast, walked around to the other side to pay homage to the statue of Sir Stamford Raffles (founder of Singapore), then headed to Singapore's biggest attraction, the Singapore Flyer. London kicked off the craze for observation wheels with the London Eye, and now every big city seems to have one plan or another for its own. The views of the city centre are pretty spectacular, though I was more impressed by the crowd of container ships and tankers, all waiting patiently to get into one of the busiest ports in the world.

Back on the ground we escaped another heavy rain storm and then headed to Bukit Pasoh, a part of Chinatown that had once been a den of vice, but had been restored to a quaint old-timey district of cafes, restaurants and boutiques. When in Bangkok, we had watched a crappy Singapore romantic film called *The Leap Years* which had been filmed there, with the most "romantic" scenes happening at the Seven On Club. Sadly it was closed, so no re-enacting for us.

Stop number three was Ho Chi Minh City, a city known more for a war that has been eulogized by Hollywood despite its abject failure. The first thing you notice about the city is the inordinate number of bikes, both motorized and pedal powered. This city, large and crowded though it is, still retains its image of French colonial grandeur, interspersed with elements of imposing Communist palatial simplicity and the flourishing of a modern high rise development.

Crossing the road was an adventure in itself, but was actually much easier than anticipated. The traffic can't go too fast at the best of times, and the bikes are nimble enough to avoid any collisions. The trick is to keep a steady pace and not be indecisive. If there is any chance of being hit, the bikers will take the necessary action for you.

We took a walk down to the mighty Mekong River and strolled through the centre, finding our way to the over-sized General Post Office, the incongruous Notre Dame Cathedral and the ornate Municipal Theatre. This part of the city was devoid of any kind of Asian identity. In fact, the only way to identify it as such was from the people's faces and the mass of cabling overhead. That evening, after some dinner, we took a walk down to the Ben Thanh Market, where I bought myself a Vietnam flag t-shirt, after my most successful bout of haggling ever.

In the morning, our first full day started with a walk to the Reunification Palace, former home to the President of South Vietnam and now a war relic that has been left largely unchanged since tanks stormed the grounds on 21st April 1975. We avoided it though, walking around its perimeter and, after getting shot of the desperate attentions of a pedalo rider, ended up at the War Remnants Museum. The grounds display captured planes, helicopters and tanks left by the Americans, but the sights inside are more striking. One section is devoted to the effects of Agent Orange, the chemical used by US forces as a weapon that has led to lasting genetic mutations in the civilian population, from mild deformities to outright retardation. We carried on with our tour, not really looking to go anywhere in particular but just taking in the crazy atmosphere.

The following day we hired a couple of pedaloes and let ourselves be carried through the craziness of the city's streets, somehow avoiding being flattened by one of the countless thousands of two-wheeled vehicles and the occasional truck. After a few miles, and what felt like countless near misses, we were dropped off at the Jade Emperor Pagoda, a temple housing a jade statue covered in luxurious robes, and with pools full of turtles, young and old.

We walked back to the city centre, crossing through a park with a stone bench branded with the familiar logo of Fisherman's Friend, and passing by a construction site with mud so thick and soggy that the tracks of the mobile crane had sunk. The arm was still extended and the site seemed to be wide open; a complete disregard for any kind of safety standards or security. We headed back to the hotel, spending a couple of hours in the rooftop pool before heading to a local French restaurant for the evening, where we feasted on some of the best chicken either of us had had in our lives (or since Bangkok).

We took a short hop by plane to Phnom Penh, capital of the Kingdom of Cambodia. This had a very similar feel to Ho Chi Minh City, but on a much smaller and more intimate scale. We took a walk up the secluded 51st Street and found our way to the Central Market, a large, yellow-domed, Art Deco building that's home to a myriad of stalls selling electronics, clothing, stationary, flowers, jewellery and curios, surrounded by a heavy mass of two-wheeled traffic.

After negotiating the motorcades, we ambled along a narrow park to Wat Phnom. This sacred Buddhist pagoda has been central to the city's religious rites since 1373 and is the tallest, standing 26m on top of a small, artificial mound. Dotted around its corners at each level are statues of fearsome looking lions, ready to rip out the throats of any non-believers who dared to set foot on its hallowed stones. The pagoda had also become home to numerous macaques, locally known as "Gangster Monkeys" because of their often aggressive and violent interactions with people. We chose not to get too close, and they seemed to give us a wide birth too.

Across the quiet river was a large and remarkably undeveloped island, just waiting for the foreign corporations to jump in and exploit it. I'm sure it's only a matter of time before they discover this property goldmine. We took in the National Museum and the Royal Palace, both displaying the Khmer-style architecture so similar to that of the temples and palaces of Thailand. In the park outside the palace, hundreds of families had gathered, with picnics and small stoves for barbequing, despite the choking fumes of the traffic all around. I didn't blame them. The heat and humidity were stifling and they probably didn't have any air conditioning at home. We had dinner in a restaurant on the riverside and then headed back for an early night, with a long and tiring day ahead of us.

In the morning we hopped on a rickety-looking bus, with seats providing the minimum of comfort and even less leg room. We settled in for our six hour trip to Siem Reap, the true heart of the country. There was no motorway, and many parts of the road were potholed and lacking in tarmac, but at least we had some air conditioning and a TV at the front that played what I assumed was Cambodian pop videos.

We passed through endless countryside, dotted with villages of stilted houses, waterlogged farmland with ox rolling around in the mud, and people on motorbikes and scooters, transporting loads that should have been impossible for two wheels. We stopped off in a small town called Kampong Thom to stretch our legs, and managed to get a quick lunch before the remaining hour or two to our destination. After arriving at the bus station, we took a short tuk-tuk ride to our hotel which, gloriously, was the nearest to the site that had drawn us there; Angkor.

In the morning we hired bicycles from the hotel. They were old and certainly not built with Western men in mind so, for the whole day, I found myself unable to get a full leg extension with each turn. We cycled along the approach road and along the banks of a lake until we arrived at one of the true wonders of the world.

Angkor was the capital of the Khmer Empire and, in 1150, construction was completed on its grandest temple. Angkor Wat. This truly is one of the most wondrous constructions in history, so much so that it is depicted on the national flag. At the heart of it is the iconic central structure, comprised of a rectangular base with a tower on each corner and a central tower standing the highest of them all. It's a staggering piece of early medieval architecture, as unique as the Pyramids of Egypt or the Great Wall of China. Inside, the walls are decorated with some of the most exquisite Hindu-inspired friezes one is likely to see anywhere in the world and even today, corners are still set aside for religious devotion.

For the whole day, we cycled around the entire Angkor site. It was hot and humid and our energy was sapped with the rapidity of a marathon runner. Everywhere we stopped there was a stall selling cold drinks, ice-cream and other snacks, and we were frequent customers. We visited every site we passed, such as Baksei Chamkrong (its entrance home to a scary hornet's nest), Angkor Thom (with the beautiful Terrace of the Elephants), Phnom Bakheng, Prasat Kravan and Neak Pean.

Every temple was a combination of imposing standing structures and piles of rubble, but nothing could detract from the awe-inspiring beauty of each stop-off we made. It was 4 o'clock by the time we got back to the approach road. We were both sticky with sweat and our arses were aching from the horrendously hard seats we'd been forced to endure.

After a dip in the hotel pool, we freshened ourselves up and headed into another of Asia's Western-focussed Bar Streets. As is typical, it was lined with a combination of local style restaurants and foreign eateries, and every one of them was full of tourists. We chose a barbeque restaurant where we indulged our more adventurous natures by trying snake, crocodile and frogs legs, the latter being the one that made me feel like retching. It wasn't the taste that did it (it was like common chicken), it was the fact that it looked like a baby's leg with webbed feet and very tiny bones.

We got ourselves an early night and somehow, despite our exertions, we dragged ourselves out of bed at half past three in the morning to catch one of the best light shows in the world. I didn't think we would make it though. It was pitch black as we cycled up the approach road to Angkor Wat, without any lights or reflectors, and we had to keep talking to make sure we didn't lose each other. Eventually we made it to the temple, where the waiting game began.

What we were treated to was easily the most beautiful sunrise we had ever seen. The temple is on an east-west alignment, with the large grass courtyard providing grounds for the spectacular view. As the sun rose behind the temple, the towers were displayed in silhouetted perfection, the glow of the rays encircling this ancient monument of devotion that had seen empires, kingdoms and dictators come and go. Thank God the Khmer Rouge had decided to keep their destructive hands off of it.

Later that morning we hopped on the bus back to Phnom Penh which, unfortunately, didn't give us as long a rest stop as we had hoped. By the time we arrived we were tired and hungry, and were in no mood for the clueless tuk-tuk driver who seemed to genuinely have no idea where he was going. I don't blame him though. The streets are numbered and in a grid pattern, like New York, but none of them are in order.

We had planned to go to a "Finnish" bar, but when we looked in it seemed pretty cheap and uninviting, so we found another restaurant on the banks of the river that catered for the tastes of the unadventurous. There was no partying, just a desire for food, cold drinks and an early night. In the morning, after another wander around the city centre, we packed up our gear and headed back to the airport and, after having to pay a surprise exit fee, settled in on the plane and headed for our final destination.

My stay in Bangkok was only a short one. I was only there for one full day, and that was spent just wandering around, soaking up the sun and humidity, sheltering from the afternoon downpour and wandering around the shopping areas along the route of the Sky Train. We had some amazing memories to treasure together, and we spent a lot of time trying to decide which the best were.

Top of the list was Angkor. Despite the sweat and the aches it left us with, cycling around that ancient city was not just the most memorable adventure of our trip, but of our lives. It was the most beautiful place we had ever visited, and every strain on every muscle had been worth it. The Petronas Towers were a close second, but there were so many others that we just couldn't decide.

The Giant Buddha of Leshan, the Singapore Flyer, Muay Thai boxing at Lumphini, the War Remnants Museum, the boating lake in People's Park in Chengdu, Chongqing Zoo and New Year on Kao San Road were just a handful of the memories that made our trips together so fantastic, even if things didn't always go according to plan. I had never travelled so much with one person, and it was certain that later in the year I would join her in Helsinki.

On our final evening we had dinner in Silom Soi and drinks in a few pubs, including one where we could watch England vs Scotland in the Six Nations. I tried to explain the rules of rugby union and, bravely, the differences with rugby league. Miisa didn't get it, which probably explains why Finland has a long history of being the lowest ranked nation in the sport (below ANDORRA!). Thankfully I didn't have an early flight to catch, but I didn't feel like doing long haul with a hangover, so we had another early night.

I loved the taxi ride through Bangkok. It was long in distance but short in time, thanks to the toll highway cutting through the middle of the city. I loved gazing out at the crazy and ever expanding skyline as it crept into the sky and encroached into more and more of the surrounding countryside. Construction cranes were as much a feature as the numerous high rises, and I wondered if Bangkok's time was coming close.

It had never been one of the "Tiger Economies", but it was still a vast and ever growing regional power, still smarting from the indignities of the Asian financial crisis in 1997. Its airport was its greatest statement of intent, and when we arrived we had to wait a little while for my check-in to open. I felt like staying, but I also wanted to go home. I wouldn't say I was homesick, but I did want to get back to see my friends and family. I had coped perfectly well just using Skype, MSN and Facebook, but I was ready for the real thing again.

Eventually I checked in and decided it was best to go straight through. We had a final goodbye and then I went through security and was airside once more, praying that this visit would not be as long as the previous. I had a Burger King and a Starbucks and, after another wander round the shops, I parked myself in my gate and waited. This time there were no delays. I had finally left Southeast Asia – the Orient – and was heading back to Europe.

The flight was perfectly comfortable, with all the necessary mod-cons for a long air trip. I managed to get some broken sleep as we crossed over the great Eurasian landmass and eventually landed in Manama, Bahrain. Thankfully, this was nothing like my trying experiences in Doha, where on two occasions I had to spend seven hours in one of the most boring terminals in the world. It wasn't a big airport, but there was a decent café and plenty to look around at. Free wi-fi was a God send too, and I fired off a few emails to let everyone know I was safe. Then it was onto the next plane for the final leg of my mighty adventure.

When I woke up we were just leaving mainland European airspace. It was grey and pouring with rain, just the kind of welcome I should have expected from my home and, as the plane descended over London, my head became clearer and clearer. Despite being just a few minutes away, I would not feel like I had arrived until I stepped over the threshold of the plane doors, onto the sky bridge and walked into the airport. It was 6:30 am, so passport control was a doddle. I grabbed a trolley and a few minutes later, it was loaded with my suitcase and I walked into departures. My sister, Caroline, was waiting for me, and she almost went into full blubber mode at the sight of her beloved, wonderful and adorable baby brother finally coming home.

The drive back to Portsmouth was pretty easy. The M25 wasn't too busy and the A3 was kind for a change, and by the time we arrived in Portsmouth the sun was out and the day was mild. We detoured to Palmerston Road, where big sis treated me to a large latte and a cake from Costa, and then we headed back to mum's.

When we parked out front, surprise surprise, mum was waiting at the door, big hug all prepared and ready for delivery. Inside, the cats got a huge hug. Sooty was her usual tiny self, and I was introduced to a new friend, Mr Sneaks, a former neighbour's cat who had adopted mum while I was away (and then they left, without him). That evening, I popped round the corner to get myself a large cod, large chips, mushy peas and a fizzy drink. Normally enough to share, I shoved it down my face in record time. I was finally home.

I wasn't quite done with Asia. The following day was chilled out. I went to a local coffee shop and got to chat to Miisa in the morning, then had a wander round Portsmouth. It had hardly changed, save for one or two new buildings of a very modest size. It was this lack of change that I struggled with, seeing as I had spent a year in a region where new builds were par for the course.

The following day was mum's birthday, and Caroline and I treated her to a day out in London. Our destination was Claridge's for a spot of traditional, English high tea. We were a bit early when we arrived at the hotel, and as we passed the front entrance we saw a crowd of people, waiting expectantly outside. On one side of the door was a crowd of photographers, all jostling for the best position. On the other was a bunch of screaming girls, some of them so young they were with their parents. Directly in front of the door was a minivan, waiting patiently. A shadow of doom descended over my soul.

We went for a little walk to kill time, doing a bit of window shopping around the local boutiques but not straying too far. Then we headed back. The photographers, girls and minivan were still there, as was my dread. A smartly dressed doorman was standing on the pavement, doing the best he could to keep order, so Caroline asked him who they were all waiting for. My feeling of despair was solidified when the doorman said the name: Justin Bieber.

That little shit wipe was following me, haunting me across the continents. It had been impossible to avoid him in Asia but I had thought he wasn't that significant back home. How naïve was I. Caroline wanted to get a pic, so we waited for a while, but eventually she gave up and we went inside. Barely a minute passed when I turned around and saw a small group heading for the exit, with the small, slender figure dressed in a track suit surrounded by heavies. We had just missed him. Thank God!

1. Hong Kong from Victoria Peak. 2. Hillside graveyard. 3. Downtown Singapore. 4. Mega Crabs. 5. Ho Chi Minh City. 6. Phnom Penh. 7. Eating snake in Siem Reap. 8. Angkor Wat at dawn. 9. Another temple in Bangkok. 10. Homecoming fish 'n' chips with mushy peas and curry sauce.

31 章三十一章

So, now comes the profundity. Did the experience change me? What did I learn about the world? What did I learn about myself? Am I a better person? Had a grown? Do I see things differently through new eyes? Did my home seem different to me?

Well, one thing I did notice was the increased number of mainland Chinese people in Portsmouth, almost all of whom seemed to be students, but some were older adults, even elderly. It's hard to explain how I could tell. Certainly Mandarin sounds different to Cantonese, but they look different too, mainly in their style.

Portsmouth seemed a bit weird for a while, but that was mainly because of how much the same it was to when I had left. There were noticeable changes in Chongqing from the day I first walked through Monument Square to the day I left, mainly due to the completion of one particularly tall skyscraper, but Portsmouth was exactly that same. I didn't need to re-acquaint myself with my hometown because I still knew it.

I did notice that KTV had started appearing. One was in an old theatre that was also a snooker club, and the other was an old pub. They weren't proper KTV's, just bars with karaoke machines, but it was nice to see a bit of Asian cultural imperialism creeping into the West. I had talked about opening one myself, a proper one in fact, but it would cost a fortune and I'm not sure suitable properties are out there.

There were two significant changes to myself. One is that I now make fewer assumptions about what should be obvious between cultures. It happened a year after I left. The newspapers in the UK reported that Swansea University had put up posters in the toilet cubicles to show their proper usage i.e. sit on them. It seemed that some students were standing on the rims and squatting. Pretty stupid don't you think?

Well, remember how I tried to find a way to sit when I first used the squat toilet? It's no different. Many students are now coming to Britain from cities that are rapidly developing, but with little to no Western influence. This means that there are many things they've never seen or used before, and one of these is the seated toilet. How many times have you seen someone taking a shit in a big Hollywood blockbuster? Like me trying to hold myself up, these students were just doing what they knew best. Sadly it gave "health and safety gone mad" cannon fodder to the *Daily Mail* and some of the idiots on *Mock the Week*.

The other is of a culinary disposition. Being brought up in England means I'm particularly conscious of how I eat i.e. not chomping my food with my mouth open like an animal, not slurping food and drink, and sitting properly. Now, when it comes to rice with chopsticks, I'm like a native. I'll either get my head down close to the plate or I'll move the plate or bowl to my face and scoop it in. No need for etiquette with rice.

Oh, and pick 'n' mix was more expensive. Before leaving for China, every time I went to the cinema I would grab a tub of sweets (mostly the jelly ones such as cola bottles, sugared cherries, strawberries and wine gums), and 500 grams would cost just over £5. On my first visit back home, it was over £7. I was fucking furious!

However, the big question is, 'Was it all worth it?' My answer can be best understood in the context of what has happened since.

My clear intention was to go to Finland and give it a real go with Miisa, but I didn't want to jump into a tricky situation work and money-wise. I took a bit of time to chill out and then looked for teaching jobs locally, sending my CV out to a few of the big language schools in Portsmouth. Three replied, and after interviews I was asked by one to give a lesson the following day. They let me use their resources and WOW, they had some resources. Their teacher's room was perhaps ten times the size of EF's and they had pretty much every teaching course book imaginable. Sadly I didn't impress them enough.

Miisa kept telling me to just get out there and we would sort something out, which was appealing and scary in equal measure. I won't say that my logic at the time made sense, but eventually I started looking for teaching jobs in Finland, securing a place at some summer camps run by Nordic School, a Russian company that specialized in teaching Scandinavian languages (although these camps were for English language students). Miisa was also annoyed with me that I had not been there for Finland's greatest sporting moment in over a decade; beating Sweden in the Ice Hockey World Championships. Looking at the public celebrations on YouTube, I have to say that I regret missing it too.

I arrived in Helsinki in late June, and after a week getting accustomed to Finland, I was on a train to a little town called Inkeroinen, to educate Russian kids in English, in Finland, for a school that teaches Finnish, Swedish, Danish and Norwegian, but not English. The town, I'm sorry to say, was pretty horrid. It looked like a typically depressed British council estate, stuck in the middle of nowhere with only one significant employer, the Stora Enso mill. Like all factories, it had laid off a lot of staff, so unemployment was a big problem, as was drinking in the two local bars.

There were two, two week camps and, despite the isolation, lack of English speakers, lack of amenities and general detachment from the world, I had a great time. The kids were awesome and their language skills were both insane and embarrassing. I made some good friends with the teachers too, and we hung out a lot. Somewhere in this world, there is camera phone footage of me miming an horrendously camp (yet perfectly timed and interpreted) version of *All I Wanna Do is Make Love to You* by Heart. I even had my first experience of foreign football, when a few of us teachers cycled to neighbouring

Myllykoski to watch the local team, MyPä, lose 1-0 to the mighty HJK Helsinki in the Finnish Veikkausliga.

After my first four weeks there I headed back to Helsinki for a bit. Miisa and I then went to her hometown, Salo, to meet her family and also visit Turku, the original capital of Finland. That summer was surprisingly hot and humid, two words that rarely get used when talking about Finland but, believe me, it gets hot there.

Sadly, things didn't work out between us, so I eventually came home, cancelling my place on a further camp. Back in Portsmouth, I got back in the job hunt and signing on (unemployment welfare), but had a quick revisit to Finland. I had decided to try and go back into the world I had abandoned two years before, but the economy was pretty tough. Miisa and I kept talking and there were still plenty of feelings there and so, at the end of the year, I decided to give it one last go. I headed back to Finland just before New Year and we had a wonderful New Year's Eve in Tallinn, Estonia. Sadly it quickly didn't work out again, and I was back home, at square one.

After a few depressing months of job hunting I finally got something. As of writing this I am still there, working as a management information analyst for an insurance services company.

So what do I think about China, and Chongqing in particular? Well, let's look at the facts. The country is heavily polluted, especially in the big cities. Sunlight is a luxury. The streets are often filthy and stink from the smell of human faeces coming from the aging sewers. Drinking water only comes in bottles because the tap water can't be trusted. Their treatment of animals leaves a lot to be desired, but their treatment of people can be worse. There is often open xenophobia, the kind that would make UKIP look like the Green Party, or the *Daily Mail* look like the *Guardian*. People are often pushy and rude. Customer service can be very frustrating. Some aspects of life are totally devoid of common sense. But you know what? I fucking love China.

In contrast, the Chinese are often the nicest and most hospitable people I have ever encountered. They are friendly and enthusiastic about visitors. Things may lack logic, but they still work. China is a country that still values the concept of making stuff, something that has been dismissed as trivial and old-fashioned by successive UK governments in my life time. It's an exciting country, with a crazy mix of the traditional and the modern that is still looking for a balance, but it's slowly getting there.

I love the food, the style, the language, the writing, the music, the folk traditions, the warmth, the modernity, the chaos, the staggering infrastructure, KTV, the nightlife, the instant noodles, the cinema, Mandopop, the countryside, the arts and crafts, the town planning and I could probably go on and on, but I need to stop somewhere. What I'm trying to say, is that I love China with all my heart, for the good and the bad.

So was it all worth it? Was it worth leaving that really well paid job for a year and a bit of low to zero-paid work experience and months of unemployment to get a job back in the environment I had been so dismissive and negative about for so long? The answer is an unequivocal *yes*.

Teaching in China is without doubt the single best thing I have ever done. It's the most important and valuable experience of my life. It's something that is genuinely meaningful and valuable in the world. It was the hardest I've ever worked, and the most stressful job too, but it was also the most exhilarating and uplifting job ever.

No piece of code, system testing or process development has challenged me more than standing in a room full of 5 year-olds and trying to get them excited about learning a bunch of new words for reasons they are too young to understand.

Nothing has been so hard as trying to get a bunch of adults to forget that they had paid for the course (and can do what they like) and remember that I had put in a ton of work for that lesson, and that they should at least turn up, let alone try.

Nothing has been as satisfying as giving young kids a task, demonstrating what they have to do, and then seeing them do it with language they'd learnt months before and hadn't been specifically shown to use that day. The experience of teaching, and seeing students actually learning, has been the greatest joy of my life.

So why, if it's so great, have I not gone back? Well, I never did it to make a new career, so it was never in my mind to carry on for long, plus I've done it now and I'm happy. I've used that experience in my current job with some training I've given and it's worked pretty well. I have thought about going back abroad to teach again, but now I'm back in Portsmouth I feel happy, and would like to make some roots again. I still have my flat in Essex, so I always have that to fall back on. I'm not saying my life has been wonderful since; there have been plenty of problems but nothing insurmountable either.

I have no regrets about what I did, just some of the outcomes since, but I look to myself first and foremost for the reasons they went wrong. There are a number of reasons why Miisa and I didn't last, and I won't ever pretend to be a saint or a victim, but what's done is done.

Everyone I worked with at EF has now moved on, some to new schools, some to new countries and some home. We haven't all been brilliant at keeping in touch, but some of the fondest and most beautiful memories of my life have come from my year working and partying with the guys at EF in Chongqing, China. It was an amazing twelve months, and looking at the photos fills me with joy every time. I sometimes find it hard to believe that I was there, that I actually did it, that I actually saw those places and tasted the food and breathed the air and walked on the land, but I did. That, for me, is what makes that year in Chongqing the best year of my life.

About the Author

 Andrew Snape was born in Portsmouth in 1975. After studying at university in Bournemouth and Sheffield, he spent nine years working for Ford Motor Company in Essex, before taking the plunge and becoming an English teacher. An avid traveller he has, as of publication, visited 48 countries and had a number of travel articles published in high-end property magazines.

Printed in Great Britain
by Amazon